The Apocalyptic Paul:
Retrospect and Prospect

Cascade Library of Pauline Studies

The aim of the series is to advance Pauline theology by publishing monographs that make original scholarly proposals in conversation with existing scholarly debates, and which have the potential to shape future trajectories in research.

As both the title of the series and the list of categories above suggests, it is their contribution to critical discussion of Pauline theology that will be the hallmark of books published in CLPS. However, the nature and scope of Pauline theology is intended to be understood in a somewhat expansive manner, with an openness to the use of methodologies (e.g., social-scientific or post-colonial approaches) that have sometimes been regarded as standing in opposition to theological modes of Pauline interpretation. The criterion by which the suitability of a study for inclusion in the series will be assessed is its theological interest. This judgment will be made on the basis of the potential benefits of a particular approach or methodology for our understanding of Pauline theology rather than on the basis of conformity to preconceived ideas of what constitutes an appropriately theological approach to Pauline interpretation. As such, CLPS will also be open both to studies that are broadly confessional in tone and to those that are more critical of perspectives expressed in the Pauline texts.

Series Editors:
Stephen Chester, Wycliffe College, Toronto
Dorothea H. Bertschmann, Abbey House Palace Green, Durham University

Editorial Board:
John M. G. Barclay, Durham University
Lisa Marie Bowens, Princeton Theological Seminary
Martinus C. de Boer, Vrije Universiteit Amsterdam
Andreas Dettwiler, Universite de Geneve
Susan Eastman, Duke Divinity School
Beverly Roberts Gaventa, Baylor University
David G. Horrell, University of Exeter
Jonathan Linebaugh, Beesen Divinity School, Samford University
Grand Macaskill, University of Aberdeen
Volker Rabens, Friedrich Schiller University Jena

The Apocalyptic Paul

RETROSPECT AND PROSPECT

Jamie Davies

FOREWORD BY John Barclay

CASCADE Books · Eugene, Oregon

THE APOCALYPTIC PAUL
Retrospect and Prospect

Cascade Library of Pauline Studies

Copyright © 2022 Jamie Davies. All rights reserved. Except for brief quotations in critical publications or reviews, no part of this book may be reproduced in any manner without prior written permission from the publisher. Write: Permissions, Wipf and Stock Publishers, 199 W. 8th Ave., Suite 3, Eugene, OR 97401.

Cascade Books
An Imprint of Wipf and Stock Publishers
199 W. 8th Ave., Suite 3
Eugene, OR 97401

www.wipfandstock.com

PAPERBACK ISBN: 978-1-5326-8192-9
HARDCOVER ISBN: 978-1-5326-8193-6
EBOOK ISBN: 978-1-5326-8194-3

Cataloguing-in-Publication data:

Names: Davies, Jamie, author. | Barclay, John, foreword.

Title: The apocalyptic Paul : retrospect and prospect / by Jamie Davies; foreword by John Barclay.

Description: Eugene, OR: Cascade Books, 2022 | Series: Cascade Library of Pauline Studies | Includes bibliographical references and index.

Identifiers: ISBN 978-1-5326-8192-9 (paperback) | ISBN 978-1-5326-8193-6 (hardcover) | ISBN 978-1-5326-8194-3 (ebook)

Subjects: LCSH: Bible. Epistles of Paul—Criticism, interpretation, etc.—History. | Bible. Epistles of Paul—Theology. | Eschatology—Biblical teaching. | Paul, the Apostle, Saint.

Classification: BS2650.2 D385 2022 (print) | BS2650.2 (ebook)

For Grant Macaskill

who taught me the intellectual virtues this book tries to practice
and who got me into this mess in the first place

Contents

Series Introduction | ix
Foreword by John Barclay | xiii
Preface | xvii
Acknowledgments | xxi
Introduction | xxv

PART ONE: Retrospect

1. The Genealogy of the Apocalyptic Paul | 3
    1.1 Johannes Weiss & Albert Schweitzer | 4
    1.2 Rudolf Bultmann | 9
    1.3 Ernst Käsemann | 12
    1.4 J. Christiaan Beker | 17
    1.5 J. Louis Martyn | 22

2. The Apocalyptic Paul in Contemporary Scholarship | 27
    2.1 Martinus de Boer | 29
    2.2 Leander Keck | 33
    2.3 Alexandra Brown | 39
    2.4 Beverly Gaventa | 42
    2.5 Douglas Campbell | 45
    2.6 Susan Eastman | 49
    2.7 Lisa Bowens | 52

3. Christian Theology and the "Apocalyptic Turn" | 57
    3.1 Walter Lowe | 58
    3.2 Nathan Kerr | 60
    3.3 Philip Ziegler | 63
    3.4 Douglas Harink | 67

CONTENTS

PART TWO: Prospects

4. Unsettled Questions for the Apocalyptic Paul | 75
    4.1 The Apocalyptic Paul and the Jewish Apocalyptic Tradition | 76
    4.2 The Apocalyptic Paul and Karl Barth | 84
    4.3 Paul's Apocalyptic Epistemology | 91
    4.4 Paul's Apocalyptic Eschatology | 99
    4.5 Paul's Apocalyptic Soteriology | 105

5. Paul's Apocalyptic Theology in Interdisciplinary Perspective | 114
    5.1 Paul and the "Age to Come" | 115
    5.2 Wisdom and Revelation in 1 Corinthians 2 | 132
    5.3 Time and Space, Continuity and Discontinuity
        in Galatians 4 | 149

Conclusion: The Tone and Tasks of the Apocalyptic Paul | 161

Bibliography | 169

Series Introduction

For the apostle Paul, his own significance rested entirely on his commission as an apostle and his proclamation of the gospel of Christ ("by the grace of God, I am what I am," 1 Cor 15:10). For this reason, the heart of Pauline studies must lie in Paul's exposition of this gospel, which is to say his theology, as it comes to expression in his surviving letters. Here Paul expresses both his deepest convictions about the significance of Jesus Christ and his perspectives on their embodiment in the life of early church communities. The Cascade Library of Pauline Studies (CLPS) will focus squarely on engagement with the theological content of the Pauline letters, along with its impact on human thought and behavior throughout the centuries. The series aims to provide a home for research efforts that produce fresh insight into Paul's theology in its original contexts, its legacies and reception, and its significance today; efforts that therefore possess the potential to shape trajectories in future research.

To stake such a claim for the centrality of Pauline theology within its discipline implies both something about the current state of Pauline studies and also an aspiration for its future. For the discipline is simultaneously marked by impressive vitality and by fragmentation. A wide range of theoretical approaches are employed, and even among those adopting a more traditional approach, the list of different frameworks within which Paul is understood is substantial: the apocalyptic Paul, the covenantal Paul, the Paul of the New Perspective, the Paul of the Old Perspective, Paul within Judaism etc. It is easy for the scholarly discourses which result to feel like separate conversations. Forums are needed within which a shared focus on Paul's theological ideas can stimulate new thinking, promote dialogue, and help to map pathways forward beyond the reassertion of incommensurate conclusions. CLPS aims to provide such a forum.

Series Introduction

Yet an insistence on the centrality of Pauline theology within Pauline studies ought not to mean imposing a forced uniformity or understanding the scope of Pauline theology in a narrow manner. For one thing, engagement with the theological content of Paul's message is impossible without the careful historical work necessary to understand Paul's ideas in their own ancient contexts. The study of Pauline theology cannot be advanced by the erection of artificial divides between theological and historical approaches to interpretation. Neither can our attempts to understand Paul's ideas in their own ancient contexts be detached from the influence upon us of our own historical location as interpreters. We are impacted both by previous traditions of interpreting Paul and by our own social and cultural contexts. They shape our concerns, and they both enable and constrain our understanding of the past. Implicit in even the most historical approaches to the study of Pauline theology are present day questions and horizons. Some theological interpreters simply take account of the impact of historical location upon their task, keeping their focus on Paul in his own time and place. Others instead embrace the constructive task of explicitly re-contextualizing Paul's theology for contemporary readers, connecting the historical study of Paul's ideas in varied ways with the Christian tradition today.

There is thus considerable and appropriate diversity within the study of Pauline theology. For this reason, exegetical studies, studies comparing Paul's ideas with those of others in the ancient world, studies exploring Paul's ideas in their canonical contexts, studies of reception history, and studies bringing Paul's theological ideas into dialogue with contemporary theological concerns are all welcome within CLPS. Some of these types of studies may employ analytical tools drawn from the Christian theological tradition. Their methodology will be theological as well as their content. However, engagement with the theological content of Paul's message can also sometimes be served by inter-disciplinary methodologies that have not typically been understood as theological or have even been understood by some of their practitioners as antithetical to theological interpretation. Post-colonial interpretation, the use of various forms of political philosophy that prioritize liberation, and various kinds of feminist interpretation all provide examples of such inter-disciplinary methodologies. Where studies use such methodologies to engage with Paul's theological ideas or to recontextualize them for the contemporary world they too will be welcome within CLPS. It is the kinds of questions asked, the quality of the theological

SERIES INTRODUCTION

reflection offered, and the depth of critical engagement that we intend to be the hallmark of CLPS.

Dorothea H. Bertschmann
Stephen J. Chester
Series Editors

Foreword

John Barclay

No one familiar with the study of Paul in the last twenty-five years can have failed to notice the frequency with which he is claimed to be an "apocalyptic" theologian, and the centrality of that claim in influential strands of interpretation. Even those of us (like me) who have avoided using the adjective "apocalyptic," because of the difficulty in defining that word, have been stimulated and influenced by scholars who promote the "apocalyptic Paul." But the complexity of the term, the variety of ways in which it is understood, and the resulting confusions and controversies frequently leave us bewildered and frustrated, and apt to complain: "Could somebody please explain exactly what the word 'apocalyptic' means, where it comes from, and why it sounds so attractive to important interpreters of Paul?" We can complain no longer. The answer is right here in this concise, clear, even-handed, and highly stimulating book.

Jamie Davies is well placed to provide the answers we seek. Right from the days of his PhD (published as *Paul among the Apocalypses?*) he has wrestled with the question of the relationship between the texts we call "apocalypses" and the mode of thinking we find in Paul. He is a sure-footed guide to the Jewish and early Christian apocalyptic literature, and an expert in the study of Paul. But more than that—and essential to the task of this book—he has made himself familiar with the theology of Barth (and with interpreters of Barth's theological development) such that he understands subtexts operative in the representation of Paul as an "apocalyptic" theologian that few have been able to grasp. This is a unique set of skills, and precisely what we have needed for many years. Both for the newcomer

FOREWORD

to this field and for the seasoned expert, this book is a highly welcome resource and a vital contribution to scholarship.

The three elements of this book may be summarized as survey, critique, and constructive proposal.

The survey of the key contributors to the "apocalyptic" reading of Paul is exceptionally helpful. Carefully unravelling who contributed what, and why, Davies avoids the over-generalizations that abound in this field, and offers a concise, clear, and accurate depiction of the main scholarly "players" in this field. Crucial here is his inclusion of the theological dimensions of this school of interpretation, without which we would fail to understand central figures such as Käsemann, Martyn, and Harink.

When he turns to critique, Davies never fails to be fair-minded and generous. At a time when arm-waving dismissals and windy rhetoric are all too common in our field, it is a delight to read this probing analysis of the key elements of the "apocalyptic Paul," conducted with precision, sensitivity, and nuance. Where "apocalyptic" readings of Paul tend to trade in dichotomies (some derived from Paul, some added along the way), Davies presses carefully to ask which of these are necessary or helpful, and to remind the Barth-influenced readers of Paul that there was more to Barth than his early, sometimes hyperbolic, commentary on Romans.

The third element of this book—constructive proposal—adds still further to its value. Davies rightly insists that the exegesis of Paul in this vein should pay attention to the most recent historical work on Jewish apocalypses (and related texts). He encourages interpreters away from reliance on outdated scholarly assumptions, while showing how newer analyses of ancient Jewish thought help us read Paul in fresh ways. Paul, of course, reworks his tradition from a distinctive, christological standpoint, but it remains important to be clear about where he fits within the ancient Jewish conversation. However, Davies also points up the value in deploying the critical tools provided by theology, recognizing what more could be achieved analytically with the aid of (for instance) nuanced theological conceptions of time and space. What is refreshing is Davies's refusal to place historical and theological approaches to Paul in a false antithesis; he rightly looks both ways for assistance in reading Paul well.

As Davies points out, the discussion of the "apocalyptic Paul" has been largely confined in recent years to Anglophone, Protestant circles. But among the many virtues of this book is its potential to open up this discussion to a larger audience and a wider range of contributors. Davies models here the kind of cross-disciplinary conversation that is badly needed right now, but also the tone of honest enquiry and respectful disagreement that is necessary if the study of Paul is to avoid getting sucked into the vortex of the culture wars and their scholarly equivalents. But he also opens up topics that need not, and should not, be confined to one quarter of the scholarly field. How can we think better about the complex constructions of time and history that we find in the ancient apocalyptic literature and in the theology of Paul? What might it mean to say that the Christ-event has changed the coordinates of reality while bringing God's creation plans and covenant promises to their fulfillment? How might we conceive of God as both immanently engaged in the events of history and radically transcendent to our space-time continuum? At a time of political, social, medical, and ecological crisis, what sort of alternative vision does Paul's theology offer, and how can this be rendered comprehensible and relevant in the twenty-first century?

These are among the many fruitful questions posed by the "apocalyptic" Paul, as here explained, critiqued, and developed by Jamie Davies. This book helps us understand where we have come from, and why we stand where we are. It also opens up further topics of conversation as we consider how to move forward in what remains one of the most stimulating inter-disciplinary conversations in Pauline studies. Everyone will learn something from this book, and everyone should be stimulated to rise to the challenge it offers. Given where we stand in history, and given the critical tools honed by historians and theologians, what are the best ways to interpret Paul's apocalyptic claim that the life, death, and resurrection of Christ have transformed reality and made possible radically new patterns of life and thought? And what might that newness look like, here and now, in practice?

Preface

I NEVER REALLY WANTED to write on Paul. This is my second book on Paul. When I began my doctoral dissertation, which I planned to write on the book of Revelation, my supervisor, Grant Macaskill, suggested I begin by reading up on what the word "apocalyptic" means. No doubt he knew exactly what he was doing, but I headed to the library blissfully unaware of the quagmire into which he had sent me. The literature on Revelation and on the apocalyptic genre was vast but fascinating, and my reading in that area yielded all sorts of insights. I read the primary texts, worked through the influential volumes by John Collins[1] and Christopher Rowland,[2] and got up to speed on the work of the *Enoch Seminar* and other recent contributions. When I turned to the discussions of apocalyptic theology in Pauline scholarship, however, I found myself perplexed by a conversation which sounded simultaneously familiar and strange. I reported this confusion back to my (clearly not surprised) supervisor, and I was rapidly drawn into the task of exploring the similarities and differences of this "other" parallel conversation. My dissertation topic soon shifted to reflect this new interest.[3] I recall that feeling of overwhelming confusion lasting about a year. The discussion about Paul's apocalyptic theology sometimes intersected with what I knew from studying Revelation and other texts in the apocalyptic genre, to be sure, but there also seemed to be another conversation going on, sometimes in the same room but more often in an adjoining one. It was a lively conversation among friends, but I was (as we all are) entering it in full swing and I wasn't sure I fully understood the talking points. Lacking an initiation to this conversation, I ended up spending a large amount of

---

1. Collins, *Apocalyptic Imagination*.
2. Rowland, *Open Heaven*.
3. It was subsequently published as Davies, *Paul Among the Apocalypses*.

time and energy trying to orient myself by distilling the key issues from a large corpus of essays, monographs, and commentaries on Paul.

Of course, that was time well spent, and the brief retrospective offered in the first part of this book should not be a substitute for the careful reading of that scholarship, a lot of which will be signaled in the footnotes of the following chapters. But there comes a point when that literature becomes so vast that it can be bewildering to the uninitiated, and significant themes and voices can too easily be missed.[4] With all of this, it can be helpful to have a guide, and that's one of the reasons I have written this book. Its intended audience is, in part, graduate students and nonspecialist New Testament scholars who are looking for a brief and accessible overview of this perspective on Paul. Perhaps it will prove useful for others, too, but it should be made clear at the outset that this is a book which is concerned with offering an orientation to the Apocalyptic Paul, its past, present, and possible futures of this fascinating interpretation of Paul's letters. A second concern of this book, however, is a desire to foster and (hopefully) to model generous interdisciplinary dialogue within and beyond the guild of Pauline scholarship, as the conversation continues about his apocalyptic theology, and to make contributions to that end. As such, I have in places signaled where I think such dialogue might bear fruit, posed some critical questions, and have offered some constructive proposals of my own.

It's impossible to say anything about the apostle Paul without it being controversial to someone. The apocalyptic reading of Paul is no different, stimulating lively debate in the guild of Pauline scholars and, as we shall see, beyond. For my own part, while affirming many of the interpretative theological insights this approach to Paul has provided, I still have questions, some of which are indicated and explored in what follows.

Though I speak unambiguously throughout this volume of *The Apocalyptic Paul*, I am keenly aware that labeling a "school" or a "movement" is always fraught with problems. For one thing, it risks imposing a false homogeneity on what is actually a subtly diverse range of interpretative proposals. For another, it can easily be complicit with a worrying fragmentation of the discipline into segregated tribes, each with its own specialized vocabulary and stock bibliographies. The guild of Pauline scholars, already too often a "silo" within New Testament studies, risks becoming further

---

4. One of the oversights of my first book was that I did not sufficiently engage with the important contributions of Leander Keck and Alexandra Brown, an omission I hope to have corrected here.

fragmented into such "schools," which threaten to shrink into ever smaller echo chambers. This is not to minimize the importance of specialist conversations taking place with agreed terminological shorthand and unspoken shared commitments—that is naturally important for any discipline if we are to avoid endless prolegomena. But an unintended side-effect of this can sometimes be that important areas of common ground between interpretations are minimized, while differences are exaggerated or skewed by those defending their tribe.

More broadly, I have had a growing sense that too often the debate is characterized by confusion over key concepts and terms, and some talking at cross-purposes. Leading figures in the discussion claim that they have been misunderstood by their critics, sometimes with good reason. Accusations of supersessionist or Marcionite errors are regularly thrown around, at times threatening to devolve into *ad hominem* attacks or trenchant stagnation. While some may enjoy the gladiatorial spectacle of theological prizefighting, to my mind this approach does poor service to the task of theology (not to mention its object of study) and can certainly make entrance into the conversation even more daunting for the uninitiated. In these pages I have tried, here and there, to clarify some of the muddy waters and to pour oil on others, to avoid partisan flag-waving, and perhaps even name some common ground. Whether I have been successful in any of this is, of course, for others to assess, but it is my sincere hope that those named in these chapters recognize themselves in my summaries and find any critiques well placed. Perhaps some of the areas where I have suggested common ground will turn out to be nothing of the sort, while others may bear fruit. But maybe even clarifying that could itself be worthwhile. Since this is a book at least partly aimed at introducing the discussion, I am conscious that some readers may be trying to figure out their own way in, and perhaps these "conversation starters" will prove helpful in that regard.

Acknowledgments

THE BULK OF THIS book was written at my home in Bristol, UK, during periods of quarantine due to the 2020–2021 coronavirus pandemic. This was not, as one might imagine, an experience of glorious scholarly isolation—far from it. The first draft was written on a hastily assembled temporary desk in the corner of our bedroom, surrounded by laundry baskets and regularly interrupted by the hurly-burly of family life as my wife and I juggled our careers with unplanned homeschooling and a thousand other things. Around a year later, as I completed the draft of chapter 5, my son was once again in quarantine, and so my morning's writing was punctuated by discussions of mathematics and Macbeth. Perhaps this is fitting for a book on the apostle Paul, who was not the ivory-tower scholar we sometimes imagine but, as Walter Lowe puts it, a writer of "theology on the run."[1] In the "apocalyptic" chaos of a global health crisis, and our own little piece of it, somehow a book emerged. I am immensely grateful to my wife Becky for putting up with a mini-library in the bedroom and a husband whose mind was sometimes elsewhere, and to the kids for their patience through all of this.

One of the unexpected gifts of this strange and difficult season was that it became a catalyst for various creative alternatives to the usual conference-based scholarly activities. In particular, I was very thankful for a small gathering, which sprang up unexpectedly during the crisis, of colleagues interested in conversation (via video) about apocalyptic theology. I am extremely grateful to Philip Ziegler for setting that up, and for inviting me along. I want to express my thanks to that group: Dorothea Bertschmann, Kait Dugan, Declan Kelly, Beverly Gaventa, Erin Heim, Joe Longarino, Chris Tilling, Jennifer Strawbridge, and Sam Tranter. Chris and Erin were particularly generous in volunteering some of their summer to look at

---

1. Lowe, "Prospects for a Postmodern Christian Theology," 18.

an early draft of the first part of the book, and their comments were immensely helpful. Our Zoom party was also happily gatecrashed by (among others) Douglas Campbell, Martinus de Boer, Lisa Bowens, Ann Jervis, and Jonathan Linebaugh, from all of whom I have learned a great deal.

A number of people helped me think about this project in its infancy and some have been extraordinarily generous with their time in correspondence. A few have gone above and beyond by looking over draft sections, offering detailed comments, and sharing their own forthcoming work. I want to express my thanks in that regard to John Barclay, Alexandra Brown, Stephen Chester, Mike Gorman, Doug Harink, Loren Stuckenbruck, Tom Wright, and Phil Ziegler. They are not, of course, responsible for how this book ended up, but it would have been worse without them.

My current and recent PhD students (Dr. Allen Hill, Ben Leighton, Dr. Matthew Moravec, Steve Whitacre, Amy White, and Calvin Williams) all deserve thanks for allowing me to think out loud with them (sometimes temporarily hijacking their supervision sessions!) and for looking over an early draft of the first part of the book and making comments. My former student Dr. Joshua Heavin deserves particular thanks for his enthusiastic and careful reading of that early draft and for his insightful reflections.

Huge thanks are owed, too, to all the team at Cascade Books of Wipf and Stock Publishers, and in particular Michael Thomson who first discussed this volume with me and who has remained an enthusiastic supporter throughout its development, which has not exactly been routine. The book was originally conceived as a brief introduction to the Apocalyptic Paul debate, but took on a life of its own, growing into this monograph and finding a home in this exciting new series. That this was possible is due almost entirely to the creative vision and adaptability of the publishing team, and particular thanks are due to Chris Spinks and Heather Carraher for their immense patience with a book (and an author) changing direction mid-stream. I'm very grateful to the advisory board and series editors of the Cascade Library of Pauline Studies, especially Stephen Chester, who greeted the book with enthusiasm, invited its inclusion in this new monograph series, and made a number of immensely valuable editorial suggestions in the final stages.

With this new home for the book came an unexpected and undeserved gift of a foreword by John Barclay. I have long been grateful for his scholarship, and in recent years it has been a joy to share collegial conversation and

Acknowledgments

correspondence, not only on the topic of apocalyptic theology in Paul but on a wide range of questions. It's an honor to share these pages with him.

One of the convictions expressed in this book is the importance of interdisciplinary theological dialogue. I am privileged to work in an environment where this is commonplace, and I'm grateful to my colleagues at Trinity College, particularly Helen Collins, Jon Coutts (now at Ambrose University, Calgary) and Justin Stratis (now at Wycliffe College, Toronto), who have been much more than colleagues, and who have helped me become a better theologian.

Last, and by no means least, I remain grateful to my former doctoral supervisor, Grant Macaskill, whose breathtaking range of scholarship continues to be a source of inspiration and, more importantly, whose approach to the theologian's vocation has left more of a mark on me than I think either of us realized. This book is dedicated to him, in gratitude.

INTRODUCTION

"Stumped by Apocalyptic"?

WHAT DOES IT MEAN to say that Paul was an "apocalyptic" thinker? As almost any introduction like this will tell you, the word is of Greek origin, deriving from ἀποκάλυψις, "unveiling." Lexically, therefore, it simply means "revelatory." Would that it were so simple. The reality is that the term has tended to become either too nebulous to be any use or so fraught with competing definitions that it is almost irretrievably confusing, even to the specialist. No wonder some have considered declaring a moratorium on its use, or even ditching it altogether.[1] In the field of biblical studies, it has generally been taken to denote the eschatological teachings of Jesus, and/or the visions recorded in revelatory literature, in particular the book of Revelation, whose first words ἀποκάλυψις Ἰησοῦ Χριστοῦ (rightly or wrongly) gave us the label for the literary genre "apocalypse." The recognition of these origins and foci has been useful but has not, however, completely cleared the "cloudiness of current definitions" of the word, as Klaus Koch lamented in 1970 in his useful little book, *Ratlos vor der Apokalyptik* ("Perplexed" or "Stumped by Apocalyptic").[2] More recently, the discussion about the apocalyptic character of the theology of the apostle Paul has become something of a storm center in this matter of definition, adding an extra layer of complexity to an already challenging question. Fifty years after Koch's lament, it is still regularly observed that there is considerable confusion over the meaning of the word. It appears that we're still stumped.

One of the main sources of this confusion is the nature of the relationship (if any) between an apocalyptic reading of Paul and the wider

1. E.g., Sturm, "Defining," 17; Wright, *Fresh Perspective*, 41.
2. Koch, *Rediscovery of Apocalyptic*, see esp. 18–22.

corpus of Jewish and Christian apocalyptic literature. For some this remains a defining feature of the term, and the apparent neglect of this relationship is one of the most frequent critiques of the Apocalyptic Paul. But others suggest that this represents a category error: the two fields of enquiry are simply using the word in different ways, one concerned with describing literary features and the other indicating a theological heritage (say, in the work of Karl Barth). As such, it is suggested that any connection between Paul and the apocalypses is, at best, of limited relevance to the Paulinist.[3] However, briefly to anticipate one of the conclusions of this book, while it is not always immediately evident, most scholars attempting an "apocalyptic" reading of Paul do in fact share a commitment to examining the apostle's thought in relation to the theology and/or worldview expressed in the Second Temple Jewish and Christian apocalypses. Despite rumors to the contrary,[4] the majority of the scholars surveyed in this book acknowledge this relationship, variously understood, in their discussions of Paul's apocalyptic thought. While it may appear, therefore, that the conversation is doomed to dissolve into a mere terminological stalemate, this should not be the case. I for one remain convinced that we should continue to use the word "apocalyptic" when talking about Paul's thought, and that we should do so while remaining mindful of the literary *and* theological connections thereby implied.

Of course, we do not find a literary apocalypse in any of the letters of Paul, though 2 Cor 12:1–10 comes close.[5] Nevertheless, it is my conviction, shared with most of the interpreters discussed below, that Paul was a thoroughly apocalyptic thinker, and that this is indicated by the architecture of his thought and by the numerous "apocalyptic expressions"[6] found throughout his letters. In this endeavor I continue to find it helpful to think of Paul as a writer not of apocalypses but very much in the "apocalyptic mode."[7] While "apocalyptic" is sometimes used substantively (likely due to

---

3. This is Campbell's position. See Campbell, *Quest*, 56–57. Cf. Campbell "Attempt," 165n6.

4. Christopher Rowland expresses concerns of this nature when he says that "it is striking that most definitions of 'apocalyptic' work with a view of the phenomenon which is only loosely related to the apocalypses." Rowland and Morray-Jones, *Mystery*, 15.

5. On which see Bowens, *Apostle in Battle*. Bowens's work will be discussed in 2.7 below.

6. This is Martyn's phrase. To name just one, Paul's use of the phrase "the present evil age" is a sign of his apocalyptic thought.

7. This is a framework borrowed from Fowler, *Kinds of Literature*, via Tigchelaar,

the influence of the German *Apokalyptik* during the word's journey from Greek to English) it is perhaps more helpful to retain it as an adjective, such that the noun it modifies must always be specified. The adjective "apocalyptic" thereby represents a distillation of the key features of the noun "apocalypse." Paul can thus be said to have an "apocalyptic eschatology," or an "apocalyptic theology." Of course, not everyone is this concerned with such linguistic precision, and it's fairly pointless to be completely dogmatic about it, but I have found it grammatically *and theologically* helpful to remain mindful of this usage. For one thing, it establishes and encodes an appropriate connection between Paul and the apocalypses and indicates the value of bringing them into the conversation, placing Paul among them to see what can be said about his apocalyptic mode of thinking while contextually anchoring the distinctive theology found in his letters. But it also recognizes that the point is not simply to engage in historical or intertextual comparison, or to reduce Paul's theology to an instance of a general pattern of thought. Labeling Paul's theology "apocalyptic" remains a theological claim as well as an historical one, as I hope this book will demonstrate.

As I have said, most of the scholars surveyed here acknowledge some kind of connection between Paul and the apocalypses in their use of the term "apocalyptic" to describe the apostle's thought. This is not to say, of course, that the challenge of definition is purely illusory. Examinations of the apocalyptic literature have routinely highlighted and discussed the themes of eschatology, cosmology, soteriology, and epistemology, and each one of these remains a source of debate among Pauline scholars. The first of these, eschatology, has been a particular focus in many discussions of the apocalyptic tradition (to the extent that the words have sometimes been used interchangeably) while the last, epistemology, has received less attention than it perhaps deserves (remarkably, given that ἀποκάλυψις means "revelation"), though that situation is changing. Likewise, as we will see in the chapters that follow, approaches to Paul as an apocalyptic theologian have largely focused on one or more of these four themes, with varying emphasis. Moreover, what must be accounted for as a matter of supreme importance is Paul's distinctively *christological* reworking of this apocalyptic theological framework. It is here that crucial questions and differences often emerge in the debate over the Apocalyptic Paul.[8] In

---

Prophets, 5–8. See the discussion in Davies, *Paul Among the Apocalypses*, 33–34.

8. See Keck, "Paul and Apocalyptic Theology," 231.

addition to making some contributions to this debate, it is my hope that this volume might also serve as an orientation to some of these questions for those new to the conversation.

The Shape of this Book

This book is arranged in two parts. Part One (chs. 1–3) offers a retrospective on the Apocalyptic Paul and charts the various contours of the contemporary conversation. While this part of the book contains some critical insights, its primary purpose is to survey the contributions of the most important voices, and to offer a compact retrospective for those who are new to the Apocalyptic Paul discussion. Part Two (chs. 4 and 5, which are somewhat longer) is more prospective, exploring some key questions, bringing in other voices, and offering some constructive proposals of my own. Those who are already familiar with the conversation about Paul's apocalyptic thought may wish to skip Part One, and turn straight to this more prospective material, though the retrospective also includes some critical analysis.

The logic of each chapter is as follows. Chapter 1 describes the origins and development of the Apocalyptic Paul movement more or less chronologically, beginning around the start of the twentieth century with Johannes Weiss and Albert Schweitzer and tracing this interpretative genealogy through to the work of J. Louis Martyn. Chapter 2 summarizes the contributions of key interpreters in contemporary Pauline scholarship, selecting what I consider to be the most important voices in the conversation about Paul's apocalyptic theology since Martyn, and their particular contributions. Since this is a description of a "live" conversation, any ordering imposed on this list of scholars is bound to be inadequate in some way. There are some clear lines of influence that can usefully be traced, but of course these often flow both ways. In any case I have done my best to arrange this material in a way I hope is helpful as an introduction to the ongoing conversation. I initially intended that this part should close with a short section on the reception of this Pauline scholarship in contemporary systematic theology, but this soon grew into a chapter of its own, chapter 3, which completes the survey. My aim throughout the book has been to offer as generous a reading as I could of the scholars listed, summarized (all too briefly) in such a way as to orient the reader to the main contours of their work and its significance for interpreting Paul's letters. As I explain further in the introduction to chapter 2, each scholar's work has been described on its own terms, rather than in comparison or counterpoint, so as to avoid overemphasizing differences at the expense of commonalities.

Chapter 4 begins the second part of the book and switches genre, moving from a retrospective survey to something more like a systematic overview of the main critiques of the Apocalyptic Paul. This material begins with consideration of two significant methodological challenges (namely, the relationships with scholarship on the apocalypses and on Karl Barth) before examining three significant theological themes: epistemology, eschatology, and soteriology. As well as introducing key critiques of the Apocalyptic Paul, this section also offers some signposts to recent constructive responses and suggests key dialogue partners in this endeavor from both "inside" and "outside" the movement. Perhaps this last section can serve, therefore, as a collection of "conversation starters" for those continuing to investigate Paul's apocalyptic theology as well as potential areas of investigation for those just joining in.

Chapter 5, which closes the book, is again longer and more constructive in its aims. There I offer a series of exegetical and theological discussions, as an attempt to build upon what has gone before and make my own contributions to the ongoing conversation about Paul's apocalyptic thought. I have selected one distributed apocalyptic motif (the "two ages") and two Pauline texts (1 Cor 2 and Gal 4) to focus the discussion and bring the Apocalyptic Paul into conversation with both recent scholarship on Second Temple Jewish apocalyptic literature and systematic theology in the Barthian tradition. No doubt this interdisciplinary work will have weaknesses (there is a reason we have specialisms, and nobody can expect to master such a range, especially when it comes to Paul) but I offer it here as an attempt to engage in the kind of generous interdisciplinary discourse for which I have advocated elsewhere in the book, and as an invitation for dialogue across our disciplinary boundaries.

PART ONE

Retrospect

CHAPTER 1

The Genealogy of the Apocalyptic Paul

GIVEN THE VIBRANCY OF the present debate over the Apocalyptic Paul, it may come as something of a surprise to those new to the conversation that the recent history of apocalyptic in Pauline scholarship began with pessimism. Published in 1970, when the debate on apocalyptic thought in Paul was heating up, the provocative title of Klaus Koch's short survey *Ratlos vor der Apokalyptik* said it all: modern New Testament scholarship had been "perplexed" or "stumped" by apocalyptic (the English title *The Rediscovery of Apocalyptic* is regrettably tame). Before charting its renaissance, Koch began with an overview of the study of apocalyptic at the start of the twentieth century, which he saw as a lamentable state of affairs. In one section, for example, he described how apocalyptic had become so thoroughly ignored in German-language research that "where treatment of the book of Daniel in Old Testament commentaries was unavoidable, or where the heading 'apocalyptic' had to be discussed in books of reference, foreign scholars had to come to the rescue."[1]

It was not that apocalyptic had been completely forgotten, of course. The late-nineteenth century German *Religionsgeschichtliche Schule* certainly did not ignore it, as the work of Johannes Weiss demonstrates. Beginning with him and Albert Schweitzer, this first chapter offers something of a whistle-stop tour through major figures in twentieth-century Pauline scholarship who have investigated the question of "apocalyptic" in relation to Paul, ending with the programmatic work of J. Louis Martyn at the close of the century. As I hope will become clear, however, this is more than a

---

1. Koch, *Rediscovery*, 38.

work of genealogical due diligence, since the contours of these founding debates continue to shape the discussions today.

1.1 Johannes Weiss and Albert Schweitzer: The Strange New World of Apocalyptic

Johannes Weiss and Jesus's Apocalyptic Proclamation

Though this is a story about interpreters of Paul, it begins with the message of Jesus. Against the prevailing consensus of nineteenth-century Protestant liberal scholarship in Germany, Johannes Weiss argued that the signature theme of Jesus's teaching, the "kingdom of God," ought not to be understood as a subjective, inward, or spiritual experience, but the expression of an objective reality rooted in and inextricably tied to Jewish apocalyptic eschatology.[2] This eschatological interpretation represented something of a turning point in New Testament interpretation more broadly, but it came into particular focus through Weiss's engagement with the views of his father-in-law, Albrecht Ritschl. Over against Ritschl's interpretation of the kingdom as an immanent and expanding "moral society" or its expression of "moral goods," Weiss argued that at the heart of Jesus's message were apocalyptic convictions concerning the radical transcendence of the kingdom. Weiss's apocalyptic Jesus espoused a cosmological dualism of a "twofold world" characterized by conflict and was driven by an imminent expectation of the eschatological *event* of God's deliverance.[3] In short, in Jesus's understanding the kingdom "is not a matter for human initiative, but entirely a matter of God's initiative."[4]

This was an apocalyptic-eschatological reading of the kingdom that threatened the foundations of the liberal Protestant account of Jesus's central message, and indeed that whole approach to modern theology, but Weiss did not press his convictions that far. He was keenly aware that his historical conclusions concerning the apocalyptic and eschatological nature of Jesus's teaching on the "kingdom of God" did not automatically answer the theological questions concerning what we might make of that today. The apocalyptic Jesus of Weiss's historical investigations was decidedly foreign to the contemporary church and its ethical challenges and stood as a

---

2. Weiss, *Proclamation*, 133.
3. Weiss, *Proclamation*, 74.
4. Weiss, *Proclamation*, 132.

rebuke of "lives of Jesus" that created him in the image of modern liberal Protestantism. While praising his contemporaries for the attention given to the kingdom of God (rather than taking Pauline theology as its point of departure), Weiss observed that this theme had not been described in historically faithful terms but had instead been filled out with distinctly modern liberal notions, transforming it into some kind of ethical ideal. "The Kingdom of God as Jesus thought of it," he insisted, "is never something subjective, inward, or spiritual, but is always the objective messianic Kingdom."[5] This, Weiss argued, required an eschatological and apocalyptic reading of the theme that contemporary readings had mitigated or even suppressed.

But this posed a problem: was this apocalyptic theology a possibility for the contemporary church? Weiss conceded that, while modern liberal interpretations of the kingdom were certainly incorrect when it comes to the historical Jesus, they remained the best viable options for contemporary theology. He thus admitted that however anachronistic Ritschl's idea of the "kingdom of God" may be as an interpretation of Jesus, it need not be completely thrown out as an expression of the gospel for today. As such, Weiss suggested a separation of the historical investigation of the thought of Jesus and the discourse of contemporary theology, and a distinction between that which was universal from the historical contingency of Jesus's message. He concluded, "that which is universally valid in Jesus's preaching, which should form the kernel of our systematic theology is not his idea of the Kingdom of God, but that of the religious and ethical fellowship of the children of God."[6] Certainly, he maintained, the phrase "kingdom of God" had enduring value in modern theology, but the result of his approach was two distinct senses in which it should be used, the historical and the theological, both of which could be affirmed as long as one remains clear which is being deployed and resists the collapsing of the latter into the former.[7] For Weiss, the "old coinage" (*Münzen*) of Jesus's apocalyptic proclamation concerning the kingdom must by necessity be issued at a new "rate of exchange" (*Curs*) in contemporary dogmatics.[8]

5. Weiss, *Proclamation*, 133.
6. Weiss, *Proclamation*, 135.
7. See, e.g., Weiss, *Proclamation*, 135.
8. Weiss, *Proclamation*, 59–60. For an evaluation of this metaphor and its limitations for contemporary apocalyptic dogmatics, see Morse "If Johannes Weiss is Right . . ." Later, Ernst Käsemann would describe this as a retreat "with all speed into the liberal conception of Jesus" (Käsemann, *New Testament Questions*, 109n2).

The Apocalyptic Paul

Albert Schweitzer and Paul's Apocalyptic "Mysticism"

Despite Weiss's efforts, however, there was little change to the general state of affairs in early twentieth-century New Testament research. Where apocalyptic was given any attention as a theme, it was treated with varying degrees of suspicion, and was more likely to be seen as an obscure or fantastical feature of "late Judaism" that should be treated with caution,[9] certainly in relation to the message of Jesus, if not Paul. Even among those who embraced apocalyptic, there remained a degree of reserve. Far from offering it as a candidate for the "center" of Pauline theology, post-enlightenment liberal theology largely saw apocalyptic as something from which the apostle, and certainly Jesus, needed to be saved.[10]

It was still against the grain of contemporary scholarship, therefore, when Albert Schweitzer described with unambiguous and consistent positivity the importance of the Jewish apocalyptic worldview for New Testament thought. Schweitzer was convinced of the immense significance of Weiss's short book, describing it as "one of the most important works in historical theology. It seems to break a spell. It closes one epoch and begins another."[11] For his own part, Schweitzer went with and beyond Weiss in arguing that early Christianity could only be understood against this Jewish apocalyptic background. Though he rarely used the term *Apokalyptik* to describe his approach, preferring to speak of *spätjüdischen Eschatologie* ("late Jewish eschatology") or *Mystik* ("mysticism"), he clearly and repeatedly anchored this idea in Jewish apocalyptic thought, and his discussion of Paul in particular was punctuated with discussions of the apocalypses.

In his earlier work on Jesus, especially his *Skizze de Lebens Jesu* and *Von Reimarus zu Wrede: Eine Geschichte der Leben-Jesu-Forschung* (ET: *The Quest for the Historical Jesus*), Schweitzer argued for the importance of "thoroughgoing eschatology" (*konsequente Eschatologie*) for understanding Jesus's message. Convinced that Weiss had stopped too short by only considering Jesus's teaching and not his actions, Schweitzer viewed not only the message of the "kingdom of God" but also Jesus's entire ministry as eschatologically determined.[12]

---

9. E.g., Gunkel in *Schöpfung Und Chaos*, cf. Sturm, "Defining," 26.

10. See Koch, *Rediscovery*, ch. 6, "The Agonised Attempt to Save Jesus from Apocalyptic" (57–97).

11. Schweitzer, *Quest*, 238.

12. Schweitzer, *Quest*, 351n1, though Schweitzer perhaps missed the importance Weiss attached to, e.g., exorcism (see Weiss, *Proclamation*, 32). See also Schweitzer, *Out*

Schweitzer's intention was to follow his work on Jesus immediately with the development of the argument in relation to Paul, but he was prevented from doing so by illness, other publishing commitments, and missionary work in Africa. Thus, his most constructive work on Paul waited until 1930 and the publication of *Die Mystik des Apostels Paulus* (ET: *The Mysticism of Paul the Apostle*, 1931). Here Schweitzer argued for the complete agreement of Paul with Jesus in relation to the centrality of a thoroughgoing apocalyptic eschatology, and he consistently drew on the Jewish apocalypses and the worldview they encapsulate (and not the Hellenistic world beloved by much contemporary scholarship) as source and context for his Pauline theology. As Schweitzer put it, "since Paul lives in the conceptions of the dramatic word-view [*Weltanschauung*] characteristic of the late-Jewish Eschatology, he is by consequence bound to the logic of that view."[13] In his analysis of this worldview, the distinctive emphases drawn out by Schweitzer can be seen, reading backwards from what came later, to anticipate the main contours of the "apocalyptic turn" in Pauline studies.

Schweitzer's discussion of Pauline "mysticism" highlights three defining characteristics. First, there was the theme, already mentioned above, of "thoroughgoing eschatology," the keystone of which is a commitment to the imminent end of the world and a dualistic contrast of two ages. Throughout his letters, Schweitzer's Paul was driven by the eschatological conviction that the new Messianic age had already dawned in the resurrection of Jesus, and that the present age would be decisively put to an end by his imminent return. Paul's consistent and thoroughgoing eschatology demanded this radical conclusion: "If Jesus has risen, that means, for those who dare to think consistently, that it is now already the supernatural age. And this is Paul's point of view."[14] The two worlds are "intermingled," and it is this fact that creates the conditions for Paul's particular form of mysticism.[15] The seemingly paradoxical implication of this eschatological conviction, however, was that the world appeared to be enduringly natural and unchanged. This appearance, Schweitzer argued, was deceptive, and this led to his second theme.

For Schweitzer, this imminent eschatology is coupled with a belief in angelic or demonic powers, signaling that redemption in the teaching

---

of My Life and Thought, 50.

13. Schweitzer, *Mysticism*, 11.
14. Schweitzer, *Mysticism*, 98.
15. Schweitzer, *Mysticism*, 99.

of Jesus and of Paul was "cosmologically conceived" not as an individual transaction but as a "world-event" in which the believer participates.[16] It was this cosmically conditioned view of salvation, he argued, that lay behind both Jesus's self-understanding and Paul's eschatological expectation. The present situation between the resurrection of Christ and his return is characterized by conflict between the powers of sin and death in the natural world and the power of the supernatural world already at work within it. The rebellion of angels and the influence of demonic powers present in the world is the source of evil and is met by the eschatological arrival of the Messianic kingdom, of which the resurrection of Jesus is the initial event.[17] Characteristic of such a view were the Jewish apocalypses, and Schweitzer here draws particular attention to angelic revolt and cosmic warfare motifs in 1 Enoch. (Though he also directs the reader to consider 4 Ezra, Jubilees, and the Psalms of Solomon, Schweitzer notes that these writings do not emphasize the angelic/cosmic dimensions of salvation and considers 1 Enoch to be closer to the teachings of Jesus and Paul.)[18]

Third, these two characteristics of Paul's "mysticism," imminent eschatology and cosmological soteriology, are bound up in Schweitzer's central theme: the doctrine of "being-in-Christ," or *Christusmystik* (Christ-mysticism). For Schweitzer's Paul, the "prime enigma" of Pauline theology is that the believer,[19] through union with Christ in his death and resurrection, participates now in the age to come and the cosmic redemption it brings. Since the present age persists, the Christian life is thus characterized by a cosmic struggle with angelic powers until the imminent eschatological consummation,[20] but their reality is one of sharing in Christ's resurrection life. In union with Christ the elect are like a submerged volcanic island in the process of rising from the waves but of which only the peak (the resurrected Christ) is presently visible.[21] Only at the consummation of that kingdom, Schweitzer argues, does this "Christ-mysticism" (being-in-Christ) give way to "God-mysticism" (being-in-God), Christ having destroyed death as the last enemy and handed over the kingdom to God in order

---

16. Schweitzer, *Mysticism*, 54.
17. Schweitzer, *Mysticism*, 98.
18. Schweitzer, *Mysticism*, 54–57.
19. Schweitzer, *Mysticism*, 3.
20. Schweitzer, *Mysticism*, 66.
21. Schweitzer deploys this image in *Mysticism*, 112. See now also Barclay's interaction with it in "The Day is at Hand."

that he may be "all in all" (1 Cor 15:26–28).²² It is this thoroughly eschatological "Christ-mysticism" that constitutes the architectonic framework of Schweitzer's Pauline theology and within which key doctrines are located.

The most significant example of this is his treatment of "righteousness by faith," which Schweitzer takes up towards the end of *Mysticism*. Deploying another geological metaphor, Schweitzer describes how "being-in-Christ" is the "main crater" of Pauline theology within whose rim the doctrine of righteousness by faith forms a subsidiary crater (*Nebenkrater*).²³ Paul speaks of the atoning sacrifice of Jesus's death, to be sure, and of the consequent forgiveness of sins, but for Schweitzer this way of speaking is circumscribed by Paul's preferred language of the cosmic abolition of sin in the death and resurrection of Jesus and, supremely, the believer's union with him in it.²⁴ Righteousness by faith is thus a consequence and "first effect" of this union with Christ,²⁵ by which believers possess in advance the righteous existence proper to the eschatological Messianic kingdom.

Weiss's and Schweitzer's works may have placed apocalyptic back on the radar of New Testament scholarship, but it nevertheless remained "an unfashionable theme,"²⁶ sidelined from Pauline exegesis and given very little specific attention in the major reference works produced in the period between the two World Wars.²⁷ However, a generation after Schweitzer, a debate began which turned the tide and brought apocalyptic front and center in Pauline theology. It is a debate which remains crucial to understanding the contours of the ongoing conversation about the Apocalyptic Paul, even today.

1.2 Rudolf Bultmann: Demythologizing Apocalyptic

Rudolf Bultmann, who completed his doctorate at Marburg under Weiss's supervision and whose ideas on the question were already taking shape in the 1920s, agreed with his teacher and with Schweitzer that the apocalyptic

---

22. See Schweitzer, *Mysticism*, 12–13.
23. Schweitzer, *Mysticism*, 225.
24. See Schweitzer, *Mysticism*, 223.
25. Schweitzer, *Mysticism*, 205.
26. Käsemann, *New Testament Questions*, 108.
27. See the discussion of Kittel, Strack-Billerbeck, and the *TWNT* in Koch, *Rediscovery*, 60–61.

mythological worldview was central to the thought of Jesus and Paul.[28] He agreed that the dominant concept of the message of Jesus was the "kingdom of God," understood as the imminent eschatological irruption of God's victory over anti-God powers, a liberating reign brought about by God alone without human effort.[29] He also agreed that the sources and proper context for this eschatological expectation were the Jewish apocalyptic writings, and in particular their discussions of the "two ages." The enduring question, however, was what the contemporary theologian was to do with all this. As we have seen, Weiss and Schweitzer had posed and answered this question in their own way, and this set the stage for Bultmann's very different contribution. Discussing Weiss's influence, Bultmann recalls the impact it had on him and others.

> When I began to study theology, theologians and laymen were excited and frightened by the theories of Johannes Weiss. I remember that Julius Kaftan, my teacher in dogmatics in Berlin, said: "If Johannes Weiss is right and the conception of the kingdom of God is an eschatological one, then it is impossible to make use of this conception in dogmatics."[30]

The apocalyptic Jesus of Weiss's investigations was a strange Jesus: not a comfortable, liberal, middle-class modern man but one whose thought was fundamentally shaped by the foreign world of first-century Jewish apocalyptic mythology.[31] And so, *mutatis mutandis*, was Schweitzer's Paul. What was today's theology to make of this strange new world of New Testament investigation? For Bultmann, the answer lay in his (in)famous program of *demythologization,* the classic formulation of which came in his 1941 essay "Neues Testament und Mythologie: Das Problem der Entmythologisierung der neutestamentlichen Verkündigung" (ET: "The New Testament and Mythology: The Problem of Demythologizing the New Testament Proclamation").[32] The pre-scientific cosmology and eschatology that characterized the New Testament apocalyptic "mythical world picture"

---

28. He also agreed with Schweitzer on the importance of Weiss's book, calling it, as Schweitzer had done, "epoch-making" (in Bultmann, *Jesus Christ*, 12).

29. Bultmann, *Theology of the New Testament*, 4.

30. Bultmann, *Jesus Christ*, 13. Bultmann goes on to note that Kaftan would be among many theologians who eventually agreed that Weiss was right.

31. See Bultmann's preface to Weiss, *Jesus's Proclamation*, xii.

32. The essay can conveniently be accessed in Bultmann, *New Testament and Mythology*, 1–43.

(*mythische Weltbild*), Bultmann argued, are simply incredible for the contemporary world. Repristinating such an understanding of the cosmos would be both impossible and pointless for the contemporary Christian. Since our thinking has been irreversibly transformed by modern science, sheer resolve will not make such a mythological worldview possible for the Christian today. As Bultmann famously put it, "we cannot use electric lights and radios and, in the event of illness, avail ourselves of modern medical and clinical means and at the same time believe in the spirit and wonder world of the New Testament."[33] The meaning of Jesus's apocalyptic message of the kingdom of God, or of Paul's apocalyptic gospel, was not to be interpreted according to such a mythological view of the world. Instead, the Christian proclamation, whether of Jesus or of Paul, must be reinterpreted and translated into the contemporary idiom—this was the task of theology. Moreover, this reinterpretation, Bultmann insisted, must be a *wholesale* treatment of all such mythology. We cannot pick and choose which myths to demythologize: "we can only completely accept the mythical world picture or completely reject it."[34] Anything else would render Christian theology either irrelevant or inconsistent.

Bultmann located this reinterpretation in an anthropological (which for him meant *existential*) approach to the interpretation of New Testament mythological worldview. Approached in this way, apocalyptic language in Paul becomes a way of understanding present authentic human existence. This approach, Bultmann insisted, can and must be applied wholesale to every doctrine and to all areas of Pauline apocalyptic theology. Pauline cosmology, eschatology, anthropology, and soteriology are thus all passed through this demythologizing translation process.[35] Language of cosmic powers, for instance, must be interpreted as way of understanding our present captivity to our own fallenness. Future eschatology must be transposed into a present eschatology located in the moment of individual responsibility, the urgent existential decision of the "day of salvation" in which "the life of the future has already become present."[36]

In this way, apocalyptic remained a central concern in Bultmann's reading of Paul, though in what Koch called a "completely negative respect."[37] In

---

33. Bultmann, *New Testament and Mythology*, 4.
34. Bultmann, *New Testament and Mythology*, 9.
35. Bultmann, *New Testament and Mythology*, 4–6.
36. Bultmann, *New Testament and Mythology*, 19.
37. Koch, *Rediscovery*, 66. The result was, in one recent assessment, a

his later defense of his ideas, Bultmann accepted that there was a negative perspective to his approach, as interpretation which critiques myth and subjects it to destruction in the light of modern scientific thinking. There was, however, also a positive way of seeing it. Bultmann contended that his hermeneutical method did not ultimately do violence to New Testament mythology, but rather was faithful to it as a process of getting to the heart of what such myth intended to elicit from the interpreter. "Demythologizing interpretation," he argued, "seeks through its criticism to bring out the real intention of the biblical writings."[38] Bultmann saw himself in this regard as following in the hermeneutical footsteps of the writers of the New Testament themselves, Paul especially, as they interpreted the message of Jesus. His program of demythologization was an attempt to respect the intention of apocalyptic language in the New Testament, and to understand this cosmological imagery in anthropological terms. It is "existentialist interpretation, in that it seeks to make clear the intention of myth to talk about human existence."[39]

1.3 Ernst Käsemann: Apocalyptic as the Mother of Christian Theology

In what has been described as a "palace revolt" the strongest challenge to Bultmann's approach came from one of his own students.[40] Ernst Käsemann agreed with his teacher about the centrality of apocalyptic for understanding Paul, but in a bombastic series of essays published in the 1960s he insisted that Bultmann's demythologizing program, fueled by an individualistic and Heideggerian existential anthropology, anachronistically

---

"deapocalypticized Paul, a Paul with no future eschatology and no cosmological powers." (De Boer, "Paul's Mythologizing Program," 5.)

    38. Bultmann, "On the Problem of Demythologising (1952)" in *New Testament and Mythology*, 99.

    39. Bultmann, "On the Problem," 99.

    40. Matlock, *Unveiling*, 129. The combative language sometimes used to describe the debate can be taken to imply animosity or disrespect between the two scholars, especially given Käsemann's penchant for dramatic turns of phrase. But this would be a mistake. The nature of Käsemann's attitude toward Bultmann, as recalled by J. Louis Martyn, was that he was both "utterly respectful and thoroughly rebellious." (Martyn, "Personal Word About Ernst Käsemann," in Davis and Harink, *Apocalyptic and the Future*, xv). See also the discussion in Way, *Lordship*, 45.

prevented the apostle from speaking on his own terms.⁴¹ Among other things, for Käsemann this was crucially a matter of historical faithfulness to early Christian self-understanding: "the earliest Christian theology," he insisted, "cannot adequately be interpreted from an existentialist starting-point, if decisive weight is to be given to its fundamental understanding of itself."⁴² Thus, where Bultmann felt the demythologizing imperative, Käsemann affirmed the opposite, insisting on the positive significance of apocalyptic in Paul, much to the concern of Bultmann and his allies,⁴³ many of whom continued to view Jewish apocalyptic mythology with suspicion.

For many involved in today's ongoing discussion regarding the Apocalyptic Paul, it was Käsemann who fired the starting gun with his famous declaration that apocalyptic was "the mother of all Christian theology."⁴⁴ While the history surveyed so far shows that the issue was already on the table before he came along, Käsemann can certainly be credited with the most substantial and focused treatment of Pauline apocalyptic theology to date. It was his disagreement with Bultmann, and the latter's responses, that fueled Käsemann's investigations and formed the context that shaped his views. To this day, the debate between the two continues to leave its mark on discussion of the "apocalyptic" nature of Paul's thought.⁴⁵

---

41. In various ways this criticism had been around for a while. In 1941, Bultmann notes it yet insists that it misses the point. He insists that Heideggerian philosophy "all by itself already sees what the New Testament says" (*New Testament and Mythology*, 23). This assessment of Bultmann has been challenged recently (see Congdon, "Is Bultmann a Heideggerian Theologian?"). See also Koch *Rediscovery*, 67, arguing that Bultmann wasn't "a flight into inwardness."

42. Käsemann, *Questions*, 117.

43. E.g., Ebeling and Fuchs, see Koch, *Rediscovery*, 79–80.

44. Käsemann, *Questions*, 102. Martyn, assessing the "tectonic shift" represented by the contemporary apocalyptic approach to Paul described it as a "relatively new view, spawned originally and centrally by the work of Ernst Käsemann" (Martyn, "Afterword," 161). So also Barry Matlock: "'Apocalyptic' interpretation of Paul does not properly begin until Ernst Käsemann announces his verdict, with Paul as chief witness, that 'apocalyptic' is the beginning of Christian theology." (Matlock, *Unveiling*, 129). See also Koch's assessment: "up to then apocalyptic had been for biblical scholarship something on the periphery of the Old and New Testaments—something bordering on heresy. Käsemann had suddenly declared that a tributary was the main stream, from which everything else at the end of the Old Testament and the beginning of the New was allegedly fed." (Koch, *Rediscovery*, 14.)

45. See, e.g., de Boer "Paul's Mythologising Program," 3–7; Davis, "Introduction: The Challenge of Apocalyptic to Modern Theology" in Davis and Harink, *Apocalyptic and the Future*, 31–36; Campbell, *Deliverance*, 188–89.

The disagreement between them can be most clearly seen in their treatments of anthropology and cosmology. Where Bultmann had transposed cosmology into anthropology, Käsemann pushed forcefully in the opposite direction, placing anthropology within an apocalyptic cosmological frame. In his 1957 essay "Neutestamentliche Fragen von Heute" (the lead essay in the 1969 collection translated into English as *New Testament Questions of Today*, a title certain to get his former teacher's attention), Käsemann argued that Bultmann's individualist anthropology was irretrievably compromised in that it denied Paul's apocalyptic vision of humanity its cosmic breadth.[46] For Käsemann's Paul, the world is not neutral ground but a battlefield in the war between cosmic powers.[47] Humankind is therefore defined, as it were, from "outside," not as individuals faced with the moment of existential decision but as combatants caught up in a cosmic war. Anthropology, for Käsemann, is thus cosmology *in concreto*.[48] The resulting apocalyptic focal point of Paul's thought, for Käsemann, is not the crisis of decision but the question "to whom does the sovereignty of the world belong?"[49] This, he argued, is what it means to understand Paul's anthropology apocalyptically.

Käsemann's thoroughly apocalyptic refocusing of the center of Paul's thought was not, however, simply a return to Weiss and Schweitzer. While he was gratefully indebted to their work on apocalyptic in New Testament thought, Käsemann went beyond them in his development of this theme and was clearly critical of the limitations of their efforts. For example, Weiss's negotiation of the historical and theological senses of Jesus's apocalyptic message of the kingdom had, in Käsemann's view, "retreated with all speed into the liberal conception of Jesus."[50] When it came to Schweitzer and his followers, Käsemann's opinion was that they had "got in their own way"[51] by restricting their enquiries about apocalyptic to historical Jesus questions rather than seeing it as generative of the earliest Christian theology, including and especially the Pauline doctrine of justification. Käsemann thought this narrowly historical-critical approach ultimately "obscured rather than

---

46. See the discussion in Käsemann, *Questions*, 14–15.

47. Käsemann, *Perspectives*, 23.

48. "On Paul's Anthropology," *Perspectives*, 27; "anthropology must then *eo ipso* be cosmology" (23).

49. Käsemann, *Questions*, 135.

50. Käsemann, *Questions*, 109n2.

51. Käsemann, *Questions*, 101.

illuminated the true state of affairs,"⁵² and considered it vital that this was integrated into theological interpretation. The depth of his concern to deploy the apocalyptic question in the realm of Christian dogmatics is no more clear than when he closed his discussion of the importance of apocalyptic to post-Easter faith by asking "whether Christian theology can ever survive in any legitimate form without this theme."⁵³

A word is due at this point on the importance of Karl Barth for Käsemann's approach to apocalyptic theology. Here and elsewhere his similarity with Barth's concerns and theological foci are clear, and Käsemann himself testifies in various places to his influence when it came to the theological exegesis of Paul, including Käsemann's own commentary on Romans.⁵⁴ He did not study directly with Barth at Münster, but he later recalled how he "devoured his writings ravenously" and found his own hermeneutical convictions particularly reflected in the prefaces to Barth's *Römerbrief*.⁵⁵ For Käsemann, it was Barth who "brought 'thoroughgoing eschatology' back out of its existence among the shades and made it the keynote of New Testament interpretation."⁵⁶ As we will see, this conviction has remained a central and generative characteristic of the Apocalyptic Paul ever since.

In developing his apocalyptic reading of Paul's theology, Käsemann placed his doctrinal emphasis not on the "kingdom of God" or on "Christ-mysticism" but on the doctrine of justification, and in particular the interpretation of this doctrine through the Pauline motif of the "righteousness of God" (δικαιοσύνη θεοῦ). This was both the "nucleus" of Pauline theology and its central problem.⁵⁷ Käsemann understood the phrase as referring not to a righteousness bestowed upon us by God but one which is proper to God himself. This Pauline doctrine of justification, he believed, could only be interpreted against a Jewish apocalyptic background, cosmologically modified.⁵⁸ When located in this cosmological-apocalyptic frame, Käse-

---

52. Käsemann, *Questions*, 113.

53. Käsemann, *Questions*, 107.

54. Way, *Lordship*, 40, cf. Ziegler, "Some Remarks on Apocalyptic in Modern Christian Theology" in Blackwell et al., *Apocalyptic Imagination*, 204.

55. Käsemann, *Nazarene*, xv.

56. Käsemann, *Questions*, 109n2.

57. Käsemann, *Questions*, 168; see Way, *Lordship*, 280.

58. Though he worked this out most thoroughly in the 1960s in various essays and his Romans commentary, this was a position Käsemann seems to have held many years earlier, as expressed in a letter to Bultmann dated April 18, 1949: "one can only understand the Pauline doctrine of justification against the background of Jewish apocalyptic

mann understood justification not as the salvation of the individual but as the militant saving power of God in recapturing the embattled cosmos for himself.[59] As with Schweitzer, then, this was an approach to redemption as liberative "world event" rather than "transaction."

Käsemann's theological concerns were not, of course, restricted to the refutation of Bultmannian demythologization and the development of a fresh reading of justification. His apocalyptic approach to this doctrine in Paul was also a challenge to Krister Stendahl and Oscar Cullmann (who were themselves challenging Bultmann's hermeneutical program in other ways) in respect of their treatment of the question of salvation history. Käsemann insisted that Paul remained an apocalyptic thinker whose belief was characterized by a future eschatology,[60] and who looked for an imminent *parousia*. In this connection, it may be tempting to think that an apocalyptic Paul according to Käsemann involves a straightforward rejection of all linear schemes of salvation-history, but this would be seriously to misread him. Käsemann was clear in his affirmation of salvation history as an indisputable horizon for Pauline theology,[61] without which it would be "impossible to understand the bible in general or Paul in particular,"[62] but he nevertheless challenged some (to his mind) dangerous definitions of the term. In particular, he remained vigorously resistant to any construal of *Heilsgeschichte* as an "immanent evolutionary process whose meaning can be grasped on earth, or which we can control or calculate."[63] At this point, Käsemann did not mask the importance of his own context and experience as one of the "burnt children" of Nazism, which he thought represented a secularized political expression of a nineteenth-century liberal progressive-evolutionary theology of history. In Käsemann's view, this particular conception of salvation history was a disease, relapsing repeatedly in a century of German theology, the vaccine for which was a proper account of the

---

and that in it one must see an adaptation of the cosmological views of this apocalyptic." (Quoted in Way, *Lordship*, 123.)

59. See "Gottesgerechtigkeit bei Paulus," 367–78 (ET: "The Righteousness of God in Paul" in *Questions*, 168–82).

60. Contra Bultmann, Käsemann thought that Bultmann performed a reduction of "God's future to man's futurity." (Käsemann, *Questions*, 96.)

61. Käsemann, *Perspectives*, 66.

62. Käsemann, *Perspectives*, 63.

63. Käsemann, *Perspectives*, 63.

doctrine of justification.⁶⁴ Salvation history in Paul, then, should not be rejected but must be subordinated to this doctrine.⁶⁵

For Käsemann, then, salvation history's importance as the indispensable horizon of Pauline thought is only defensible if such progressive-evolutionary continuities are rejected, and history is instead understood as an apocalyptic battlefield between the powers of death and life, sin and salvation, and therefore as the locus of the promise and triumph of God.⁶⁶ Käsemann's approach to salvation history, therefore, contrasted sharply with the version advocated by Cullmann, who saw the Christ-event as D-Day, with V-Day just ahead, the result of the church's inexorable triumphant progress. As such, though history measured by "human criteria" is nothing short of disastrous, salvation-historical continuity may nevertheless be affirmed theologically. Käsemann concluded that this affirmation of both continuity and discontinuity meant that "the Pauline proclamation of the reality of salvation history is deeply paradoxical."⁶⁷ Perhaps for the first time, these signature concerns of Käsemann's Pauline theology brought into coherence the principal themes of what would become the apocalyptic reading of Paul and, as we will soon see, his work continues to exercise profound influence over the contemporary discussion.

1.4 J. Christiaan Beker: Apocalyptic and the Triumph of God

Ever since the debate between Käsemann and Bultmann, the motif of God's cosmic triumph has left an indelible mark on apocalyptic treatments of Paul, and an example of this is found in the work of J. Christiaan Beker. In 1980, Beker published his most expansive treatment of Pauline theology, *Paul the Apostle: The Triumph of God in Life and Thought*. In two short opening chapters, Beker outlined the dominant architectonic question of his Pauline theology, that of the contingency and coherence of Paul's letters. In seeking to describe the "center" of Paul's thought in which to anchor its coherence, Beker argued that, despite a history of scholarship that had suppressed it,

---

64. I am here summarizing Käsemann's "personal reminiscence" in Käsemann, *Perspectives*, 63–64. Here Käsemann sounds like Barth, who describes his own earlier reading of Paul as an "antiseptic" against these views in German political life (Barth, *CD* I/2 §14, 50).

65. Way, *Lordship*, 285.

66. Käsemann, *Perspectives*, 67.

67. Käsemann, *Perspectives*, 68.

an apocalyptic framework for Paul's thought offered the best option. His dramatic conclusion is that "only a consistent apocalyptic interpretation of Paul's thought is able to demonstrate its fundamental coherence."[68]

Beker largely followed Käsemann in protesting against an introspective distortion of Paul's gospel, offering as a correction an exposition of the Christ-event as "the reversal of the ages" and the righteousness of God as "God's liberating act for his creation."[69] He also echoed and joined Käsemann in challenging Bultmann, insisting that Pauline apocalyptic is oriented toward the cosmological rather than the anthropological pole. In Beker's view, this eschatological and liberative proclamation of the triumph of God was the only viable solution to the jaded quest for the Pauline "center." However, he also posed a challenge to Käsemann in the form of a different approach to this question. This "center," he stressed, must not be understood as a dominant theme or symbol in Paul's thought. That, Beker suggested, was a methodological error at the heart of Käsemann's apocalyptic reading of the righteousness of God. Rather, the "center" should be construed not as a theme but as a "symbolic structure," the linguistic expression of Paul's encounter with the risen Christ. This language, which therefore expresses Paul's thought, is the language of Jewish apocalyptic, christologically intensified and modified. Understood in this way, Christian apocalyptic constitutes the "heart of Paul's gospel."[70] Beker saw in this approach a way through the impasse created by the Bultmann-Käsemann debate. Bultmann had identified the apocalyptic theme and dismissed it as an existential projection of the human plight, using obsolete mythological language, rather than the reality of God's triumph and the core of Paul's gospel.[71] Käsemann fused apocalyptic with the theme of the righteousness of God, and identified this theme as the Pauline center. Both were mistaken, Beker thought, in being caught up in a conceptual fallacy, namely the search for a dominant central theme or symbol, and they therefore failed to identify that apocalyptic is not a concept, even a central one, but the very "texture of Paul's thought."[72]

---

68. Beker, *Paul the Apostle*, 143.
69. Beker, *Paul the Apostle*, 7.
70. Beker, *Paul the Apostle*, 17.
71. Beker, *Paul the Apostle*, 140–41.
72. Beker, *Paul the Apostle*, 16–17.

The Genealogy of the Apocalyptic Paul

Given the significance Beker attaches to the apocalyptic texture of Paul's theology, it is a surprising fact (noted by various readers)[73] that Beker's work provided very little by way of his own direct engagement with the apocalyptic literature. This was likely not due to a methodological commitment, since Beker was clearly convinced that Paul's apocalyptic gospel derives its various components from the Second Temple Jewish apocalyptic literature.[74] Apocalyptic, for Beker, is a language, a "symbolic structure" taken from the Jewish apocalypticism in which Paul lived and thought and which, once christologically nourished, intensified, and modified, is the "indispensable means for his interpretation of the Christ-event."[75] Yet instead of offering his own exegetical exposition of these components from the Jewish apocalypses, or from Paul, Beker relied on the definitions provided by Philipp Vielhauer and Klaus Koch,[76] preferring the latter due to his greater emphasis on the linearity of salvation history. From these two scholars Beker distilled his own definition of the apocalyptic worldview, beginning his major discussion of Paul's apocalyptic theology by boiling down their descriptions of the apocalyptic worldview into three essential components: "(1) historical dualism; (2) universal cosmic expectation; and (3) the imminent end of the world."[77] The result of this approach is that apocalyptic is, in Beker's view, sharply (and almost exclusively) focused on eschatology. When Beker turned to Paul, he explored how the apostle's apocalyptic gospel modifies these essential eschatological ideas in the light of the Christ-event.

First, the stark historical dualism of the "two ages" of the Jewish apocalyptic worldview is, for Beker, both tempered and intensified in Pauline apocalyptic. The "old age" is not straightforwardly an age of sin and death but contains the "hidden presence of God's promises."[78] It is crucial to Beker's approach, therefore, that an apocalyptic interpretation of Paul marries the liberative core of his gospel, the triumph of God, to a salvation-historical scheme, properly understood as God's faithfulness to his

---

73. See, e.g., Matlock, *Unveiling*, 247; Sturm, "Defining," 36; de Boer, *Defeat of Death*, 33.

74. Beker, *Paul's Apocalyptic Gospel*, 30.

75. Beker, *Paul the Apostle*, 19. See the whole discussion in pages 15–19.

76. See Vielhauer, "Apocalypses" and Koch, *Rediscovery*. As we will see in section 4.1, this reliance on the definitions of Vielhauer and Koch remains, in the view of some, an ongoing limitation of the Apocalyptic Paul.

77. Beker, *Paul the Apostle*, 136.

78. Beker, *Paul the Apostle*, 151.

promises and the climax of his plan of redemption.[79] However, like Käsemann before him, Beker did not allow this tempering of historical dualism to lead to a smoothly continuous understanding of redemptive history, since the Christ-event also represents the "incursion" of the age to come into the present,[80] intensifying an eschatological crisis of conflict between the powers of death and life. While they are in agreement on this essentially disruptive point, Beker nevertheless remained committed to the essentially linear salvation-historical framing of this divine incursion, and this represented a distinctive contrast to Käsemann's approach. Where Käsemann had rejected Cullmann's linear analogy of Pauline inaugurated eschatology as D-Day and V-Day, Beker embraced it as a helpful way of thinking "bifocally" about Pauline eschatology.[81]

Second, the universal cosmic expectation characteristic of Beker's Pauline apocalyptic theology is a result of his twin emphases on the divine cosmic triumph and (again with Käsemann) the cosmological understanding of the human person, inextricably involved in that cosmic conflict. In Beker's view, the Jewish apocalyptic expectation of God's triumph was rooted in the particularity of the election of the people of Israel, a vision Beker describes as "introverted rather than extroverted."[82] In Paul's christological modification of that expectation, however, the locus of judgment and the horizon of expectation are both cosmic and universal. Though he recognizes that Paul stops short of an unequivocal universalism, Beker is clear on where the emphasis lies. "Because the person is viewed from a cosmic perspective," he argues,

> a profound solidarity and interdependence exists among the people in the world, a solidarity which even reaches into the realm of nature . . . This means that, until all of God's creation comes to its destiny of glory, neither God himself is vindicated nor the human being completely or fully "saved."[83]

Third, Beker considers the Pauline modification of the apocalyptic-eschatological theme of the imminent end of the world. Faced with the stark reality of continuing chronological time, Beker refuses to follow the

---

79. Beker, *Paul's Apocalyptic Gospel*, 30–40. Here, Beker shows his preference for Koch over Vielhauer; see 136.
80. Beker, *Paul's Apocalyptic Gospel*, 40.
81. See Beker, *Paul the Apostle*, 159, 177, 179. See also de Boer, *Defeat of Death*, 33.
82. Beker, *Paul's Apocalyptic Gospel*, 35.
83. Beker, *Paul's Apocalyptic Gospel*, 36.

Bultmannian path of demythologizing or neutralizing Paul's statements about eschatological imminence. As modified in Pauline apocalyptic, Beker argues, "imminence" means only "the sense that, with apocalyptic authors, Paul expects the future to entail a definitive closure/completion-event in time and space, rather than a continuous, open-ended process."[84]

Beker's identification and development of apocalyptic as the coherent center of Pauline thought does not mean, of course, that the matter of contingency had been left behind. For Beker, the letters of Paul demonstrated considerable variety in the deployment of the apocalyptic texture of his thought according to their different contextual situations, and consideration of Paul's contextual expressions of his thought in different letters was essential to the task of Pauline theology. The two letters given closest attention in Beker's work, Romans and Galatians, are not viewed as abstract doctrinal treatises but as highly situational and contingent expressions of Paul's gospel and are to be interpreted as such. Thus, the apocalyptic "indicative" of God's triumph in Christ is indexed in various ways to the "imperative" of Paul's epistolary arguments to diverse audiences. In his first letter to Corinth, for example, this apocalyptic texture is clearly imposed on the situation as Paul responds to Hellenistic enthusiasts who, in Beker's view, thought "in spatial-vertical categories rather than in the temporal-historical categories of apocalyptic thought."[85] This logic is clearly what drives Beker to locate his most detailed exegetical discussion of Pauline apocalyptic theology in his discussion of 1 Cor 15.[86] When it comes to Galatians, however, the virtual absence of the resurrection and the paucity of future eschatological language suggests to Beker that the apocalyptic texture of Paul's thought is here significantly suppressed in response to a different contextual challenge,[87] namely the threat to his gospel from "Judaizers and Jews" who have created a situation which restricts Paul's full expression of his apocalyptic-eschatological gospel.[88]

The significance of Beker's work did not take long to be recognized. Two years after its publication, *Paul the Apostle* was reviewed by another Pauline scholar whose name has since become synonymous with the Apocalyptic Paul: J. Louis Martyn, to whom we now turn.

---

84. Beker, *Paul's Apocalyptic Gospel*, 50.
85. Beker, *Paul the Apostle*, 165.
86. Beker, *Paul the Apostle*, 163–76.
87. Beker, *Paul the Apostle*, x.
88. Beker, *Paul the Apostle*, 151.

1.5 J. Louis Martyn: Apocalyptic Invasion

Martyn's review of Beker's *Paul the Apostle* hailed it as "the strongest and the most compelling" attempt in recent years at a comprehensive treatment of Paul's thought.[89] In particular, he agreed heartily with Beker's central conviction that the best hope for coherence was to be found in a "consistent apocalyptic interpretation" of Paul's contingent letters.[90] This agreement was in large part due to the two scholars' shared indebtedness to Käsemann, as Martyn observed. His review took issue, however, with one of the points of friction between Beker's approach and that of Käsemann, namely the question of Pauline apocalyptic and salvation history. Martyn noted Beker's "marriage between apocalyptic (as core) and salvation history (as structure?)"[91] and challenged it as an unwelcome suppression of the disjunctive apocalyptic eschatological dualism of the two ages in favor of a more linear-progressive approach to history. Martyn's opinion was that this combination of salvation history and apocalyptic was a marriage "rather more arranged by Beker than discovered in Paul" and that it owed more to a distillation of Koch than to exegesis of Paul's letters.[92] Nevertheless, the question of the relationship of salvation history to apocalyptic (and the proper definition of both terms) had been posed afresh in relation to Paul, and Martyn took up this challenge in his own work.

Martyn's apocalyptic approach to Paul was developed over the next three decades, but is best encapsulated in two volumes published in 1997, both of which have proven programmatic for the contemporary discussion: the Anchor Bible commentary on Galatians (which Martyn dedicated to Käsemann), and the edited collection of essays published as *Theological Issues in the Letters of Paul*, which also gave considerable attention to that letter and included the Beker review as an appendix to an essay on the Abrahamic covenant in Gal 3–4.[93] No doubt Beker would have considered Martyn's focus on Galatians a less than promising decision for an apocalyptic reading of Paul; he had, after all, considered that letter an example of a contingent Pauline suppression of the apocalyptic theme of his gospel.

---

89. Martyn, "Review," 194.
90. Martyn, "Review," 196.
91. Martyn, "Review," 196.
92. Martyn, "Review," 196.
93. "The Abrahamic Covenant, Christ, and the Church" and its Appendix, Martyn, *Theological Issues*, 161–82.

Käsemann, likewise, had made almost no reference to Galatians in his various essays on Pauline apocalyptic thought. Martyn, however, made it the keystone of his discussions of Paul's apocalyptic theology. In his view, both Beker and Käsemann had relied too heavily on making an eschatology of imminent expectation and future triumph the *sine qua non* of apocalyptic thought, and this had the effect of blinkering their vision when it came to Galatians, in which such themes are largely absent. Crucial to removing these blinkers was allowing that letter to inform a fresh reconsideration of the apocalyptic heart of Paul's gospel. Martyn sought to demonstrate that Pauline apocalyptic, properly defined, is emphatically not suppressed in Galatians. After all, as Martyn had earlier said to Beker, it is a letter "in which Paul says with unmistakable emphasis that the truth of the gospel is a matter of apocalypse."[94] But what did Martyn mean by that?

In a number of exegetical-theological comments punctuating the Galatians commentary, as well as in many of the essays gathered in *Theological Issues* and elsewhere, Martyn outlined his understanding of Paul's apocalyptic theology. A proper account of Pauline apocalyptic thought, in Martyn's view, should be oriented not around an imminent *parousia* but around the theme of *invasion*, a ubiquitous category in Martyn's discussions which has profound implications for his reading of Paul's apocalyptic eschatology, epistemology, cosmology, and soteriology.

Let us begin with eschatology. Despite voicing concerns about the weight attached to imminent eschatology in Beker and Käsemann's definitions, Martyn certainly does not play down the eschatological features of Paul's apocalyptic theology, and nor does he find those features completely suppressed in Paul's letter to the Galatians. The signal expression τοῦ αἰῶνος τοῦ ἐνεστῶτος πονηροῦ, "the present evil age" (Gal 1:4b) is, in Martyn's view, the first clear indication of the letter's apocalyptic theology, for the eschatological motif of the "two ages" indicated by this expression was "a scheme fundamental to apocalyptic thought."[95] For Martyn, a crucial step in allowing Galatians to inform our understanding of Pauline apocalyptic was recognizing that the interrelationship of the present evil age and the new creation is best understood through the motif of invasion, not an imminent *parousia*. What this allows us to see, Martyn argues, is that the disjunctive apocalypse of Jesus Christ results in "a radically new perception

---

94. Martyn, "Review," 196. Beker would later accept Martyn's critique regarding the value of Galatians (see *Paul the Apostle*, xix).

95. Martyn, *Galatians*, 98.

of time"⁹⁶ best understood in a punctiliar, rather than linear, mode. The apocalyptic eschatological question "what time is it?" receives its answer as God sends Christ "onto the scene" of history "at a time selected by him" (Martyn's preferred rendering of τὸ πλήρωμα τοῦ χρόνου in Gal 4:4).⁹⁷ It is therefore the end of the "present evil age" and "the dawn of the new creation."⁹⁸ In this way, Martyn rejects all redemptive-historical schemes which view the two ages in linear terms of "before" and "after" or which see the "fullness of time" as a point that lies at the end of a line. His particular focus in this rejection, however, is on evolutionary schemes which view salvation history as an immanent, gradual maturation. "For Paul, therefore, as for all thoroughly apocalyptic thinkers, this liberating redemption does not at all grow out of the present scene. Redemption is a matter of God's invasive movement into that scene."⁹⁹ In the place of all such linear schemes, Martyn argues in favor of a polemically punctiliar and singular liberative invasion, insisting that this polemic is crucial to Paul's apocalyptic gospel in Galatians.

The revelation of Jesus Christ at the turn of the ages constitutes not only an eschatological irruption but also an "epistemological crisis." In his Galatians commentary, Martyn notes Paul's repeated use of revelatory vocabulary (Gal 1:12, 16; 2:2, 5, 14) as an indication of his apocalyptic epistemology. Perhaps his most influential discussion of Pauline apocalyptic epistemology is, however, an early essay on 2 Cor 5:16–17 entitled "Epistemology at the Turn of the Ages."¹⁰⁰ In that essay, Martyn argued that Paul's use of the expression κατὰ σάρκα in 2 Cor 5:16a is adverbial, which is to say it denotes not the object of knowledge but a fleshly "way of knowing," which is operative in the present age within which the Corinthians used to regard Christ. Correspondingly, since the death and resurrection of Christ have decisively launched the new age, Paul advocates a new "way of knowing." The turn of the ages brought about by the apocalyptic invasion of God in Christ separates these two incompatible ways of knowing. However, importantly for Paul's purposes in addressing the enthusiastic excesses in Corinth, this epistemology is not located as an unambiguous arrival of the

---

96. Martyn, *Galatians*, 104.
97. See Martyn, *Galatians*, 388–89.
98. Martyn, *Theological Issues*, 122.
99. Martyn, *Galatians*, 100.
100. Martyn, "Epistemology" (reproduced in *Theological Issues* 89–110). See also Martyn, *Galatians*, 104.

"new age" way of thinking according to the Spirit (as if the antithesis to knowledge κατὰ σάρκα were straightforwardly knowledge κατὰ πνεῦμα) but a way of knowing characteristic of the point at which the ages meet. For Martyn, Paul's apocalyptic epistemology is κατὰ σταυρόν, a way of knowing that confronts both the fleshly knowing of the present age and an enthusiastic claim to unambiguous "spiritual" epistemology with a way of knowing according to the cross. This apocalyptic epistemology, Martyn argues, is inadequately captured by language of "unveiling" mysteries, but is better seen in more radical irruptive terms, a "disjunctive apocalypse" constituted by the dawn of the new creation. This is an epistemological earthquake, whose aftershocks are felt throughout Paul's theology, not least due to its illustration that, for Martyn's Paul, there is "an inextricable connection between eschatology and epistemology."[101]

This apocalyptic invasion is not only an epistemological and eschatological irruption but a cosmological one, and one which therefore shapes Paul's apocalyptic soteriology. Alongside the eschatological question "What time is it?" is the cosmological question "In what cosmos do we actually live?"[102] The answer, for Martyn, is that the present cosmos is enemy-held territory, and thus the invasive Christ-event launches an offensive which commences "the war of liberation from the powers of the present evil age."[103] The result is that the old cosmos which God has invaded has itself been altered by that invasion, with far-reaching theological implications. Paul's argument in Galatians does not proceed, therefore, "on the basis of a cosmos that remains undisturbed."[104] The antinomies that characterized the present evil age (Jew/Greek; slave/free; male/female) have been dissolved, and new antinomies (Flesh/Spirit; faith in Christ/Law) have emerged.[105] The cross of Christ, as the invasion that launches a war against the enslaving powers of the present evil age, results in an anthropology and soteriology oriented "not towards personal guilt and forgiveness but toward corporate enslavement and liberation."[106] Here Martyn's indebtedness to Käsemann is most clear, in their shared emphasis on the nature of justification as liberative

---

101. Martyn, "Epistemology," 92.
102. Martyn, *Galatians*, 23.
103. Martyn, *Galatians*, 105.
104. Martyn, *Galatians*, 22.
105. Martyn, *Galatians*, 570–74 and *Issues* ch. 7.
106. Martyn, *Galatians*, 101.

event, with the attendant understanding of Paul's apocalyptic cosmology and anthropology.

In his earlier expression of this apocalyptic soteriology, Martyn drew a sharp dichotomy between juridical and liberative approaches to justification, as the above quotation shows. In his later discussions, however, Martyn articulated a more nuanced view than the stark dualism implied by the "not . . . but" of this earlier statement, arguing for the interrelationship of "guilt" and "deliverance."[107] While still seeing the motif of slavery/deliverance as "primary" and that of guilt/forgiveness as "secondary," he saw them not as a strict dichotomy but bound up together in tension. Interpretative help in this regard, he suggested, might be found in the category of human "complicity" with enemy powers,[108] a suggestion which other scholars have since taken up, as we will soon see.

Martyn's influence on the contemporary discussion of the Apocalyptic Paul is hard to overestimate. Before he passed away in 2015, it was clear that this group of conversation partners were becoming something of a "school," and now it is regularly recognized that it constitutes a distinct interpretation of Paul worthy of its own place at the table of Pauline perspectives. In the second section of this book, our attention turns to this contemporary discussion.

---

107. Martyn, "Afterword," 163.
108. Martyn, "Afterword," 163.

CHAPTER 2

The Apocalyptic Paul in Contemporary Scholarship

A NUMBER OF CONTEMPORARY Pauline scholars have taken up Martyn's theological framework and extended or nuanced his main lines of enquiry. Many of these were his former students and colleagues, as attested by the important contributions to the discussion made through *Festschriften* and other volumes in Martyn's honor.[1] The circle, however, is certainly wider than this, and broadening rapidly as more voices enter the conversation, including those (as chapter 3 will show) of systematic theologians. Much of this interdisciplinary work has been carried out through the SBL/AAR working group "Explorations in Theology and Apocalyptic," which first met in Montreal in 2009, discussing the influence of Martyn's work as its inaugural theme.

Though Martyn's *Galatians* remains enormously influential for its theological convictions and interpretative contours, and valuable additional work has been done on that letter (e.g., Martinus de Boer's *New Testament Library* commentary), the discussion has also rippled out to the other Pauline epistles. As will become clear, Romans (especially chapters 1–8) unsurprisingly features as a regular locus for discussion of Paul's apocalyptic thought (e.g., in the work of Beverly Gaventa and Douglas Campbell). There have also been important contributions to scholarship on 1 Corinthians (e.g., Martinus de Boer, Alexandra Brown), 2 Corinthians (Lisa Bowens), and Philippians (Susan Eastman). It is something of a surprise, given

---

1. Fortna and Gaventa, *Conversation Continues*; Marcus and Soards, *Apocalyptic and the New Testament*; Davis and Harink *Apocalyptic and the Future*; Gaventa, *Apocalyptic Paul*.

their obviously apocalyptic content, that the Thessalonian letters have yet to have their time in the spotlight, but perhaps this too will come in time.

What follows is a roughly chronological account of the main contributions to scholarship on the Apocalyptic Paul in the decades since Martyn's *Galatians*. However, since all the scholars named here are active participants in an ongoing discussion, this section is necessarily part "historical survey" and part "snapshot" of the contemporary state of play. To borrow the title of one of Martyn's *Festschriften*, "the conversation continues."[2] This being the case, this section of the book will probably be out of date very soon, as the scholars surveyed here continue to refine and develop their various contributions, and new voices emerge.[3] As will no doubt become obvious, in addition to a shared indebtedness to Martyn, there are numerous threads of mutual influence in the work surveyed below (we have, as it were, both the "vertical" and the "horizontal" to describe). As a result of this situation, there is a large amount of agreement on core themes, but also some important and theologically generative distinctives.

Two options immediately present themselves for how to structure an introduction to a live discussion such as this. The first is to survey the key themes and areas of agreement, noting each scholar's contribution to a shared apocalyptic perspective on Paul. This option, however, runs the risk of imposing a false homogeneity on what is actually a subtly diverse family of interpretations. As with any scholarly movement, no matter how clear the lines of genealogical influence, there is no singular "party line." The convention of labeling a "school" or a "perspective" is always something of a two-edged sword, simultaneously helpful and unhelpful, and the Apocalyptic Paul is no exception.

The second option for approaching this descriptive task would be to emphasize the distinctive contributions of each scholar through contrast with others. This, however, courts the equal and opposite danger of caricature, skewing the account too much toward what is different rather than what is held in common. To deploy a somewhat tired (but suitably apocalyptic!) image, we have here a Scylla and Charybdis situation.[4] In the

---

2. Fortna and Gaventa, *Conversation Continues*.

3. A summary of the work of Lisa Bowens has therefore been included here, by way of hearing one of these emerging voices, though of course more could be added from among what Alexandra Brown has called the "fourth wave" of scholarship on Paul's apocalyptic thought (Brown, Review of Davies, *Paul Among the Apocalypses*, 330).

4. Perhaps it's my interest in the book of Revelation, but I'm tempted to explore further the surplus of meaning in this imagery. Is Charybdis the vortex of homogeneity,

section that follows I have attempted to chart a course between both dangers, and to offer an account of each contributor to the discussion on their own terms. It is my hope these brief accounts of the various voices in the continuing conversation about the Apocalyptic Paul allow both the important theological similarities and the distinctive emphases of each scholar to emerge naturally, and in proper proportion.

2.1 Martinus de Boer: Two "Tracks" of Apocalyptic Eschatology

Among the names regularly appearing in Martyn's footnotes is that of Martinus de Boer, whose contribution to the debate about the Apocalyptic Paul began in his doctoral dissertation completed under Martyn's supervision at Union Theological Seminary in 1983. Subsequently revised and published under the title *The Defeat of Death: Apocalyptic Eschatology in 1 Corinthians 15 and Romans 5*, it was an important first statement of what would become de Boer's signature contribution to the discussion, outlining an analysis of Paul's apocalyptic thought which he then developed in a number of essays (including one on Paul for the *Encyclopedia of Apocalypticism*[5]) and his own commentary on Galatians, in which Martyn's enduring influence can clearly be seen. In *Defeat of Death*, de Boer traced the line of thought on Paul's apocalyptic theology from Schweitzer to Käsemann's debate with Bultmann, and on to Baumgarten and Beker. However, in addition to examining this genealogy, de Boer also developed his own lines of enquiry back to the Jewish apocalyptic literature. This corpus was and is frequently cited by de Boer, who regularly expresses the conviction that, when applied to Paul, the scholarly construct "apocalyptic eschatology" signals the presence of "conceptual affinities" between the apostle and the Jewish apocalypticism of his day.[6] Running through two decades of de Boer's work is the conviction that it is "difficult if not impossible to discuss Paul's apocalyptic eschatology apart from Jewish apocalyptic eschatology."[7] Of particular

---

sucking everything in, while Scylla, a monstrous caricature, stands the other side ready to devour the inattentive writer?

5. De Boer, "Paul and Apocalyptic Eschatology." This and numerous other essays on the subject have now been helpfully collected in *God's Apocalypse*.

6. De Boer, *Defeat of Death*, 7, 181.

7. De Boer, *God's Apocalypse*, 3, repeating the sentiment of "Paul and Apocalyptic Eschatology," 347.

concern are the eschatological expectations characteristic of the apocalypses, especially the distinctive commitment to a "two ages" eschatological dualism. When placed against this background, Paul's distinct expression of this eschatology, de Boer argues, can be found in the contrast between death and resurrection/eternal life in the christologically determined apocalyptic eschatology of 1 Corinthians 15 and Romans 5.

Throughout his analysis, de Boer has been relatively consistent in his use of "apocalyptic" as an adjective modifying the noun "eschatology," not a noun in itself.[8] Apocalyptic, as de Boer uses the term, is a form of eschatology.[9] This usage reflects a conviction that what is in view in this discussion is Paul's particular form of eschatology as a defining characteristic, rather than other apocalyptic motifs such as the revelation of mysteries.[10] De Boer's focus, as with Schweitzer and Käsemann, is on God's eschatological activity, rather than (say) a seer's mystical revelatory experiences. In this connection de Boer disagrees with scholars of the Jewish apocalyptic tradition (such as Christopher Rowland) who advocate examining apocalyptic thought with a broader scope that includes "communication of heavenly mysteries in all their diversity" rather than the narrower focus on eschatology preferred by Vielhauer, Hanson, and Collins.[11] That said, de Boer's particular eschatological approach to Paul's apocalyptic thought is by no means restricted to chronology, as we will see.

Perhaps de Boer's most enduringly significant contribution to the Apocalyptic Paul debate is his analysis that the Jewish apocalyptic literature is characterized by two eschatological "tracks," which he labels "forensic apocalyptic eschatology" and "cosmological apocalyptic eschatology."[12] This analysis was subsequently deployed by Martyn in his commentary on Galatians, and hailed as "extraordinarily perceptive" and "essential to the reading of Galatians."[13] While both apocalyptic "tracks" demonstrate the

---

8. Though he is content to deploy the word "apocalyptic" nominally, as a shorthand for 'apocalyptic eschatology' See de Boer "God's Eschatological Activity," 45 and *God's Apocalypse*, 1n1.

9. De Boer "God's Eschatological Activity," 51.

10. De Boer "God's Eschatological Activity," 51.

11. Rowland, *Open Heaven*, 14. De Boer's investigation of apocalyptic has frequently had cause to challenge Rowland (e.g., de Boer, "Paul, Theologian of God's Apocalypse" (now republished as ch. 2 of *God's Apocalypse*).

12. De Boer, "Paul and Jewish Apocalyptic Eschatology," 180 (now republished as ch. 1 in *God's Apocalypse*).

13. Martyn, *Galatians*, 97n51.

importance of a revelatory epistemology and an eschatological dualism, there are considerable differences between them.

"Forensic apocalyptic eschatology" is fundamentally characterized by a view of sin as human transgression against God's law, resulting in death in the present age and awaiting a final judgment in the age to come, with reward for the righteous and punishment for the wicked. The attribution of evil to cosmic forces such as rebellious angelic powers is largely absent, or even explicitly challenged, in this "track." Here the "two ages" are construed as linear and successive epochs of world history. Examples of this judicial form of apocalyptic eschatology can be seen in many places in the corpus of Jewish apocalypses, but it is particularly clear in two texts written in the wake of the destruction of the Jerusalem temple, 4 Ezra and 2 Baruch.

By contrast, "cosmological apocalyptic eschatology" takes these themes of sin, divine judgment, and the eschatological "two ages" and drives them in a completely different direction. This "track" plays down human transgression and forensic judgment and instead attributes sin and death to primordial angelic rebellion, resulting in cosmic warfare between God and his enemies. Accordingly, the eschatological expectation is not one of divine assize in the heavenly courtroom, but an imminent divine invasion and final battle ending in God's triumph and the deliverance of his world from captivity to these powers. De Boer detects this version of apocalyptic eschatology in its "purest form" in 1 Enoch,[14] particularly the Book of the Watchers (chapters 1–36). This "cosmological" framework of Jewish apocalyptic eschatology is still characterized by the motif of "two ages" but, in contrast to the "forensic" variety, these ages are not primarily understood in sequential chronological terms but as two radically opposed and discontinuous "spheres" or "orbs of power" which are both temporal and spatial and which have rival claims for sovereignty over the world.[15]

Among the possibilities for the analysis of Paul's apocalyptic theology, this definition allows de Boer, with Martyn before him, to account for the apocalyptic character of Paul's theology in Galatians where strictly temporal frameworks had been insufficient. It is important to note that, in describing this two-track model of apocalyptic eschatology, de Boer was careful to insist that this is a heuristic device, not to be crudely deployed in

---

14. De Boer, *Galatians*, 32.

15. De Boer, *Galatians*, 33. De Boer saw the *Book of the Watchers* as an example of this martial approach to apocalyptic, with 2 Baruch and 4 Ezra characterized by the forensic approach.

support of assigning texts straightforwardly to one track. He is clear that, while his analysis presents descriptions of internally consistent patterns of thought, the two tracks are not mutually exclusive but may be found running in parallel or intersecting in any given apocalypse. This is a significant but often overlooked nuance.[16] However, when turning to his examination of Paul's christologically determined apocalyptic eschatology, it is clear for de Boer that, while Paul adapts both patterns of Jewish apocalyptic thought, one track (the "cosmological") decisively circumscribes the other (the "forensic").

One of the repeated features of de Boer's analysis and his subsequent explorations of Pauline apocalyptic theology is his observation that the two tracks of apocalyptic eschatology bear a striking resemblance to the debate between Bultmann and Käsemann over "anthropological" and "cosmological" accounts of Paul's thought.[17] De Boer notes how this discussion affects interpretation of Romans, with Bultmann preferring the predominantly "forensic" language of chapters 1–4, while Käsemann highlighted the "cosmological" features of chapters 6–8. In this way, chapter 5 represents for de Boer a location where the two soteriological narratives interpenetrate,[18] or even are (to use the more antithetical conflict metaphor de Boer sometimes adopts) "contested territory" within the argumentative flow of the letter,[19] as Paul transitions from the forensic eschatological language of the early chapters to the motifs of the cosmological eschatology that will circumscribe and overtake it.[20] In evaluating the views of Bultmann and Käsemann, it is clear that de Boer prefers the latter, arguing repeatedly that Paul's distinct apocalyptic logic is of the *cosmological* type, christologically modified. To be sure, Paul makes use of themes more obviously associated

---

16. For example, N. T. Wright has described this as a "*split* between two types of 'apocalyptic' theology" (Wright, "Paul in Current Anglophone Scholarship," 373 [emphasis mine]). Again, Simon Gathercole labels the two "tracks" in Martyn (though Martyn gets it from de Boer) as "two opposite systems" ("'Sins' in Paul," 147). In my own earlier analysis, I noted this nuance but also questioned the validity of the "tracks" metaphor on these grounds (Davies, *Paul Among the Apocalypses*, 186–91), though see sections 4.1 and 4.5 below for further discussion.

17. This has led some critics (e.g., N. T. Wright and Jörg Frey) to question whether this debate, and not the evidence of the apocalyptic texts, is driving his dichotomous analysis of the "two tracks." This is a charge he has now rejected. See *God's Apocalypse* 34–38 and the references to Frey and Wright's criticisms therein.

18. De Boer, "Paul and Apocalyptic Eschatology," 365.

19. De Boer, "Paul's Mythologizing Program," 6–7.

20. See "Paul's Mythologizing Program," 3–7.

with the "forensic" track, such as the references to Adam's disobedience in Rom 5 and 1 Cor 15. However, in de Boer's analysis, the presence of "forensic" elements in Paul's letters (for example, in Rom 2:5–8) is explained not as an integral feature of his own thought but a rhetorical tactic deployed against his opponents.[21] These forensic motifs, de Boer insists, are present in Paul's letters for rhetorical-argumentative reasons and are decidedly overtaken or circumscribed by his cosmological apocalyptic eschatology.

There are a number of theological commitments that result from de Boer's analysis of Pauline apocalyptic eschatology. The exclusive temporal emphasis on imminent eschatology that de Boer observes in the work of Käsemann or Beker is judged to be inadequate. A "cosmological" spatio-temporal analysis, he argues, provides a better framework for Paul's apocalyptic eschatology. The two ages, thus construed, are understood to be in a starkly dichotomous relationship. Temporally, the Christ-event represents a "clean break" with the past, evil age.[22] Spatially, it represents a decisive conflict between two opposing orbs of power and the locus of the divine triumph. This strict dualism signals a profound disjunction between the "ages," with no human possibility of moving from one to the other (for example through law observance), and thus no occasion for human boasting. Salvation is a pure gift brought about through God's victory over his enemies. Paul's gospel, for de Boer, is that in the cross of Christ, precisely at the moment where they seemed to have won, God destroyed the (personified, mythologized, and hypostasized) powers of Sin and Death. The cross thus reveals the hegemony of these inimical powers while simultaneously rectifying the cosmos and bringing it into the sphere of life. The revelatory (apocalyptic) force of the cross is in its power to defeat Sin and Death, and through faith the believer can be liberated from these enslaving powers and participate in this singular event of divine incursion onto the world stage.

2.2 Leander Keck: Paul's *Ex Post Facto* Logic

In Leander Keck's opinion, the question of Paul and apocalyptic theology is ultimately not one that can find an historical answer. However, that does not diminish its importance as a theme to be explored in Paul's thought, and Keck has offered a number of contributions to that endeavor. Despite being skeptical of any attempt to trace the historical genealogy between

---

21. See de Boer, *Defeat of Death,* 183, and "Paul and Apocalyptic Eschatology," 365.
22. De Boer, *Galatians,* 262.

Paul and the contemporary Jewish and Christian apocalyptic writings, Keck is clearly committed to exploring Paul's apocalyptic theology within that matrix. In an essay on the subject in 1984, he made this a matter of first principle. Though admitting (as many do) that the word can be tricky to define, Keck states plainly that "'apocalyptic' is an adjective which should be used to characterize the thought and imagery of those texts regarded as apocalypses."[23] This commitment carries through into the rest of the essay, where citations of 1 Enoch, 4 Ezra, and others are offered in comparison to Paul, and in his commentary on Romans, where Keck characterizes Paul's theology as rooted in "biblical and Jewish apocalyptic thought."[24]

Paul, of course, did not write any apocalypses, which is why it is important for Keck that we recognize that, beyond its foundational importance as a genre, apocalyptic is also "a type of theology" that characterizes Paul's letters.[25] Of course, that is emphatically not to say that Paul slavishly follows the contours of this theology or only makes minor adjustments to it. For Keck, Paul's apocalyptic theology, though rooted in the apocalyptic literature of his day, has been transformed by the pivotal event that is the death and resurrection of Christ,[26] and it is this christocentric transformation of apocalyptic thought that generates the apostle's distinctive theological vision. Though the apocalyptic theology of his time forms the framework for Paul's thought, the disjunctive and revelatory event of Jesus's resurrection was its point of departure.[27]

There is a generative tension inherent in this double commitment. For Keck, Paul does not only think "new thoughts" but also thinks the "old thoughts" differently.[28] Both must be grasped and properly ordered if Paul is to be intelligible. At this point Keck defines this theological point of departure with precision: "Jesus's resurrection was not the absolute starting point, of course; it was *the starting point for Paul's rethinking the theology he inherited*. Paul's Christian theology is the result of thinking on this side

---

23. Keck, "Paul and Apocalyptic," 230. This has been reprinted as "Paul and Apocalyptic Theology" in Keck, *Christ's First Theologian*, 75–87. Subsequent citations of this essay will be to this more recent version.

24. Keck, *Romans*, 33, see also 58–59, 210.

25. Keck, "Paul and Apocalyptic," 79. Here Keck describes apocalyptic theology as something that "emerged from the covenantal theology" and is "on the basis of covenantal theology" (79–80).

26. Keck, "Paul and Apocalyptic," 77.

27. Keck, "Paul and Apocalyptic," 87; Keck, *Echoes*, 56.

28. Keck, *Romans*, 35.

of the Jesus-event. Paul's theology is *ex post facto* theology."[29] Here Keck expresses an important epistemological theme that runs throughout his explorations of Paul's apocalyptic theology: its fundamentally retrospective logic. Paul's thinking starts with the resurrection of Jesus and works backwards, not only *after* this event but *because of it*. What is more, he argues, readers of Paul must do likewise if we are to understand the complex interactions of this "new thought" and the "old thoughts" of his apocalyptic matrix.

In a 1993 essay entitled "Paul As Thinker,"[30] Keck offered a more expansive account of this Pauline *ex post facto* logic, and the way the apostle reasons from the resurrection of Jesus to his deployment of apocalyptic themes, chief among which is his eschatology. Paul's apocalyptic epistemology, Keck argues, is inseparably bound up with an apocalyptic eschatology of "two ages" inherited from the Jewish apocalyptic tradition and transformed in the light of the Christ event.[31] This forms the nexus of Paul's apocalyptic theology.[32]

A crucial transformation of this "two ages" tradition that Keck observes in Paul is that because the resurrection of the crucified Jesus launches the new age "there is in Paul an irreducible tension between the 'already' and the 'not yet,' which is generally absent from apocalyptic theology."[33] There are a number of corollaries to this. First, because history's decisive event lies in the past, what must result is a theology of history fundamentally opposed to any forward-moving utopian vision of history as progress. Keck's account of Paul rejects any notion of "salvation history" that views this age as a prelude to its consummation in the Christ event. Rather, viewed retrospectively, Paul's account of history is not tied to a *telic* narrative of salvation history but to the scriptural witness to the "constancy of God."[34] Second, because the Christ-event was an eschatological event, Pau-

---

29. Keck, *Romans*, 34 (emphasis mine).

30. Keck, "Paul as Thinker," reprinted in *Christ's First Theologian*, 89–101. Citations of this essay will be to this more recent version.

31. Keck, "Paul as Thinker," 98.

32. Some of Keck's more forceful statements of the importance of the two ages come in his Romans commentary, not least when commenting on chapter 8 (Keck, *Romans*, 210).

33. Keck, "Paul and Apocalyptic," 86.

34. Keck, "Paul as Thinker," 97. Keck goes on to say that "salvation history as an epic of God's saving acts toward and through Israel's experience across centuries was simply not within the scope of Paul's thinking" (97). His language is imprecise at this point. If

line apocalyptic eschatology reckons with a future that is already underway, exposing the present age and the human condition for what it really is. That is to say, Paul's apocalyptic *ex post facto* thinking is "solution-to-plight" thinking, with far-reaching consequences for Christology and soteriology.[35] Third, Paul's apocalyptic theology is a theology of discontinuity, since the in-breaking of the new age in Christ in no way represents a progressive ameliorating influence on this present age but its radical, invasive alternative. Here, Keck is in dialogue with Martyn, whose discussion of "apocalyptic antinomies" in Paul is cited at this point.[36]

In affirming the essentially discontinuous nature of Paul's thought, however, Keck is careful to avoid overplaying this in cosmically dualistic terms. Paul's commitment to a theology of discontinuity does not entail such a thoroughgoing world-denying dualism, since (despite the false claims of anti-God powers) the present age remains under God's rule. For Keck's Paul, Jesus's resurrection is not the end *of* history but the end *in* history.[37] As such, the age to come, while being an absolute contrast to the present age, is not a substitute for it: "new creation" (καινὴ κτίσις, Gal 6:15; 2 Cor 5:17) is renewed creation.[38]

The eschatological framework of Paul's thought leads to a holistic evaluation of the defining realities represented by both "ages." Keck's christologically modified two-age eschatology, and the retrospective mode of thinking that comes with it, is the pivot upon which a whole host of Pauline themes turn. Among them, as noted above, is his soteriology. It is surely not an accident that in the recent collection of his various essays on Paul, the chapter that immediately follows "Paul and Apocalyptic Theology" and "Paul as Thinker" is "The Logic of Paul's Soteriology."[39]

---

this salvation-historical "epic" is understood as an immanent account of history's development, the point is consistent with Keck's rejection of *Heilsgeschichte*. But if the accent falls on "*God's* saving acts" this does not contradict his affirmation of Scripture's witness to God's constancy.

35. See Keck, "Paul as Thinker," 98.
36. Keck, "Paul as Thinker," 95.
37. In fact, this formulation is Beker's (*Paul the Apostle*, 149). Keck suggests a modification, adding that the resurrection is not only an end but a new beginning in history, but Beker's point still stands, and Keck considers the formulation apt. ("Paul as Thinker," 94n11). Keck would later go further: "the age to come is neither a mere new phase *in* history, nor the fulfilment *of* history, but the alternative *to* history" (105).
38. Keck, "Paul as Thinker," 95. Keck sees such a view in Revelation.
39. Keck, "The Logic of Paul's Soteriology" in *Christ's First Theologian*, 103–15.

Paul, Keck notes in this essay, does not give us a definition of σωτηρία. As such, an account of Paul's soteriology must work inductively, making inferences from his account of the effects on the human condition of the Christ event. As we have seen, in Keck's Pauline apocalyptic theology, the resurrection of the crucified Christ is the generative event for his coherent system of thought. Paul reasons *ex post facto* from his own encounter with the risen Christ and his soteriology is a reflection on the consequences of that experience.

When it comes to sin and the human condition, Keck's assessment is that Paul's "*ex post facto* soteriology"[40] is less concerned about "sins" as human acts of transgression than "sin" as a power, a structured reality which holds sway over the present age. Thinking backward from the eschatological event of the resurrection, what is revealed is not the relative differences of particular human sins but the reality of sin itself as a cosmic opponent, and of Christ's lordship over it. Keck argues that Paul's christologically transformed apocalyptic theology has, as result, a more radically pessimistic account of the human condition than that found in the Jewish apocalyptic theology, for Paul views sin as *bondage*. Keck finds nothing comparable to this in the apocalyptic literature. Some apocalypses come close, he argues, but "it is Paul who views sin as a power to which one is enslaved."[41] The logic of Pauline soteriology implied by this view of sin therefore requires a fundamentally liberative account of the Christ event. Through faith the believer participates in death to the old age and life to the irruptive new reality of Christ's lordship over sin and is thereby freed from its dominion. Commenting on Rom 6:18, Keck summarizes his argument: "rectitude is not an achievement; it is seen as a new reality structure."[42]

Once again, however, Keck resists allowing his account to grow into dualistic distortion. In addition to this participatory and liberative paradigm, he recognizes that Paul's soteriology also deploys forensic categories. This forensic soteriology is not, he argues, incoherent with Paul's liberative categories; nor does one need to become "embroiled in the 150-year-old argument" about which is more important,[43] so long as one recognizes the na-

40. Keck, "Logic," 104.
41. Keck, "Paul and Apocalyptic," 83–84. Here Keck compares this view with both the "rebellious angels" of 1 Enoch and the "evil inclination" of 4 Ezra. When it comes to the former and the question of sin, Keck observes that people are "not prisoners of the angels but accomplices." (83)
42. Keck, "Logic," 112.
43. Keck, *Romans*, 144.

ture of Paul's coherent logic. The liberative and participatory soteriological paradigm described above is directed at the ontological problem of sin as a hostile power, the lordship of Christ over it, and the deliverance of humankind from its bondage. But this emphasis on "sin" as a power does not entail, for Keck, a complete rejection of "sins" as misdeeds. Working together with the liberative paradigm in Keck's interpretation of Paul's apocalyptic soteriology is a forensic paradigm of justification dealing with universal human accountability for transgression and a resulting wrong relationship to God, the impartial judge.[44] Both the condition of bondage and the resulting human dilemma in relation to God are the result of sin, each addressing a particular aspect of the human condition. In the former, humanity is seen as a victim, in the latter a responsible agent.[45] Carefully framed in this way, these two soteriologies are not contradictory, and are deployed by Paul without confusion. In Keck's interpretation of Romans, Paul views both paradigms retrospectively, generated by the inauguration of the new age in the Christ event, and "moves easily from one to the other."[46] In Rom 1:18—5:11, Paul largely deploys forensic soteriological categories because he is there dealing with the human *dilemma*, having done wrong and now facing the judgment of the God to whom we are wrongly related. In Rom 5:12—8:30, liberative and participatory language comes to the fore, as Paul deals with the underlying cause: the enslaved human *condition* (and, by the end of chapter 8, the condition of the whole creation) under the tyrannical power of sin.[47] Thus Keck traces a theological rationale for the shape of Romans, moving from the largely anthropological concerns of its first movement to the more fundamental theological condition causing this human dilemma, and why the eschatological event of Christ addresses it. This, again, is an example of Paul's theology moving from "solution" to "plight," even if the argument of his letters sometimes moves in the other direction.[48]

---

44. See, e.g., the summary of this point in Keck, *Romans*, 99–102, discussing Romans 3:19–20.

45. See Keck, *Romans*, 107, commenting on Rom 3:22.

46. Keck, "Logic," 113.

47. See Keck's introduction to his commentary on Rom 1:16—8:39 in *Romans*, 50, and also the comments on the transition to 5:12 on 142–44.

48. Keck, "Paul and Apocalyptic," 85, at this point endorsing the views of Sanders.

2.3 Alexandra Brown: Paul's Apocalyptic Word

The weight of discussion in the Apocalyptic Paul conversation has largely been placed (as so often in Pauline studies) on Galatians and Rom 1–8, and on questions of eschatology, cosmology, and soteriology. In her 1995 book *The Cross and Human Transformation: Paul's Apocalyptic Word in 1 Corinthians*, however, Alexandra Brown brought to the conversation a sustained attention to Paul's first letter to Corinth, with its particular emphasis on apocalyptic epistemology and anthropology.

As the title of the book indicates, Brown is committed to reading Paul as an apocalyptic thinker, which for her means an essential connection to the other Jewish apocalyptic writers of his time.[49] The apocalyptic eschatological expectations found in the writings of these seers left their mark on Paul, who draws ideas and imagery from this deep well, while radically transforming them. In addition to exegesis of 1 Corinthians, therefore, Brown's study examines texts such as 1 Enoch, 4 Ezra, and 2 Baruch. Nevertheless, the term "apocalyptic" is not limited to questions of literary dependence or generic similarity. It is also a theological concept, signaling the presence of motifs such as the "two ages," the sovereignty of God, his imminent eschatological triumph, and future reign. Paul's encounter with the risen Christ profoundly transformed these apocalyptic categories, notably in regard to his inaugurated eschatology. No longer is the "age to come" a matter of merely future hope; for Paul the longed-for new world was present here and now in the coming and crucifixion of the Messiah and the power of the Spirit. As such there is a distinctive eschatological transformation in Paul's apocalyptic thought.

However, it is in the area of epistemology, rather than eschatology, that Brown's analysis breaks the most significant ground. In her focus on the revelatory heart of Paul's apocalyptic thought, Brown notes the apostle's connection to the essential theological insights expressed in the Jewish apocalypses, while also drawing attention to his radical christological extension and transformation of them. However, Paul's relationship to his context, for Brown, is more complex still. Alongside his familiarity with the language and thought-forms of Jewish apocalypticism, Brown also detects in Paul's letter to Corinth clear evidence of familiarity with the Hellenistic Jewish wisdom tradition. Thus, alongside the Jewish apocalypses, her study examines the search for knowledge in texts such as Sirach, Baruch, and

---

49. Brown, *Cross*, xviii.

the Wisdom of Solomon. These two Jewish traditions, apocalyptic and wisdom, collide and combine in Paul's letter, an interaction most keenly felt in his epistemology, as he addresses the Corinthian concern with wisdom and knowledge. How do these interact and what force does the *kerygma* have on their construal in Paul? It is at this point that Brown's analysis of Pauline apocalyptic theology presses most firmly. In assessing the epistemological question of revelation and wisdom, central to 1 Corinthians, Brown is careful not to rely on a sharp, dichotomous distinction between the apocalyptic and sapiential streams of Jewish theology. Sometimes they operate in conflict, but sometimes they flow together.[50] The complex created by the joining of these two streams, and the transformation of both in the light of the decisive event of the cross, are what generates Paul's distinctive apocalyptic epistemology.

In seeking to describe this aspect of Pauline apocalyptic thought, Brown acknowledges a cumulative debt to Käsemann, Beker, and Martyn. The last of these three is particularly significant for Brown's endeavor due to his handling of Paul's apocalyptic "antinomies." Just as Martyn was, Brown is careful not to say that all theological dualities are dissolved by the apocalypse of Jesus Christ: indeed, some are created. But this is not to say that her analysis of 1 Corinthians and its emphasis on the revelatory word represents the creation of a strict epistemological antithesis between apocalypse and wisdom, the triumph of one meaning the demise of the other. To be sure, in Brown's reading of Paul and his context, there are two profoundly antithetical ways of knowing, but these are carefully and specifically defined as the *human wisdom* of the present age and the *revealed wisdom* and power of God (not, as one might have expected, an antithesis of "wisdom" and "folly" or, straightforwardly, of "wisdom" and "revelation"). In the light of the revelation of Jesus Christ, wisdom is not simply set aside. After all, as Paul says, "among the mature we do speak wisdom . . ." (1 Cor 2:6), but this is immediately qualified as being ". . . not a wisdom of this age or the rulers of this age, who are doomed to perish." Paul's epistemological endorsement of wisdom must, therefore, now be understood as "apocalyptic wisdom," hidden and revealed in the cross.[51] A new pair of opposites has been brought into being by Paul's apocalyptic transformation of the sapiential tradition:

---

50. Brown, *Cross*, 30.
51. Brown, *Cross*, 103.

the "wisdom of this age" versus the "wisdom of God." This is a qualitative distinction driven by distinctly apocalyptic and eschatological categories.[52]

Martyn's influence on Brown's reading of Paul can be seen most clearly in their shared commitment to unpacking the epistemological consequences of the Christ-event in Paul's thought. Building on Martyn's important essay on 2 Cor 5 and its discussion of Paul's apocalyptic "epistemology at the turn of the ages," Brown develops the claim that, in addressing the situation at Corinth, Paul's apocalyptic battleground is the "realm of human perception."[53] The revelatory word of the cross has invaded the epistemological landscape with the power to transform the Corinthian perception of the world and thus their way of being in it. In Brown's view, the proclamation of the gospel is an apocalyptic "speech act" (here she draws on analytic philosopher J. L. Austin's famous work on performative utterances) that not only communicates but transforms its hearers' minds and hence their world. Through the proclamation of the revelatory word of the cross, Paul (as it were) speaks God's new world into being. In this way, the apocalypse of the cross effects a new way of human knowing and, therefore, a transformed way of being human.

Here Brown's analysis of Pauline apocalyptic epistemology reaches its anthropological and ethical conclusions, in something of a departure from Martyn, for whom apocalyptic was not an ethical category. In Brown's reading of Paul, the proclamation of the word of the cross creates a cognitive dissonance and subsequent re-location in the minds of its hearers, effecting simultaneously the collapse of the old world and the birth of the new, an epistemological irruption at the juncture of the "ends of the ages." The foundation of ethics in 1 Corinthians is not, therefore, to be found in an alternative series of claims to human wisdom, but to the reversal of such wisdom brought about in the foolishness of the cross, which is the power of God, the redefinition of true wisdom, and a new creation. This reversal, Brown argues, lies at the heart of the apostle's apocalyptic ethics. Paul's claim in 1 Cor 2:16 that "we have the mind of Christ" is, for Brown, a defining statement of his apocalyptic epistemology,[54] and one with important soteriological implications.[55] As those who have the "mind of Christ," believers enter into the new world brought into being by the performative

---

52. Brown, *Cross*, 112.
53. Brown, *Cross*, xvii.
54. Brown, *Cross*, 108.
55. On which see now Brown, "Battlefield."

utterance of the word of the cross. The human consciousness, blinded by the corrupting power of Sin, is liberated from captivity to the powers and transformed through this irruptive Word. Paul's proclamation of the gospel, with its alternative apocalyptic epistemology, does more than reflect another world, it actually creates it. Paul's apocalyptic ethics, for Brown, thus involves just this combination of epistemology and anthropology, of "both perception and action."[56] The connections between perception and action have implications, too, for Brown's construal of S/sin in 1 Corinthians and Paul's apocalyptic soteriology, to which we will return.[57]

2.4 Beverly Gaventa: The Singularity of the Gospel

Another contemporary scholar who has emphasized the martial-cosmological tenor of Paul's apocalyptic theology is Beverly Gaventa. After being initially reticent to adopt the term, due in part to the confusion that surrounds it, Gaventa describes her interpretation of Paul as apocalyptic, not least because this nomenclature represents a clear statement of her indebtedness to Martyn, Beker, and Käsemann. Gaventa's apocalyptic reading of Paul has three emphases, each of which acknowledges and demonstrates this theological legacy while developing her own particular account.

First, Gaventa highlights Paul's cosmic soteriology, a commitment to the divine salvific invasion of the contested territory that is the present world in the death and resurrection of Jesus Christ. In particular, she explores Paul's language of sin in Romans, observing that, in that letter in particular, the apostle does not confine his comments to human misdeeds, but that there is an active role played by (upper-case) Sin as an enslaving anti-God power.[58] Sin entered the world through Adam and established a "base of operations" (Gaventa's rendering of ἀφορμή in Rom 7:8, 11), subjugating humanity. Not only does the power of Sin enslave human beings, but also the holy Law itself is made subject to Sin's control and as such used against its purpose, producing death instead of life. Paul's apocalyptic gospel, then, is that the cosmic power of God revealed in Christ has defeated the enslaving cosmic power of Sin. As such, for Gaventa, what is needed to make sense of the soteriology of Romans is a wider apocalyptic-cosmological narrative of God's invasive battle with, and victory over, the

---

56. Brown, *Cross*, 168.
57. See section 4.5 below.
58. See Gaventa, "Cosmic Power of Sin."

anti-God powers of Sin and Death. Over against accounts of salvation (whether individual or corporate) that are limited to forensic descriptions of transgression and forgiveness, this cosmological deliverance is conceived in fundamentally liberative terms. The community of Christ are those who have been rescued by God's invasion of the present evil age and who therefore join with creation (itself held captive by these powers) in groaning for the birth of the age to come.

Secondly, this is an apocalyptic invasion with epistemological consequences, revealing the extent of the world's captivity to the powers of Sin and Death, which seek to enslave and separate it from its rightful sovereign, but from which God has delivered it. This is not, in Gaventa's view, merely the public revelation of something hitherto kept secret, but an epistemological event that radically disrupts the world. These epistemological consequences are, for Gaventa, "writ small" in Paul's own life,[59] as attested in her reading of Gal 1 and 2. Paul's defense of his apostleship found in those chapters, she argues, is not merely a matter of apologetics but of Paul expounding the epistemological reversal brought about by the gospel through his autobiography. His comments about his own past indicate, for Gaventa, not merely a concern to defend himself against critics, but an occasion for the explication of his apocalyptic gospel and are therefore more tightly integrated into the theology of Galatians as a whole. In short, the revelation (apocalypse) of Jesus Christ effected for Paul a retrospective reading of his past in a new light. Turning her attention to Romans, Gaventa further argues that the same retrospective epistemology with which Paul reads his own story is also applied to his understanding of Israel's past, present, and future in chapters 9–11. There, Paul's retelling of Israel's story is not one that moves forward from Abraham, but instead works backward from the Christ-event. For Gaventa, this retrospective rethinking of Israel is a feature that Paul's apocalyptic theology shares with the Jewish apocalyptic tradition, though for Paul this is decisively transformed in the light of God's action in the Christ event.[60] Moreover, what was true of Paul and of Israel is paradigmatic for all humankind and of the whole world and its value systems. The cosmos itself is retrospectively re-cast by the apocalypse of Jesus Christ, simultaneously rendering visible its enslavement to malevolent powers and proclaiming its liberation from those powers.

---

59. Gaventa, *Mother*, 88.
60. See "Thinking from Christ to Israel" esp. 244n11 and 247.

Thirdly, Gaventa's reading of Paul highlights his apocalyptic eschatology. One of the signature contributions to the discussion of Gaventa's work is her examination of the maternal metaphors in Paul, found in the various essays collected in her 2007 book *Our Mother Saint Paul*. At first glance this might appear an unlikely locus for an exposition of such a dramatic, irruptive, and martial vision of Paul's gospel. However, far from being an exposition of cozy motherly imagery, Gaventa's work with this theme provides the context for her exposition of Paul's apocalyptic theology. Apocalyptic eschatological expectation is frequently connected to the anguish of childbirth, not only in the imagery deployed by Paul and other apocalyptic writers but also, Gaventa argues, in the apocalyptic logic of his thought. Reflection on the maternal imagery in Paul's theology began, for Gaventa, with his statement in Gal 4:19: "My little children, for whom I am again in the pain of childbirth until Christ is formed in you . . ." Far from being a merely poetic description of Paul's pastoral concern for his churches, Gaventa takes this expression to signal the apostle's eschatological anguish. Moreover, reading Gal 4 with Rom 8 (as well as the deployment of the birthing metaphor elsewhere in the NT, in the OT, and in the pseudepigraphal writings), the labor pains of Paul's own eschatological expectation can be seen to be integrally connected to those of the whole world in the framework of apocalyptic theology, as both Paul and creation eagerly await the apocalypse of Jesus Christ. It is, as Gaventa puts it, a "metaphor squared."[61]

One of the reasons for being initially cautious about adopting the label *apocalyptic* for this reading of Paul is that Gaventa felt this term did not do justice to the continuity found in Paul with the Old Testament and the history of Israel.[62] One might think, therefore, that a strong sense of continuity would characterize her reading of the eschatology presented through the maternal metaphors, but this is far from the case. Gaventa's analysis of these metaphors is again instructive on this point.

The present creation's groaning for the birth of the new creation does not mean, in Gaventa's apocalyptic reading of Paul, that it participates in the arrival of that new creation. There are labor pains in Rom 8, but no birth. Not only humanity but all of the present creation is subject to futility and so cannot give birth to this new world. This is why Paul, when speaking about his own labor pains, theologically adapts the logic of childbirth to place the agency elsewhere: he is in the pain of childbirth until *Christ* is

---

61. Gaventa, *Mother*, 5, 62.
62. Gaventa, *Mother*, 111.

formed in the Galatian church. The birthing of the new creation remains wholly God's unilateral act in the cross and resurrection of Jesus Christ, and for Gaventa this christocentric and irruptive logic is indispensable to Paul's apocalyptic theology, arguing against any possible "evolutionary" continuity in his eschatology. For Gaventa, the apocalyptic character of Paul's theology has been undermined by the way some scholars have insisted on a strong sense of continuity between Paul's articulation of the gospel and the history and Scriptures of Israel.

2.5 Douglas Campbell: Against Foundationalism

Like Gaventa, Douglas Campbell was initially tentative in his adoption of the word "apocalyptic" to describe his Pauline theology, but his theological concerns nevertheless express similar commitments to the genealogy described above. In his 2005 book *The Quest for Paul's Gospel,* he eschewed this label for his grand strategic vision of Pauline theology, suggesting instead the acronym PPME (Pneumatologically Participatory Martyrological Eschatology).[63] However, without making it bear too much argumentative weight, his subsequent descriptions of Paul's theology have cautiously embraced the term. Campbell is sensitive, as are many, to the complexities of the use of this highly contested word, and while his approach does note that it signals an implicit link to the Jewish apocalypses, he ultimately questions the value of this background for Pauline theology, judging it a species of arguing from the general to the particular and less than helpful in settling important Pauline debates.[64] For Campbell, if there is value in using the label it is to be found in a) highlighting an emphasis on Paul's revelatory epistemology and b) denoting a broad orientation to a particular approach to Pauline theology, namely an alignment with Käsemann, Beker, Keck, and (especially) Martyn.[65] In particular, Campbell develops his interpretation of Paul in line with Martyn's emphases on the unconditional, revelatory, and invasive nature of the gospel. Where Campbell parts company with these scholars, however, is in respect to the question of the role of the apocalypses in defining the term "apocalyptic." For Campbell, the possibility of

---

63. An acronym and a phrase Gaventa considered "more obstructing than illuminating" (*Mother,* 82).

64. See Campbell, *Quest,* 56–57n3.

65. Campbell, *Deliverance,* 191, though Campbell seems to have now stepped away a little from Käsemann's and Martyn's usage (Campbell, *Pauline Dogmatics,* 22n14).

a broader category of "revelations," within which the Pauline apocalypse might be said to take place, is too troublesome a prospect that threatens to undermine the uniqueness of the Christ event.[66] Campbell's deployment of the term "apocalyptic" represents an insistence upon the revelatory character of Paul's gospel, but downplays this broader literary connection much more firmly than the scholars upon whom he builds.

In his development of Martyn's insights regarding apocalyptic theology in Paul, Campbell places greatest emphasis on the conviction that Paul's christologically reworked apocalyptic epistemology is decidedly *retrospective*. As for Gaventa, for Campbell Paul's reasoning about the cosmos and the (hi)story of Israel is conditioned by and proceeds backwards from the revelation of Jesus Christ. There are clear echoes here of the *ex post facto* logic of Keck's apocalyptic reading of Paul, but it is Martyn's important essay on 2 Cor 5, discussed above, which has proven particularly influential on Campbell at this point, as it was for Brown. More significantly, however, Campbell's argument for an apocalyptic epistemology owes its greatest debt to the early work of Karl Barth, with his revelatory and christological emphases, and his protest against the prospective epistemology inherent in natural theology. Campbell is regularly explicit about his theological genealogy in this regard. In one essay outlining this retrospective epistemology in dialogue with Martyn and Barth (provocatively entitled "Apocalyptic Epistemology: The *Sine Qua Non* of Valid Pauline Interpretation"), Campbell suggests that one might even describe the apostle as "in effect, an early Barthian."[67] The methodological starting point of a retrospective epistemology is repeatedly insisted upon, not only as a reconstruction of Paul's own approach to the knowledge of God, but also as the proper mode of enquiry for the contemporary Pauline scholar.[68]

This retrospective epistemology is starkly contrasted in Campbell's work with what he considers its incompatible opposite, the "deadly methodological heresy" of theological *foundationalism*.[69] In this epistemological

66. Campbell, *Pauline Dogmatics*, 22.

67. Campbell, "Apocalyptic Epistemology," 71.

68. In *Pauline Dogmatics*, Campbell expounds his conviction that this epistemological imperative ("the truth gambit") has purchase not only on Paul's thought but also on those who would read him: "We are Christians, located by the work of God within the central truth that explains all of reality. We are in the truth already. Why step outside of this circle into a place where we no longer belong? Why accept being a non-Christian for the sake of argument?" (38).

69. Campbell, "Apocalyptic Epistemology," 78.

paradigm, reasoning is *a priori* and moves forwards, the knowledge of God being the result of reflection on the created cosmos. This, Campbell argues, is an epistemology predicated on an essentially philosophical and rationalistic view of humanity, acquiring the knowledge of God not through revelation but through observation of and reflection on the world. The two approaches to epistemology, retrospective and foundationalist, are, in his view, diametrically opposed, and his "apocalyptic" reading of Paul emphatically rejects the latter in favor of the former.[70] In his most recent argument for this position, Campbell pulls no punches with his rhetoric: to desire anything other than Christ as an epistemological starting point is to desire a share in the original sin.[71]

One doctrine in particular Campbell singles out as potentially captive to the foundationalist heresy is the doctrine of justification, which receives sustained attention in his monumental book *The Deliverance of God: An Apocalyptic Rereading of Justification in Paul*. In Campbell's analysis, the structure of what he dubs "Justification Theory" deploys both a prospective and a retrospective epistemology, relied upon in turn at the two "phases" of the logic of its soteriological system. In the first phase, the epistemology is universal, anthropocentric, and foundationalist: an omnipotent and just God is known to rational, self-interested humans by reflection on the cosmos and the human conscience. But when the soteriological model moves to its second phase, in which this God acts to save sinful humanity, the mode of epistemology shifts to the particular and historical revelation of Jesus Christ and works from there. This epistemological shift represents, for Campbell, an intrinsic difficulty in the logic of the soteriological paradigm. This is a dual epistemology, the unavoidable result of which is an internal incoherence in the "Justification Theory" model. It is an incoherence, moreover, that has serious systematic repercussions beyond soteriology into almost every area of Pauline theology. As a solution to this complex problem, and to many of the various contemporary interpretative debates generated in one way or another by it, Campbell expounds his "apocalyptic" approach to Paul's soteriology which accounts for the deployment of apparently prospective arguments in his writings (e.g., Rom 1:19–20) without subscribing to a foundationalist epistemology.

---

70. This argument for a retrospective epistemology has since been developed and expanded at length by Campbell in *Pauline Dogmatics,* Part One.

71. Campbell, *Pauline Dogmatics,* 32.

Along with his insistence on a retrospective epistemology, Campbell's reading of Paul is characterized by a second dominant theme, namely his insistence on a stark contrast between "covenantal" and "contractual" soteriological paradigms. Campbell is explicit early on that his reading of Paul at this point is indebted to the analysis of Scottish Calvinist theologian J. B. Torrance, for whom "Federal Calvinism" demonstrated a fundamentally contractual logic. In Torrance's view this represented a distortion of Calvin's own covenantal approach and was generative of important theological difficulties. This contrast between covenant and contract was essentially the genesis of Campbell's project in *Deliverance*. His argument there is that an apocalyptic soteriology construed in invasive, liberative, and unconditional-covenantal terms is fundamentally incompatible with traditional views of salvation bound up with an irretrievably forensic, individualistic, and retributive-contractual paradigm. In Campbell's view "Justification Theory" (in both its "phases") is characterized by the latter cluster of convictions, and it is a model of the atonement that has fundamentally distorted many Protestant readings of Paul, and which must therefore be subjected to a full-scale critique.

One particular feature of his re-reading that has drawn a great deal of attention is his explanation for the presence of forensic motifs in Rom 1:18—3:20, which Campbell judges to be indicative not of Paul's own views but those of his opponents, in an instance of *prosōpopoeia*, speech-in-character. This approach to this material has generated some controversy and has been met with robust challenges, leading Campbell to revise his proposal and abandon the more specific designation of *prosōpopoeia* while maintaining a broader view that Paul is here deploying Socratic irony. The attention received by this exegetical detail must not, however, be allowed to distract from the broader contours of Campbell's "apocalyptic" challenge to Pauline "Justification Theory," namely the critique of what he sees as its twofold problem of a foundationalist epistemology and a contractual soteriology. To understand Paul in a consistently apocalyptic way, for Campbell, means to endorse a liberative and retrospective model of the atonement over against the forensic and foundationalist approach of "Justification Theory."

2.6 Susan Eastman: Language, Identity, and Agency

Another Pauline scholar who owes a great intellectual debt to Martyn is Susan Eastman,[72] whose work, like that of Gaventa, explores the maternal language of Paul's letters as a window onto his apocalyptic theology. Based on her doctoral dissertation (completed under Richard Hays at Duke University Divinity School) Eastman's 2007 monograph *Recovering Paul's Mother Tongue* examines how the letter to the Galatians sheds light on the question of how God's work of new creation establishes patterns of relationship in Pauline churches. In this connection, Eastman goes with and beyond Gaventa in exploring how the maternal metaphors Paul uses at key points in this letter (particularly in 4:12—5:1) might allow for a fresh understanding of Paul's apocalyptic theology.

While Eastman's volume offers little by way of a programmatic definition of "apocalyptic," her approach clearly has an affinity with Martyn's use of the term to indicate the singular invasive act of God in Christ.[73] However, Eastman also shares with Martyn (and with de Boer)[74] a commitment to describing Paul's apocalyptic worldview and theology in conversation with the Jewish apocalyptic and prophetic literature, not least because there one often encounters similar maternal metaphors to those deployed by Paul.[75] One of Eastman's major contributions lies in her discussion of the echoes of Paul's language in the prophets, and the framing of his apostolic vocation in continuity with the prophetic tradition. When it comes to the specific question of Paul's labor pains imagery in Gal 4:19, Eastman turns to a broad textual tradition in the prophetic and apocalyptic literature for interpretative guidance,[76] and finds that a responsible theological account of this language will involve *both* the radical discontinuity of the birth of the gospel *and* the continuity of divine promise.

---

72. Though, as she says in one place, "Martyn himself would no doubt scoff at such a statement, because, as he repeatedly reminds us, there is no *quid pro quo* in the arena of God's grace in Christ" (Eastman, "Apocalypse and Incarnation," 165).

73. See Eastman, "Apocalypse and Incarnation," 166, and *Recovering*, 65n7.

74. Both are cited in Eastman, *Recovering*, 65n7.

75. For example, on maternal metaphors in apocalyptic literature, Eastman cites Humphrey, *Ladies*, in *Recovering*, 19n44. The work of John Collins is also cited (in *Recovering*, 65n6) in relation to the links between wisdom and apocalyptic literature.

76. The relevant section of *Recovering* (114–16) cites a wide range of texts, particularly from Isa 40–66 and those in the apocalyptic literature that connect birth imagery to messianic eschatological hope, such as 1 En. 62, 4 Ezra 4, Mark 13, and Rev 12.

As in the Jewish apocalyptic tradition, one of the central features of Paul's apocalyptic worldview is this question of temporal continuity and discontinuity. In the preface to this first book, Eastman indicates that Martyn was particularly helpful in helping her think through this question in the letter to the Galatians. As we have seen, in his view the key to solving this puzzle was to recognize the radical "anthropological discontinuity" of the gospel's invasion while maintaining the "theological continuity" of God's faithfulness to Abraham. Eastman considers this is a helpful analysis as far as it goes but argues that the sharp distinction between anthropological and theological frames of reference becomes problematic once we start speaking of the actual concrete history of the Pauline churches. Here we can see that the two threads of identity and continuity/discontinuity, which run through her work, cannot be teased apart. The question of (new) identity in the Galatian churches, which is an important concern in Paul's letter to them, is at the same time a question of continuity and discontinuity. Without a sense of continuity, it is difficult to speak of a community, or of its transformation. But without a strong sense of discontinuity, a "radical break with the past,"[77] the gospel loses its singularity and Paul's apocalyptic message is reduced to a form of historical evolution. How these two emphases can be maintained when speaking of the actual lives of the Pauline communities is a challenge that occupies much of Eastman's work.

Eastman also goes "with and beyond" Martyn in exploring his characterization of the Christ event as an anthropologically discontinuous "invasion" in its implications for the logic of the incarnation.[78] Martyn's consistent focus on the cross as "*the* singular, punctiliar, apocalypse" of liberating divine invasion has, Eastman argues, left unexplored the anthropological implications of the incarnation of Jesus.[79] Eastman suggests that moving beyond Martyn's martial language of invasion to that of incarnation allows a fuller christological picture that encapsulates Christ's identification *with* humanity, not just his action *for* us, with important implications for theological anthropology. This is a theological theme to which her work has recently returned in depth, as we will see shortly.

Throughout Eastman's work one hears the refrain, again echoing Martyn, of the theological geometry of "horizontal" versus "vertical"; "linear" and "punctiliar." What is clear is that Eastman is convinced these

---

77. Eastman, *Recovering*, 3.
78. The latter is explored in detail in Eastman, "Apocalypse and Incarnation."
79. Eastman, "Apocalypse and Incarnation," 166 (emphasis original).

coordinates cannot be accounted for in an overly neat scheme. Viewed in the context of his pastoral and community-forming concerns, Paul's childbirth language requires that we speak of the punctiliar event of birth, to be sure, but it also bespeaks a continuous formative process. Here Eastman detects a deficiency in both Martyn's and Gaventa's accounts of Paul's language and theology, in that neither had sufficiently addressed the relationship between the "punctiliar" and the "linear" elements of Paul's language.[80] Martyn had emphasized the apocalyptic invasion of the gospel and had sharply contrasted it with any salvation-historical linearity. For Eastman, however, the Pauline language of maternity requires that we speak of both sides of this apparent dichotomy. In the light of his gospel, Paul's theological reframing of the community identity of the Galatians requires *both* a linear/horizontal narrative *and* the punctiliar/vertical in-breaking of the apocalypse of Jesus Christ. It requires theological *as well as* anthropological continuity.[81] For this reason her argument closes with four reflections on how the creation of Christ-centered communities indicates "the power of the gospel to create a history."[82] The apocalypse of Jesus Christ, while radically discontinuous with this world, does not simply negate its history, but embraces it with "continuity as well as transformation."[83] The nature of this continuity, and of this transformative "history creation" is at the heart of Eastman's argument. To put it briefly, there is a temporal continuity in the history created by the gospel, not in an endorsement of a continuous forward progression, but in an affirmation of divine call, mediated through participation in Christ[84] and displayed in the communities and individuals formed by the gospel.

More recently, Eastman's work has pressed further into the question of participation and identity formation by placing the old (and somewhat neglected) question of Pauline anthropology in an apocalyptic light.[85] Like Bultmann, Eastman has insisted on addressing the question of theological anthropology in dialogue with contemporary scientific understandings of

---

80. See Eastman, *Recovering*, 112.

81. Eastman, *Recovering*, 16.

82. Eastman, *Recovering*, 184.

83. Eastman, *Recovering*, 185.

84. In addition to the relevant argument in Eastman, *Recovering*, see also Eastman, "Apocalypse and Incarnation."

85. In addition to *Paul and the Person* see "Ashes on the Frontal Lobe" and "Double Participation."

personhood, so that the Pauline anthropological language might be comprehensible in today's world. Unlike Bultmann, however, Eastman does not view apocalyptic as a myth to be translated into existentialist and individualist terms. Rather, Eastman's forays into philosophical anthropology and contemporary neuroscience lead her in the opposite direction, to an understanding of the self that is irreducibly relational. Eastman does not anachronistically impose this modern framework onto Paul, nor does she "demythologize" Paul into contemporary psychology or psychotherapy, but rather explores how Paul's apocalyptic theological anthropology can be brought into fruitful conversation with such insights.

Eastman's interdisciplinary investigations generate conclusions which resonate strongly with Käsemann's apocalyptic and cosmological reframing of Pauline anthropology.[86] Human persons, in Eastman's view, are not autonomous individuals but are "relationally constituted agents who are both embodied and embedded in their world."[87] The person, for Paul, is thus conceived in a relational matrix of "cosmic and corporate powers,"[88] which is to say within an apocalyptic cosmology. Under the enslaving power of sin and death, human agency is radically diminished. When brought into the liberating dominion of the power of grace, however, human beings find a new divinely gifted agency. The liberating action of God in Christ thus reconstitutes the person, hitherto constituted by the cosmic powers of sin and the flesh. This newly constituted personhood is anchored in the new creation, not the present world, and as such there exists an eschatological tension in Paul's experience of selfhood. This apocalyptic reframing of anthropology, Eastman argues, is what we find expressed in the Pauline "I" of Rom 7, and similar statements in Philippians 2 and Galatians 2.

2.7 Lisa Bowens: Epistemology, Heavenly Ascent, and Cosmic Warfare

We conclude this survey and bring it (almost) to the present day with one example of an emerging voice in the conversation about Paul's apocalyptic theology, that of Lisa Bowens. Though other scholars could also have been included, Bowens's work is particularly useful here in that she has added to the discussion a sustained reading of Paul's apocalyptic theology in 2

---

86. A connection noted in Eastman, "Apocalypse and Incarnation," 170.
87. Eastman, *Paul and the Person*, 2.
88. Eastman, *Paul and the Person*, 20.

Corinthians. Furthermore, what makes her work particularly appropriate here is that she demonstrates a commitment to the kind of interdisciplinary scholarship for which I have been advocating in these pages.

This commitment can be seen quite clearly in her doctoral dissertation, written at Princeton Theological Seminary and published in 2017 under the title *An Apostle in Battle: Paul and Spiritual Warfare in 2 Corinthians 12:1–10*. A case in point is her opening definition of "apocalyptic," which represents one of Bowens's most interesting contributions to the discussion so far. Her contention that Paul's thought qualifies as "apocalyptic" not primarily because of his eschatology but his emphasis on human and cosmic/spiritual beings "sharing social space," a notion Bowens borrows from Loren Stuckenbruck.[89] "Paul," she explains, "has a view of the world in which the human and the supernatural realms interpenetrate and intermingle in a manner that shows the two spheres are inextricably linked" and "in which each realm and the actions within that realm affect the other."[90] The character of this cosmic interaction is, as we will see, fundamentally one of conflict. First, in relation to the broader discourse on Paul's apocalyptic thought, it is interesting to note Bowens's recognition that her definition of "apocalyptic," which draws upon Stuckenbruck's analysis of Jewish apocalyptic literature, also has a great deal in common with Martinus de Boer's reading of Paul, and especially his account of a "cosmological" pattern of apocalyptic, discussed above.[91] While Bowens's reading of Paul regularly demonstrates her affinity with the line from Käsemann to Martyn and de Boer (as well as others in this genealogy), she also works with the primary texts of the Jewish apocalyptic tradition and a range of recent secondary scholarship on them.

Bowens brings this cosmological-apocalyptic lens to Paul's argument in 2 Corinthians, with a particular focus on his account of an ascent to "the third heaven" in 12:1–10. As many have observed, this is where Paul is perhaps at his most clear in his affinity with the Jewish apocalyptic tradition and its wealth of similar "heavenly ascent" narratives.[92] Bowens works closely with a number of these texts, and the secondary scholarship on

---

89. Bowens, *Apostle in Battle*, 35, citing Stuckenbruck "Prayers of Deliverance," 163. Cf. 227, where she applies the label "apocalyptic" (thus defined) to her own reading of Paul.

90. Bowens, *Apostle in Battle*, 35–36.

91. De Boer, "Paul and Apocalyptic Eschatology," cf. Bowens, *Apostle in Battle*, 36n149.

92. On which see, e.g., Himmelfarb, *Ascent to Heaven*.

them, in giving an account of Paul's apocalyptic thought in relation to this apocalyptic "cultural encyclopedia."[93]

Bowens's work gives particularly focused attention to the Qumran *War Scroll* and the *Treatise on the Two Spirits* (1QS 3:13—4:26) and their depiction of cosmic conflict, but her exegesis of 2 Cor 12 also weaves in discussions of a range of other apocalyptic and heavenly ascent texts, such as 1 Enoch (in particular the Book of the Watchers and the Book of Parables), Daniel, the Apocalypse of Abraham, Jubilees, and more. For Bowens, these texts are the evidence of a "complex web of traditions" in which Paul's apocalyptic thought participates.[94] She is careful to note that these intertextual connections do not require the assertion of direct literary influence or derivation between the apocalyptic tradition and Paul but are nevertheless part of his "conceptual environment" and evidence of "conceptual affinities" he shares with the Jewish apocalyptic tradition.[95]

Bowens's reading of 2 Cor 12 focuses on what is, by her account, an often-neglected theme: its language of cosmic warfare. Such martial language is commonly found in Paul, including elsewhere in 2 Corinthians,[96] but it is in the opening verses of chapter 10 that we find his clearest and most sustained use of such imagery. What Bowens's work demonstrates is that this warfare motif does not end at 10:6 but continues through the rest of the letter, including in the heavenly ascent of 12:1-10. Reading Paul's ascent account within this martial and theological context allows Bowens to bring a new and important layer of meaning to this most apocalyptic of Pauline texts. In almost all readings, this passage is interpreted (in different ways) as part of Paul's defense of his ministry in the face of opponents in Corinth. While not denying the insights of such readings, Bowens problematizes and deepens the analysis in theological terms by relating 12:1-10 to the wider context of chapters 10-13, a context in which cosmic warfare features heavily. Thus, the heavenly ascent account serves to locate Paul's ministry, and the lives of his Corinthian audience, within a cosmic-apocalyptic frame of reference. Paul's account of his ascent to the third heaven may well be in service of defending his ministry in some sense, but, as with

---

93. A category borrowed from Umberto Eco, *The Limits of Interpretation* (Bloomington: Indiana University Press, 1990). See Bowens, *Apostle in* Battle, 40-41; 225-26, and esp. ch. 2.

94. Another of Loren Stuckenbruck's phrases, cited in Bowens, *Apostle in Battle*, 39.

95. Bowens, *Apostle in Battle*, 40; 97, noting de Boer's use of this category.

96. As argued in Bowens, "Apocalyptic Texture."

Gaventa on Gal 1 and 2, it is much more than that: it serves to reveal that this ministry (and by extension the lives of the Corinthian believers) is part of a larger cosmic and apocalyptic battle.

Bowens argues, on the basis of the flurry of cognitive terms in the immediate context, that the primary arena of this battle in 2 Corinthians is epistemological: the cosmic war indicated by Paul's martial language is located in the human mind.[97] This conjunction of apocalyptic cosmology, anthropology, and epistemology (which Bowens also traces in the other Second Temple literature she surveys) runs through the whole of 2 Corinthians. Paul speaks of "the god of this age" (ὁ θεὸς τοῦ αἰῶνος τούτου, 4:4) who has blinded the minds of unbelievers, the "strongholds" and "obstacles" erected against the knowledge of God (10:4–5), and the deceit of the primordial serpent which is analogous to corrupt thinking (11:3). In Paul's apocalyptic thought in 2 Corinthians, all of these "anti-God powers"[98] war against the knowledge of God. Read in this cosmological framework, Bowens concludes, the ascent narrative in 12:1–10 is not merely the apostle's rhetorical defense of his authority in the face of earthly opposition, nor only a means of revelation, but an account of an "apostle in battle."[99]

Epistemology and cosmology are also interrelated in the manner of Paul's participation in this war, which is focused on his "thorn" (σκόλοψ, a word which, Bowens argues, has military connotations[100]) and his contest with a "messenger of Satan" (ἄγγελος Σατανᾶ, 12:7). Following the same logic as J. Louis Martyn's argument concerning epistemology in 2 Cor 5:16, Bowens notes that Paul's warfare in this battle is not waged κατὰ σάρκα, "according to the flesh," but by the power of God.[101] Paul's two ways of know-

---

97. Bowens, *Apostle in Battle*, 36, 70–84.

98. Martyn, *Galatians,* 370–373, cf. Bowens, *Apostle in Battle*, 84.

99. For a broader theological assessment of this idea, see Bowens "Divine Desire." For an interpretation of Paul's martial "powers" imagery in the context of a similar range of Second Temple texts, but that is critical of the Apocalyptic Paul, see Wasserman, *Apocalypse as Holy War*. In Wasserman's view, this imagery is a rhetorical device deployed to indicate a relatively stable world of "divine politics" in which the theme of cosmic battle does not speak of metaphysical realities but of "inner struggle, heroic submission, and ethical solidarity" (15). The Apocalyptic Paul's readings of such language, Wasserman insists, are hampered by "uncritical, hodge-podge conceptions ... shaped to suit certain theological agendas." (203)

100. See the word study in Bowens, *Apostle in Battle*, 156–58, which suggests that Paul's "thorn" is more like a "stake" or palisade, used on the battlefield to impede advancing armies.

101. Again, see Martyn, "Epistemology at the Turn of the Ages." Bowens's connection

ing in chapter 5 are here paralleled by two ways of waging cosmic war, as his apocalyptic theology intertwines epistemological, cosmological, and anthropological themes.

Another implication of Bowens's emphasis on Paul's martial language is that it brings the theme of *liberation* closely into the discussion of Paul's apocalyptic thought. Since Paul participates in a cosmic war that intersects with the earthly realm, his apocalyptic gospel is, in some sense, a gospel of liberation in the face of the "powers" of systemic Sin and injustice. As such, liberation theologies should be drawn into the orbit of the Apocalyptic Paul conversation. In this manner, Bowens follows the line of thinking initiated by Käsemann, for whom "apocalyptic theology always and everywhere denotes a theology of liberation in an earth that is dying and plagued by evil powers."[102] This intersection of cosmological warfare and anthropological resistance to the "powers" is a theme that has been particularly emphasised in African American reception of Paul, which Bowens has recently surveyed and to which she has already made a significant contribution.[103]

With Bowens we arrive (more or less) at the present day, and thus the end of our survey of the main contemporary contributors to the Apocalyptic Paul. In chapter 4, we will return to some of the more important themes and insights highlighted in this survey in relation to critiques of the movement. Then, in chapter 5, I will draw on these threads in responding to these critiques and offering a few case studies in interdisciplinary Pauline interpretation. Before that, however, we will take a (somewhat briefer) tour through some of the voices entering the conversation on Paul's apocalyptic thought from the field of systematic theology.

---

to Martyn is clearest at this point, as she affirms his adverbial reading of κατὰ σάρκα and develops it in relation to its martial significance in ch. 10 (Bowens, *Apostle in Battle*, 56).

102. Käsemann, "Beginning of the Gospel: The Message of the Kingdom of God" in *Crucified Nazarene*, 8. On apocalyptic literature and resistance, see also Portier-Young, *Apocalypse Against Empire*.

103. In Bowens, *African American Readings of Paul* (esp. 288–89).

CHAPTER 3

Christian Theology and the "Apocalyptic Turn"

ONE OF THE MORE stimulating aspects of the recent conversation about Paul's apocalyptic thought is that, unlike many contemporary Pauline debates, it is not a discussion that remains within the confines of the guild of Paul specialists, or even those of the New Testament. In many and diverse ways, it has established itself as a conversation between New Testament scholars and systematic theologians. This should hardly be surprising by now—if it is anything, the conversation about the Apocalyptic Paul is an irreducibly *theological* one, not least because of the profound influence Karl Barth has had on almost every scholar named so far. And Barth, of course, was no respecter of the artificial boundary regularly erected to separate the domains of exegete and theologian.[1]

An interesting example of how this interdisciplinary concern characterizes the Apocalyptic Paul conversation is the working group "Explorations in Theology and Apocalyptic" established in 2009 at the joint annual meetings of the *Society of Biblical Literature* and the *American Academy of Religion*. This group brought together New Testament scholars and systematic theologians, choosing as its inaugural theme the significance of the Pauline scholarship of J. Louis Martyn for contemporary biblical studies and theology. For more than a decade it has been something of a home to this discussion and has always attracted participants from both guilds.[2]

---

1. As Martyn notes in "God's Way of Making Right what is Wrong" in *Issues*, 144n8.

2. Their steering group still includes both Pauline specialists and systematic theologians, and both fields are well represented in their recommended reading list. See https://theologyandapocalyptic.wordpress.com.

A comprehensive treatment of the "apocalyptic turn" in contemporary systematic theology belongs in a different book and would certainly be better written by a different author, but it would be a serious error not to include at least some of these voices in the present study. As such, I offer here a few summaries, shorter still than the others, on a limited selection of Protestant theologians who have been explicit in their indebtedness to scholarship on Paul's apocalyptic thought, and who have explored its significance for contemporary Christian systematic theology and ethics.[3]

3.1 Walter Lowe: Why Theology Needs Apocalyptic

Ten years before the "Explorations in Theology and Apocalyptic" group first met, Walter Lowe wrote an article describing what he saw as the prospects for a postmodern theology in the twenty-first century. The future of theology, he argued, was a commitment to "apocalyptic without reserve."[4] His reflections on what that may mean, and why it should prove to be the hope for a Christian postmodern theology, were programmatic in the early stages of the thinking of many in this group of theologians.

As Lowe so powerfully puts it, Christian theology wasn't supposed to happen, for there wasn't supposed to have been time. The imminence of the eschatological return of Christ, expressed in the Synoptic Gospels in passages such as Mark 13 and Matthew 24, meant that there may have been "time for theology on the run, perhaps; but not for theology as we now have it, theology with footnotes."[5] At this point, Lowe, like many others, equates "apocalyptic" with imminent eschatology. The resulting urgency of the required response to the gospel, and the problem of the "delay of the *parousia*" mean, for Lowe, that an essential feature of apocalyptic theology is a challenge to historical continuity and the myth of progress.

---

3. It does seem to be largely a protestant conversation at present. D. Stephen Long, reflecting at length on the question of apocalyptic in New Testament studies, and also on the current "apocalyptic tone" in theology, describes it as the product of "some ardently Protestant theologians" (Long, *Hebrews*, 207). Cyril O'Regan has suggested that one might even say "the category of 'Catholic apocalyptic theology' is an oxymoron" (O'Regan, "Two Forms," 31). As an example of the apparently irreducibly protestant character of apocalyptic theology, Long and O'Regan both cite the work of Nathan Kerr, discussed below. See also Macaskill, *Intellectual Humility*, 113.

4. Lowe, "Prospects."

5. Lowe, "Prospects," 18.

Lowe views this early Christian apocalyptic tenor as having a parallel in twentieth century theologies of crisis, and Barth's *Romans* in particular represents a place where these concerns combine. For Lowe, what Barth achieved was something of a "postmodern" commentary ahead of its time. Though conversant with the Derridean emphasis on a postmodern philosophy with an "apocalyptic tone,"[6] Lowe begins not in postmodern philosophy but in Barth's turn away from liberal progressivism and the modernist foundations which postmodernism later challenged. Lowe's programmatic essays thus offer a distinctly Barthian account of the prospects of apocalyptic for contemporary postmodern theology.

The distinctive feature of apocalyptic theology, for Lowe, is that it "cuts across human time" as "the ultimate interruption."[7] It therefore offers the best critique to the hegemony of metanarratives, a critique famously characteristic of postmodern philosophy. The modernist tendency is to contextualize the gospel: to inscribe it by, and contain it within, the immanent frame of history. In contrast, Lowe argues, an apocalyptic theology of history considers history as such to be "headed for the dustbin."[8] Apocalyptic theology reverses this logic, insisting that it is not we that inscribe the gospel but the gospel that inscribes us, and in such a way as to make it impossible to historicize apocalyptic onto an assumed unbroken timeline. For Lowe, all continuous timelines (whether narrative or historical, earthly or heavenly) suppress the force of the apocalyptic tone in Christian theology and are therefore to be rejected.[9] Barth's theology of crisis saw this, according to Lowe, and he would have us retrieve and rethink it, lest it too be claimed by an assumed historical timeline. This, he argues, is what makes apocalyptic necessary for contemporary theology.

Lowe's subsequent work continues to demonstrate a close and extended engagement with Barth, not only in the *Römerbrief* but also in the *Church Dogmatics*. In an article entitled "Why we need apocalyptic,"[10] Lowe engages *CD* II/1, and Barth's endeavors to avoid liberal theology's fixation on experience and existentialism, and its problematic espousal of an immanent view of history as "processionalist advance."[11] Again, the central

6. See Derrida, "Apocalyptic Tone."
7. Lowe, "Prospects," 22.
8. Lowe, "Prospects," 23.
9. Lowe, "Prospects," 23.
10. Lowe, "Why We Need Apocalyptic."
11. Lowe, "Why We Need Apocalyptic," 48.

insight is that the gospel contextualizes history, not the other way around. Lowe marks this as perhaps the most crucial claim for contemporary theologians to grasp from Barth's apocalyptic theology. Though Barth is not completely averse to using the "classical language of apocalyptic,"[12] Lowe admits that the term does not appear in the index to the *Church Dogmatics*. His main argument, however, is that it remains an appropriate description of Barth's project as a whole.[13] Barth's mature theology, Lowe argues, offers a view of time and history which locates time within eternity in a manner analogous to the "traditional" apocalyptic visions in their depictions of time and history in the context of a heavenly court or divine plan.[14]

It is not clear whether Lowe was familiar with the distinctly Barthian tone of Martyn's 1997 Galatians commentary when he wrote his 1999 article on the prospects of apocalyptic for the future of theology. Certainly, though, it had an influence on his later explorations of theology and apocalyptic. In one essay, published in 2009, Lowe cites Martyn's *Galatians* with approval for bringing back into the frame the apocalyptic vocabulary of "invasion, conflict, powers, triumph" which theology had too often downplayed.[15] Lowe suggests that the Pauline cosmological apocalyptic language of new creation, especially as indexed to the "past" event of the death of Christ, offers the most potent antidote to the problems of modern liberal theology. The continued presence of Martyn's Pauline scholarship in Lowe's essays from then on indicates his importance for shaping Lowe's definition of apocalyptic.[16] His own programmatic essays, spanning more than a decade, were of foundational importance for much of the discussion of apocalyptic theology in the years that followed.

3.2 Nathan Kerr: Apocalyptic, History, and Theopolitics

Another theologian who recognizes the presence of a particularly apocalyptic tone in contemporary philosophy is Nathan Kerr. His much-discussed 2008 book *Christ, History and Apocalyptic* sought to give an account of "a

---

12. Lowe, "Why We Need Apocalyptic," 50, citing Barth *CD* II/1, 171.

13. Lowe, "Why We Need Apocalyptic," 50.

14. Lowe, "Why We Need Apocalyptic," 53. Lowe doesn't say which sources he has in mind here, but the context seems to imply Jewish and Christian visionary texts.

15. Lowe, "Why We Need Apocalyptic," 52.

16. In a 2012 volume assessing the importance of Martyn's work for the future of Christian theology, Lowe's essay is chapter 1 (Lowe, "Nearer to Us").

distinctively *Christian* apocalyptic vision" for contemporary theology.[17] Kerr developed this in relation to the political theology of Troeltsch, Barth, Hauerwas, and Yoder, before offering his own constructive apocalyptic account of Christian politics and mission. What is clear throughout the work, however, is that though its primary interlocutors are drawn from the guild of systematic theology and Christian ethics, Kerr's framing approach to the question of apocalyptic has been profoundly shaped by Martyn's scholarship on Paul. This connection to Pauline scholarship is most clearly seen in Kerr's opening "thematics" of Christian apocalyptic.

In Kerr's account, the first and most important theme for a distinctively Christian apocalyptic theology (here echoing the driving concerns of Barth's early work) is the priority of God's action and his radical otherness to this world. This "otherness" of God and the essential priority of his action means that Christian apocalyptic theology will be characterized by the motif of divine "invasive action" into a world that is passing away. Here, Kerr cites Martyn's commentary and essays on Galatians,[18] from where he borrows the language of "invasion." What is particularly interesting in Kerr's articulation of this first and fundamental point is his clear conviction that this is a theme "most clearly dependent on the conceptual framework inherited by early Christianity from Jewish apocalyptic."[19] Here he explicitly cites John Collins's work on the Jewish apocalyptic literature and his emphasis on the "radical contrasts" characteristic of that genre.[20]

The second core theme of a Christian apocalyptic theology, for Kerr, is that God's invasive action finds its particular locus (its "center of gravity") in the singular event of the history of Jesus Christ. This theme is second, however, only in terms of Kerr's outline of the thematics of Christian apocalyptic theology. In terms of logic, it is one and the same with the first point, which is to say that the concrete history of Jesus precisely *is* the invasive divine action, and thus the controlling factor in any apocalyptic reasoning. Kerr judges deficient any account of history, of God's activity within it, or of any theological principles not oriented to this christological starting point.

---

17. Kerr, *Christ, History and Apocalyptic*, 12.

18. Namely, his 1997 Anchor Bible commentary and his essay "Apocalyptic Gospel in Galatians," cited in Kerr, *Christ, History and Apocalyptic*, 13.

19. Kerr, *Christ, History and Apocalyptic*, 12.

20. Collins, *Apocalyptic Imagination*, 1–42, cited in Kerr, *Christ, History and Apocalyptic*, 12.

The third theme Kerr highlights is that a Christian apocalyptic theology recognizes that the invasive divine action in the singular history of Jesus Christ is both cosmic and historical in scope. In the death and resurrection of Christ, God brings about a new cosmos, delivered from slavery to the powers of this present evil age. This cosmic deliverance, again, is unintelligible apart from the concrete act of God in Christ. It is, as such, historical. The transformative work of God's reign within ongoing history is brought about by the Spirit, performing the reality of Christ's victory in the contingencies of history.[21] This cosmic and historical scope, rooted in the event of Christ and worked out pneumatologically, leads Kerr via a theological route to the same commitment found in most apocalyptic Pauline scholarship, namely an eschatological tension between the "already" and the "not yet."

These first three foundational theological commitments lead Kerr to two more themes, expressed by the subtitle of his book, regarding an apocalyptic account of Christian politics and mission, and of the church as the operation of God's in-breaking lordship in history. At this point the connection with apocalyptic is explained as, essentially, another name for the death and victory of Christ in which the church participates by the Spirit in the contingencies of history. Since this apocalyptic, invasive divine rule must be understood christologically, this is a lordship characterized by Jesus's victory through self-giving, and his priestly and prophetic roles, in which the church participates. The mode of this participation in the apocalyptic action of God, Kerr argues, is through mission and worship. God's invasive action in the world in Christ has liberated his people from the powers of the present age and results in praise and mission, that is, in the church's response to God's action in worship and their being sent as a witness and sign of his in-breaking reign. Martyn's commentary on Galatians is again cited at this point, as this emphasis on mission completes Kerr's survey of Christian apocalyptic thematics: "God's apocalypse of Jesus Christ . . . was the birth of the gospel mission."[22]

A driving agenda throughout Kerr's monograph is the centrality of an apocalyptic Christology understood as "a sustained response to the crisis of modern immanentist historicism."[23] This apocalyptic account of history springs from similar ideological concerns in Barth's early work, particularly

21. Kerr, *Christ, History and Apocalyptic*, 14.
22. Martyn, *Galatians*, 99 cited in Kerr, *Christ, History and Apocalyptic*, 15.
23. Kerr, *Christ, History and Apocalyptic*, 17.

his commentary on Romans, though Kerr is not uncritical of Barth at this point. Kerr deploys his apocalyptic account of history as a challenge to Troeltsch (who represents, for Kerr, the "eclipse of apocalyptic"[24]), and is variously invoked in dialogue with Barth, Hauerwas, and Yoder, and then developed in Kerr's own contribution. The question of apocalyptic theology and history is an abiding concern throughout. In short, what Kerr seeks to develop (at this point seeing a shortcoming in Barth's account and attempting to go beyond him) is an "apocalyptic historicism,"[25] and a concomitant theology of politics and mission that addresses the weaknesses of the modern immanentist view of history without slipping into the opposite error of effacing the historicity of the Christ event and its impact on our "real history." For Kerr, Christian apocalyptic theology offers the solution to this problem.

3.3 Philip Ziegler: Grace and Discipleship in the "Three-Agent Drama"

Another systematic theologian who has both learned from and contributed to the discussion of Pauline apocalyptic theology is Philip Ziegler, whose 2018 volume *Militant Grace: the Apocalyptic Turn and the Future of Christian Theology* is dedicated to Martyn. Ziegler's book gathers together various essays on theological and ethical themes, as well as focused engagements with Calvin, Kierkegaard, and Bonhoeffer. At first glance, the book may appear to be a somewhat disparate collection of a decade's worth of previously published and revised essays, but the underlying coherence of the volume is found in the apocalyptic theological convictions that drive each piece.

These convictions are explicitly developed in Ziegler's introduction to the volume, and its first two essays, outlining the "shape and sources" as well as the "background, tone, and tasks" of an apocalyptic theology.[26] For Ziegler, the "apocalyptic eschatology, language, and imagery of the New Testament is integral to its witness to the accomplishment of God's salvation in Jesus Christ."[27] Apocalyptic is no mere "husk" to the New Testament witness, an incidental external framework, but is essential to its theological

---

24. Kerr, *Christ, History and Apocalyptic*, 19.
25. Kerr, *Christ, History and Apocalyptic*, 92, 161.
26. Titles of chs. 1 and 2, respectively, in Ziegler, *Militant Grace*.
27. Ziegler, *Militant Grace*, xiii.

message and thus requiring a thoroughgoing and responsible theological account.

Ziegler notes that the most important discussions of this apocalyptic New Testament theology have come from the guild of Pauline scholars, and names a list of contemporary figures and their heritage in the line from Käsemann through Beker to Martyn. The conversation about apocalyptic theology is therefore, for Ziegler, very much a Pauline one. The theology of *Krisis* found in Karl Barth is certainly a clear influence throughout Ziegler's account of an apocalyptic Christian theology, and he names the Swiss theologian's early work (especially the second edition of his commentary on Romans) as a pioneering account of apocalyptic dogmatics, though this is usually as received through the Pauline scholarship of Käsemann and Martyn.

Ziegler seeks to take this Pauline apocalyptic theology in a systematic theological direction, rethinking Christian theology's method, shape, and foci in an apocalyptic and eschatological mode. The nature of the commitments involved has far-reaching consequences for Christian dogmatics, which Ziegler explores in his various essays. At the heart of each, however, is the conviction that for Christian theology to make this "apocalyptic turn" is to recognize that the theologian must eschew thinking according to "the world that is passing away," captive as it is to powers inimical to God, and embrace not only new thematic emphases but new forms of thought appropriate to the world made new in the liberating apocalypse of Jesus Christ.

In much the same manner as Kerr's Christian apocalyptic "thematics," and after having offered his own summary of and engagement with Kerr's project, Ziegler outlines six programmatic theses for an apocalyptic theology.[28]

First, the New Testament apocalyptic language presents, in Ziegler's view, a particularly powerful idiom with which theology can express the scope of the gospel. The scope of the claims made about the cosmological and anthropological power of God revealed in Christ expressed by the apocalyptic language of the New Testament has a particular power for articulating "the gratuity of divine sovereignty and the sovereignty of divine grace."[29] Moreover, it is well suited to describing the cosmic opposition to that sovereignty in the present age, and the essentially militant nature of the

---

28. I am here largely summarizing Ziegler, *Militant Grace,* chapter 2, previously published as "Some Remarks on Apocalyptic."

29. Ziegler, *Militant Grace,* 26.

Christian Theology and the "Apocalyptic Turn"

Christian life in this contested present time. As such the language of apocalyptic is a language uniquely suited to the task of Christian dogmatics.

Secondly, New Testament apocalyptic offers the task of Christian dogmatics a discourse that is irreducibly christological in its focus. The revelation of Jesus Christ in his incarnation, crucifixion, and resurrection is the event on which the two ages turn and is as such *the* apocalyptic event. The concrete historical shape of this apocalyptic event and its significance is thus, as Ziegler puts it, the "center of gravity" for any Christian dogmatics.[30] Theology done in an apocalyptic mode will be funded and governed by a thoroughgoing christological orientation.

Thirdly, the distinctive emphases of New Testament apocalyptic discourse on the irruptive and disjunctive nature of the divine act of salvation in Christ offer Christian dogmatics a powerful way to speak of the "newness" of the gospel. Here Ziegler signals his indebtedness to Martyn in his deployment of the motif of an "invasion" that overthrows existing distinctions (such as Jew/gentile) and the establishment of new contrasts ("militant antinomies" in Martyn's language)[31] that signal the dualistic nature of the gospel in relation to the present age. Apocalyptic theology, Ziegler argues, insists on this essentially discontinuous tenor, expressing the gospel's radical break with the present age.

Fourthly, and again drawing on Martyn's work, Ziegler finds in New Testament apocalyptic theology "an account of salvation as a 'three-agent drama' of divine redemption."[32] An apocalyptic soteriology involves speaking not only of two agents, God and humanity, but also of the inimical powers (sin, death, the devil), which threaten to hold humanity in bondage. The human situation into which God's redemptive action breaks is thus construed not merely as one of legal transgression but also of cosmic slavery under the power of this "third agent." A comprehensive, apocalyptic account of sin, therefore, will endeavor to speak both of guilt/forgiveness and of slavery/deliverance. To borrow Martyn's metaphor, it must have "bifocal vision."[33] Ziegler's most recent work is thus particularly invested in the challenge of developing a fresh account of this anti-God "third agent"

---

30. Ziegler, *Militant Grace*, 27.

31. Martyn, *Galatians*, 101, cited in Ziegler, *Militant Grace*, 28.

32. Ziegler, *Militant Grace*, 28. The phrase "three-agent drama" was developed and regularly deployed by Martyn. See "Epilogue" and "Gospel Invades Philosophy."

33. Martyn, *Issues*, 284, cited in Ziegler, *Militant Grace*, 29.

in Christian dogmatics,[34] newly funded by the explanatory power of this aspect of a New Testament apocalyptic discourse. Ziegler's apocalyptic account of Christian soteriology speaks of humanity as both agents of sin and its slaves. Crucially, the dogmatic ordering of these two truths is important: the latter logically precedes the former. In respect of sin, human beings are "first its victims and only then its recruits."[35] This leads to an account of sin not only in the moral but also the ontological register, and thus to an appropriately ontological account of God's redemption.[36] What is more, this must also lead to the question of the "apotheosis" of sin, the Devil.[37] If, as Paul so pointedly claims at the end of his letter to the church in Rome, "the God of peace will soon crush Satan under your feet" (Rom 16:20), then Christian theology must give a robust account of the dogmatic location and the ontology of this "third agent." Ziegler finds in the work of Barth and in the labors of the Apocalyptic Paul a language eminently suited to this task.[38]

What results, fifthly, is an apocalyptic and bifocal account of God's act of deliverance with a cosmic scope, not one limited to the church or even to humankind. New Testament apocalyptic has a "widescreen" view on the scope of sin and salvation,[39] in which the whole of creation is the object of God's salvific action in Christ. The church is not the sole object of God's attention but recognizes its role as the witness to the world of this broader cosmic salvation of which it is the firstfruits. Reframed in this apocalyptic mode, Christian discipleship will be shaped by militant resistance to the powers of this age that contest God's present and coming lordship, and by the task of witness to the reality of this world's true Lord, as developed in the final thesis below. New Testament apocalyptic language and thought is uniquely suited to the shaping of the Christian imagination for this vocation.

Finally, the New Testament apocalyptic eschatology, which underpins this view of the Christian vocation, means that the church's mission will be

---

34. See, e.g., "Bound Over" and "First and Final."

35. Ziegler, "Bound Over," 97.

36. Here, Ziegler's account of the ontology of sin is aided by Barth's analysis of sin as 'nothingness' (*das Nichtige*). See Ziegler, "Bound Over," 99, and cf. Barth CD III/3 §50.

37. Ziegler, "First and Final."

38. See the fuller argument of Ziegler, "First and Final" for his most recent exploration of this. In brief, Ziegler points to Barth's distributed location of this doctrine, and to the fundamental incoherence of this "third agent", again citing CD III/3 §50.

39. I am borrowing the "widescreen" metaphor from Gaventa, "Cosmic Power of Sin."

shaped by an eschatological tension between "this age" and the imminently expected "age to come." Christian theology, for Ziegler, thus adopts "a posture of prayerful expectation" of this future.[40] Christian mission, framed apocalyptically, will not be comfortable with the structures of this present world. It will be the mission of a "pilgrim" church ill at ease with this world, knowing that it lives in "the time that remains" and looking to the horizon for God's coming kingdom. The task of Christian mission, and of a Christian apocalyptic theology more generally, is thus framed by an imminent eschatological expectation.

3.4 Douglas Harink: Time and Politics in the Apocalyptic Paul

Douglas Harink is another systematic theologian who has been very clear about the indebtedness of his own work on apocalyptic theology to contemporary Pauline scholarship. Martyn is again especially praised for his programmatic influence as the "foundational figure in the contemporary understanding of the 'Apocalyptic Paul'"[41] without whom Harink's own theological work would be impossible.[42] Harink co-chairs (with Philip Ziegler) the "Explorations in Theology and Apocalyptic" working group, which began its work with a reflection on the importance of Martyn's work on Paul for systematic theology. Harink was also the co-editor (with Joshua Davis) of a volume of essays on "Apocalyptic and the Future of Theology," which explored the potential of going "with and beyond" Martyn not only in New Testament studies, but in Christian theology and ethics.[43] Harink's own essay in the volume turns to Martyn's commentary on Galatians for a framework for an apocalyptic account of hermeneutics, history, and human political agency.

The contours of Martyn's work on Paul, and behind that the thought of Käsemann, can be clearly traced in Harink's definition of "apocalypse" (a word Harink uses as both a noun and a verb).[44] The task of defining

40. Ziegler, *Militant Grace*, 30.
41. Harink, *Resurrecting Justice*, xi. Harink also names Gaventa and Campbell here.
42. Harink, "Partakers," 73.
43. Davis and Harink, *Apocalyptic and the Future*. This volume can serve as a valuable onramp to the discussion of apocalyptic after Martyn in systematic theological circles, though there are a number of Pauline scholars in the contents, too.
44. Harink, *Resurrecting Justice*, 16.

the term means, among other things, thinking biblically by going to the canonical apocalyptic texts Ezekiel, Daniel, and Revelation as well as more overtly apocalyptic material in the gospels such as Mark 13.[45] Here, Harink argues, we see the revelation of hidden things, to be sure, and that surface meaning of "apocalypse" remains. But restricting the meaning to this revelatory significance is insufficient for Harink. What we find in these texts is that God is not only pulling back a curtain to reveal mysteries but also, and perhaps more importantly, acting decisively to deliver the world from slavery and create it anew. This is most clearly seen in Revelation, which opens with a claim to be an "apocalypse of Jesus Christ" and closes with a vision of that new creative divine act. At its heart, then, Harink's view of Christian apocalyptic theology is an emphasis on the invasive divine action in Christ to liberate an enslaved cosmos and bring about new creation.[46]

In the letters of Paul, of course, we do not find this same genre of writing, though Harink notes the apocalyptic tenor of 1 Thess 4–5 and 2 Thess 2,[47] but at crucial points in Paul's letters, he does speak of his gospel as an "apocalypse." In this way Paul signals a commitment not only to the revelation of the mystery of the Christ-event but to the reality of the power of God at work in that event to destroy and remake the world (meaning the κόσμος of Gal 6:14–15, which Harink understands as something like the "present evil age," creation in bondage to the powers, contrasted with κτίσις, creation as such). Working this apocalypse out in the Christian life, Paul can therefore speak of the death to self and new life to God (e.g., 2 Cor 5:17), and in Harink's view it is this new-creative reality that constitutes Paul's apocalyptic gospel. There is also a dark side to this, however. The world-renewing act of God in Christ is also and simultaneously the revelation of God's justice against human iniquity and all that is wrong in this present world,[48] and Harink has recently explored this theme through his own theological commentary on the letter to the Romans.[49]

This focus on justice will come as no surprise to those who have followed Harink's particular contribution to the Apocalyptic Paul conversation. One of the distinctive characteristics of his various essays on apocalyptic theology has been an ongoing concern for working out its theopolitical

---

45. Harink, *Resurrecting Justice*, 13.
46. Harink, "Partakers," 74.
47. Harink, *Resurrecting Justice*, 14.
48. Harink, *Resurrecting Justice*, 15.
49. Harink, *Resurrecting Justice*.

implications, particularly as they relate to the question of human agency. Here again Martyn's influence is clear as Harink, like Ziegler, enthusiastically endorses the framework of a "three-actor moral drama," exploring its potentialities for an apocalyptic political theology. In this apocalyptic framework, there is no "neutral ground" on which the human moral agent might stand in order to make political choices. Humankind may have been created with the moral competence to make such choices, but they have, since Adam, chosen disobedience and have as a result become enslaved to the "third agent" in this moral drama, the anti-God powers. This results in a bifocal soteriology, since "the human agent must be delivered not only from disobedience, but also from enslavement" by the invasive power of the gospel.[50] In all this, Harink closely follows Martyn. His signature contributions, however, develop this apocalyptic dynamic, particularly the emphasis on the "third agent," in relation to political theology. This deliverance from enslaving powers is the only thing that can create competent human moral agency and is therefore the basis of Harink's apocalyptic account of political theology.

A political theology is necessary at precisely this point because the apocalypse of Jesus Christ not only establishes individual moral agency but creates a new corporate, and therefore political, order. The new creation does not only create new individual agency but a new community, with a new political agency. This community will find that the choice between "conservative" and "progressive" is impossible, neither will it be identified with any empire, king, or would-be "Christian" political party.[51] But nor is it straightforwardly a revolutionary politics. None of these remain theological options because of the apocalyptic basis of the new political order, not found in this present world, which is passing away, but in the new creation God is bringing about. It is thus not a community that seeks to achieve its ends or measure its accomplishments by the standards of this age, which remain part of a world in bondage. Rather, this political reality arrives, by participation in the divine apocalypse, as the invasive act of God into this world as a "*hidden* but politically *explosive* divine power."[52]

Inseparable from Harink's apocalyptic political theology is his view of time and history. In Harink's apocalyptic framework, all "times" are present in the apocalypse of Jesus Christ. This irreducibly christological perspective

---

50. Harink, "Partakers," 90–91.
51. Harink, "Partakers," 95; Harink, "Who Hopes," 164.
52. Harink, "Who Hopes," 164 (emphasis original).

on time challenges any view of history (and, as we saw above, any associated political philosophy) that views it as a linear progression leading or building up to the Christ-event. The apocalypse of Jesus is not one more event, even if the greatest, in history. It is, rather, an event invading history from without. Harink's account of apocalyptic leaves no option for any immanentist account of salvation history, since "the straightforward tracks of Scripture and tradition all arrive at a dead end."[53] His argument on this point is repeatedly framed in the most polemical language, since it strikes at the heart of his apocalyptic theology. For Harink, the invasive apocalypse of Jesus Christ cancels history, tradition, and Scripture "as far as their *messianic epistemological 'potential'* goes."[54] As such, in various places Harink argues that Paul never appeals to historical continuity in his discussion of Israel. If there is a trajectory that joins Scripture to the gospel, it is one that flows backward, not forward; the gospel does not arise from the potentialities of history but conditions and reconstitutes it. Therefore, it must not be made to conform to the logic of "linear historical causality."[55] Martyn's view, as we saw above, was that Galatians was written *against* such a view of salvation history, and here Harink agrees.

History, Harink insists, is not "going somewhere"; it has no "saving trajectory" and is therefore nothing but wreckage.[56] What the apocalypse of Jesus Christ reveals about history is that it is in bondage to the powers of sin and death. The story of Israel has some value, however, inasmuch as it is the locus of the divine promise. This is not a value inherent in the history of Israel in and of itself, of course, but names it as the place of divine election and promissory perdurance.[57] Moreover, this claim is as relevant for history after Jesus as it is of the history before him: there is thus no possibility of tracing a saving trajectory forward toward the kingdom of God. The history of the church, just as much as the history of Israel, needs to be redeemed from its bondage to the powers of sin and death.

In this connection, Harink particularly singles out the work of N. T. Wright as the prime contemporary example of this problematic approach to history. Harink rejects what he sees as Wright's narrative account of

---

53. Harink, "Partakers," 83.
54. Harink, "Partakers," 84 (emphasis original).
55. Harink, "Paul and Israel," 367.
56. Harink, "Partakers," 86, citing Walter Benjamin.
57. Harink, "Partakers," 89–90.

redemptive history, which, he thinks, falls into this progressivist trap.[58] Harink's view (again with Martyn, and both relying on their reading of Barth's *Romans*) is that such a view represents the position of Paul's opponents in Galatia rather than Paul himself. Harink suggests that the attempt to make this part of the apostle's thought is driven by a worthy but misplaced desire to protect him from an anti-Judaic hermeneutic that might lead to Marcionism or supersessionism. Harink's view, however, is that it is the progressivism of the redemptive-historical position (as he sees it) that is really supersessionist, being a species of an evolutionary developmental view of history that presumes the superiority of the later over the earlier. In Harink's view, only the apocalyptic reading of history avoids this supersessionist error.[59]

Much of the debate in the Apocalyptic Paul continues, for good reason, to focus on the question of history, and we will shortly return to this matter in the final section of this book. A final comment must be made, however, about Harink's brief explorations of the significance of apocalyptic theology for hermeneutics. Again, the catalyst for his thought is Martyn's Galatians commentary, which Harink considers one of the two most important theological commentaries of the twentieth century (the other being Barth's *Romans*).[60] What it means to speak of a "theological commentary" on Scripture is of course a contested issue. For Harink, apocalyptic theology has profound implications for defining this task.

The reality of the apocalypse of Jesus Christ is not only a theme in Paul's letters but a hermeneutical standpoint from which to read them. In Harink's view, the commentator does not work exegetically towards an apocalyptic perspective but stands within it *ab initio*. A consequence of this is that the task of theological commentary should be done from a perspective within the apocalypse of Jesus Christ.[61] This, Harink suggests, gener-

---

58. Harink says that it's not possible to speak, as he thinks Wright does, of God "quietly and steadily working his purposes out" (Harink, "Partakers," 85, quoting Wright, *Paul* 50–51), though Harink has probably misunderstood Wright here. In any case Wright's most recent work suggests that something more subtle is happening in his theology of history (see 4.4 below).

59. Harink, "Partakers," 89. For more on supersessionism and Harink's view on the relationship between Israel and Paul's apocalyptic theology, see Harink "Paul and Israel."

60. Harink, "Partakers," 75.

61. There are obvious similarities here with Campbell's most recent claims examined in 2.5 above.

ates an approach to that task that is defensibly *theological*,[62] and Martyn's *Galatians* is considered the prime contemporary example.[63] The invasive act of God in Christ has revealed that there is no "neutral ground" for the commentator either, since this world is captive to the "third agent" anti-God powers. As with politics, the message of a Pauline letter doesn't allow such a "neutral" standpoint from which the commentator may operate, even if only as a first stage in the process. It is logically impossible, therefore, to think of theological interpretation of Scripture as some kind of "second step" to be undertaken after the historical work has been done. The apocalyptic event of Christ conditions everything, including the hermeneutical process. Commentary, like politics, is first and foremost participation in this apocalyptic event.[64]

With this we come to the end of our necessarily brief and fragmentary survey of the apocalyptic turn in contemporary systematic theology, and the end of the survey of the Apocalyptic Paul movement as a whole. In chapters 2 and 3 the attentive reader may have already noted a number of points of friction and controversy it has generated. The second part of this book will now explore some of these, as well as some areas of common ground, in more detail.

---

62. I allude here to the work of John Webster, who Harink cites with approval and whose doctrine of Scripture lies behind this definition of the task of theological commentary. See Webster, "Reading Scripture."

63. Harink, "Partakers," 79.

64. Harink, "Partakers," 78.

PART TWO

Prospects

CHAPTER 4

Unsettled Questions for the Apocalyptic Paul

HAVING COMPLETED A RETROSPECTIVE survey of the movement's main voices in Part One, the aim of this penultimate chapter is to offer a more prospective orientation to some of the challenges that have been brought to the Apocalyptic Paul in a way that hopefully allows for further creative engagement with this school of Pauline scholarship. I do not propose to engage here in a detailed evaluation or critique (such books already exist)[1] but rather to offer something more along the lines of questions and conversation starters for what I hope will be constructive discussion in the future.

The first two sections of this chapter will examine questions of a more methodological nature, concerning the ways in which the Apocalyptic Paul engages in dialogue with two other guilds. First, there is the question of the interaction with scholarship on the Second Temple Jewish and early Christian apocalyptic literature. Second, there is the matter of dialogue with systematic theologians, particularly those working in the Barthian tradition. Since the Apocalyptic Paul claims variously to have connections with both of those fields, it will be important to listen to the questions that have been asked about this reading of Paul from those working in these specialisms. After examining those two interdisciplinary challenges and potential areas for further conversation, the remaining three sections of the chapter summarize some of the significant lines of critique that have arisen from within the guild of Pauline scholarship. These are arranged

---

1. Matlock *Unveiling* is a thorough critique but now quite dated. A useful introduction can be found in Blackwell et al., *Imagination* and an extensive though critical discussion is found in Wright, *Interpreters,* part 2. See now also Shaw, *'Apocalyptic' Paul.* My own contribution is Davies, *Paul Among the Apocalypses.*

thematically, examining in turn questions of epistemology, eschatology, and soteriology. I take these themes to be a reasonable distillation of the core commitments of Martyn's analysis of Pauline apocalyptic thought, as well as being important thematic concerns shared by others in the contemporary discussion. They also constitute, in my view, a helpful taxonomy for examining the principal features of the Jewish and Christian apocalyptic literature. This section thus aims to introduce some of the main critiques of the Apocalyptic Paul before offering summaries of scholarship that might offer constructive ways forward.

I have aimed throughout for a balance of affirmation, constructive contribution, and critique, and to make sure that the latter is appropriately placed. This discussion, as much as any, has at times been characterized by misunderstandings and misdirected criticisms, and important nuances are often missed. Clearing these up and signaling what I take to be somewhat illusory or misplaced disagreements is therefore one of the goals of the remaining chapters of this book. No doubt important debates will remain, but it is vital that these are pressed with precision, care, and generosity in the right places, and not pursued on the basis of misunderstandings or (worse) caricatures of positions.

4.1 The Apocalyptic Paul and the Jewish Apocalyptic Tradition

One of the more commonly heard broad-spectrum challenges to the Apocalyptic Paul movement is that its account of apocalyptic thought bears little resemblance to what is seen in the Jewish and Christian apocalyptic literature. The consideration of apocalyptic themes in Paul, it is regularly argued, attempts a definition of this key term without appropriately contextualizing him in relation to this corpus of texts, cutting the definition's historical roots.[2] In reply, it is sometimes suggested that the word "apocalyptic" is simply being used differently when it comes to Paul (as a nod to an early-Barthian theology of revelation, for example) and that no connection to the apocalyptic literature is intended or necessary.[3] Thus framed, the debate

---

2. See, e.g., Rowland and Morray-Jones, *Mystery of God*, 15; Wright, *Interpreters*, 138; Macaskill, "Review"; Stuckenbruck, "Some Reflections," 141.

3. One regularly hears this sort of comment in discussion, but rarely do any commit it to print. Some (e.g., Sturm, "Defining" and Way, *Lordship*, 131) speak of two ways of using the word ("literary" / "historical" and "theological"), but their analyses do not

threatens to dissolve into a mere terminological dispute, and a resulting stalemate.

What we have seen, however, is that both this critique and the response may well be largely off-target. It does not always come to the surface as a primary concern, but consideration of the apocalyptic literature contemporary to Paul has almost always been the stated conviction of most in the Apocalyptic Paul movement. Variously understood, a connection to the Jewish and Christian apocalyptic literature is repeatedly affirmed by almost all of these Pauline scholars, or at least by those upon whom they rely. Richard Hays is therefore correct to note that the Apocalyptic Paul, while using the word primarily to denote theological claims, nevertheless sees these claims as indicators of a "a family resemblance," a shared "apocalyptic DNA" between Paul and the apocalypses.[4] As the above discussion has shown, only Douglas Campbell stands as a possible exception to this basic position.[5] The important concern, then, is not rival terminological claims, but the question of how much the analysis of the theological themes is attentive to that corpus, and (importantly) what the apostle Paul's christologically shaped deployment of those themes looks like.

It is vital, therefore, that alongside Paulinists and Christian theologians, the voices of specialists in the Second Temple Jewish and early Christian apocalyptic literature are heard in the continuing conversation about Paul's apocalyptic theology. This would facilitate appropriate contextualization of the contours of Paul's thought, and would result in a richer and less misleading use of the term. Regrettably, while there have been numerous gains in the distinctively cross-disciplinary nature of this conversation between Paulinists and theologians, the same cannot be said of its inclusion of specialists in the apocalyptic literature. Where this scholarship does appear in the footnotes, too often it is superficial or a generation out of date. Scholars of the New Testament regularly bemoan the fragmentation of the theological disciplines, and the resulting limitations of guild overspecialism, and here as much as anywhere these limitations are keenly felt.

---

ultimately conclude that this is a mere terminological confusion. One person who does is Douglas Campbell (Campbell, "Attempt," 165n6, and the broader comments in this vein in *Quest,* 56–57n3 and *Pauline Dogmatics,* 22).

4. Hays, "Apocalyptic *Poiēsis* 202–3.

5. But even Campbell, who finds them unhelpful for settling Pauline theological questions (see *Quest,* 56–57n3) and a potential threat to the uniqueness of Christ (*Pauline Dogmatics,* 22) continues to signal his reliance upon and affinity with Käsemann, Martyn, Keck and others, who did not share that view.

It is important to state from the outset that recognizing the Jewish matrix in which Paul's christologically transformed apocalyptic theology takes shape is in no way a threat to the uniqueness of his gospel. Insisting on the presence of the voices of apocalyptic literature specialists is not to say that these voices must set the terms of the debate, that corpus then becoming the epistemological starting point, such that the logic is made to flow from the apocalypses to Paul. Moreover, it is not an insistence that this Jewish apocalyptic background must be understood prior to examining his letters (whether "prior" is taken logically or chronologically). Such a move could suppress Paul's distinctive voice, and potentially underplay the force of the "apocalypse of Jesus Christ" in his theological vision. However, the opposite danger also threatens, of restricting the scope of enquiry to Paul's letters alone such that our account of his apocalyptic theology drifts free of the Jewish and Christian literary world in which he wrote, and to which he is said to relate. The danger here is that the resulting account of Pauline apocalyptic theology is isolated from the apocalyptic witness of, for example, the books of Daniel and Revelation, effectively treating the Pauline letters as a canon within the canon. Concerns such as these have been voiced by numerous New Testament scholars, those of Second Temple Judaism, and (as we will see below) systematic theologians.[6] If we are aiming to describe the christologically transformed apocalyptic eschatology of the early Christian witness, the book of Revelation would seem to be a natural and important place to look.[7] It is important, then, that there is also dialogue with scholarship on Revelation. It is a peculiar feature of contemporary Pauline scholarship that we do seem to be much more ready to relate Paul to extra-canonical sources than we are to relate him to the other NT writings.

What fruit might come from such an interdisciplinary engagement between readers of Paul and the apocalypses? One of the first things a scholar of Second Temple Jewish and early Christian apocalyptic literature will tell you is that it is a very diverse corpus. There is considerable range of emphases represented among these various texts, representing a large diversity of (sometimes competing) theological concerns. As such, we are presented with the question of discerning which apocalyptic themes are affirmed by Paul and which are absent, explicitly denied, or reframed. As we

---

6. See section 4.2, and Jenson, "Dogmatic/Systematic Appropriation," 159; Macaskill, *Intellectual Humility*, 108, 113, cf. Macaskill, "Providence."

7. As suggested, for example, by de Boer, *God's Apocalypse*, 7–8.

saw in the survey above, Martinus de Boer has been particularly concerned with tracing some of these threads in the apocalyptic writings and teasing out their complex connections to Paul. While most of the contemporary scholarship on Paul's apocalyptic thought affirms this goal, there has so far been too little careful exegetical work following it through. I offer here, in dialogue with de Boer, just three areas where such constructive engagement might be attempted, though other suggestions will be made in the sections that follow.

Does "Apocalyptic" Mean "Eschatological"?

One of the most enduring and important debates in scholarship on the apocalypses is the question of whether that literature is irreducibly eschatological in nature. In short, is "apocalyptic" effectively synonymous with "eschatological"? There is certainly broad agreement that eschatology is a major theme of the corpus, and perhaps even the most important. But is it an essential theme?

Earlier scholarship on the apocalyptic literature, since Weiss and Schweitzer, saw eschatology as the defining characteristic of the genre, and focused particularly on the two-age scheme and the question of eschatological imminence. When Käsemann offered his own discussion of the subject, it was to Schweitzer that he turned. Though he was critical of Schweitzer's project, the definition of apocalyptic that we find in Käsemann's work is an irreducibly eschatological emphasis on the expectation of an imminent *parousia*. The work of Philipp Vielhauer in the 1960s and John Collins in the late 1970s further developed this eschatological line of enquiry, leading to Collins's much-quoted definition:

> "Apocalypse" is a genre of revelatory literature with a narrative framework, in which a revelation is mediated by an otherworldly being to a human recipient, disclosing a transcendent reality which is both temporal, insofar as it envisages eschatological salvation, and spatial insofar as it involves another, supernatural world.[8]

Many in New Testament scholarship have continued to build on this earlier work and have therefore placed an emphasis on Jewish "two age" eschatology as an essential and defining feature of apocalyptic thought.[9]

8. Collins, "Morphology," 9.
9. See de Boer, *God's Apocalypse*, 8.

Since the early 1980s, however, an alternative approach has been offered, largely through the work of Christopher Rowland. Rowland questioned the defining role played by eschatology in discussions of apocalyptic thought, suggesting that this has distorted interpretations, and explored instead how the epistemological category of "revealed mysteries" might be a better candidate for the "heart" of apocalyptic theology. Though this discussion has run for decades since, there are signs in recent years that, even if consensus remains elusive, Rowland's epistemological emphasis may be gaining in significance. In any case, the picture emerging in scholarly discussions of apocalyptic theology is certainly a more nuanced one than the earlier definitions of Collins and Vielhauer might suggest. Though eschatology remains a major concern in apocalyptic literature, it is by no means the only one.[10] In a recent volume entitled *The Jewish Apocalyptic Tradition and the Shaping of New Testament Thought*, editors Benjamin Reynolds and Loren Stuckenbruck voice a concern that the earlier eschatological focus continues to dominate New Testament scholarship, despite the developments in recent scholarship of Second Temple Judaism and its broader range of themes.[11] The volume gathers a wide range of scholarship on the apocalyptic character of the New Testament writings. It offers no fresh definition of "apocalyptic" of its own, but the essays explore the implications of this more nuanced approach to the term for the New Testament corpus. In addition to eschatological matters, questions of revealed wisdom and cosmology are given more weight as aspects of New Testament apocalyptic thought. This indicates that contemporary scholarship from Second Temple Judaism specialists has much to offer the Apocalyptic Paul, not least since the two disciplines share a broader concern with matters of epistemology, cosmology, and soteriology.[12]

Clearly, it will not do simply to re-state the definitions of a previous generation if it has been shown this would impoverish any account of apocalyptic thought in Paul or elsewhere. The signs are, however, that there is some way to go in regard to this methodological matter. The Apocalyptic Paul continues largely to build upon the earlier foundation of eschatology as the essential characteristic of apocalyptic thought, following and adapting

10. DiTommaso, "Apocalypses and Apocalypticism (Part I)," 241.

11. Reynolds and Stuckenbruck, *Jewish Apocalyptic*, xi. This is a concern also voiced by Frey, who challenges de Boer's reliance on "handbook knowledge" of the apocalypses (Frey, "Demythologising," 509). See now de Boer's response in *God's Apocalypse*, 34–35.

12. This potential is illustrated well in the recent work of Bowens, *Apostle in Battle*, discussed in 2.7 above.

Käsemann's conviction that apocalyptic denoted the expectation of an imminent *parousia*. De Boer's "two tracks," for example, are two tracks of apocalyptic *eschatology*. Though he rightly develops this also in cosmological terms, the eschatological emphasis drives the terminology and analysis. For the most part, definitions of apocalyptic in Second Temple Judaism offered by the Apocalyptic Paul continue to appeal to Vielhauer and Collins before moving on without consideration of more recent scholarship.

De Boer is something of an exception in this regard, however, in that he has carefully considered Rowland's proposal and, more recently, its influence on the contemporary discussion.[13] In his engagement with Rowland, de Boer praises the insight that apocalyptic is not only concerned with the future. Nevertheless, he remains largely critical of Rowland's definition, returning to Vielhauer and Collins in defense of the view that eschatology, and specifically eschatological dualism, remains an essential feature of apocalyptic thought. Scholars of the apocalyptic literature have noted that this surface level reliance on outdated analyses is one of the weaknesses not only of de Boer's work but of the Apocalyptic Paul conversation more broadly.[14] There is a clear need for more recent investigations of the defining features of apocalyptic thought to be brought into the conversation.

The Two Ages and Inaugurated Eschatology

This is not to say that eschatological concerns should be suppressed in discussions of apocalyptic thought—far from it. There continues to be a vibrant discussion of apocalyptic eschatology among scholars of the Jewish apocalyptic tradition, and much could be learned from that conversation for Pauline eschatology. In particular, such a dialogue between Paulinists and scholars of the Jewish apocalyptic tradition might allow a more nuanced and careful discussion of the ubiquitous matter of the "two ages."

It is regularly claimed, for example, that the *inaugurated* nature of his two-age eschatology is a feature distinctive to Pauline thought. For example, in Keck's and de Boer's readings of the apostle, the recognition that the "age to come" had already arrived in the Christ event results in an eschatological tension between the "now" and "not yet," perhaps the

---

13. See de Boer, "Theologian of God's Apocalypse," reprinted in *God's Apocalypse*, 39–54. In that volume, de Boer notes Reynolds and Stuckenbruck's recent work on 7–8n31.

14. E.g., Frey, "Demythologising," 509.

signature christological modification of Jewish apocalyptic eschatology in the writings of Paul.[15] Jewish apocalyptic thought is regularly offered as something of a foil to this construal of Pauline eschatology: whereas the Jewish apocalyptic tradition construed the two ages in terms of a static framework awaiting a future decisive event, for Paul that event had already happened in Christ, and this generates his distinctive eschatological vision. The "now and not yet" of inaugurated eschatology is thus seen as a Pauline innovation.

Of course, the Apocalyptic Paul conversation is by no means the only place one will find inaugurated eschatology as one of the distinctive elements of early Christian theology: similar claims are made in many Pauline theologies and introductions to the New Testament. It is practically a standard feature of such books. For some scholars of Second Temple Judaism, however, this represents a worrying trend of oversimplifying the Jewish apocalyptic tradition into simplistic dichotomies, in order to make Paul the heroic theologian who transcends them.[16] The consensus about the Christian uniqueness of an "inaugurated two-age eschatology" has been subject to challenge on a number of fronts, as neither sufficient nor necessary. For one thing, N. T. Wright has often reminded us that the "two ages" is a theme found in a wide variety of Jewish texts, not only apocalypses, and is therefore insufficient as a defining feature of apocalyptic thought.[17] For another, some specialists in the Jewish apocalyptic tradition have asked whether the "two age" scheme as such is actually found in the Jewish apocalyptic literature, or whether it is a later rabbinic pattern unhelpfully overlaid on a corpus of texts which, in fact, displays a much broader range of eschatological frameworks. Careful reading of the apocalypses reveals that they deploy a range of temporal schemes, including the periodization of history, cyclical patterns of time, and notions of *Urzeit* (primordial time) and *Endzeit* (end time), and sometimes combinations of these frameworks within the same text.[18] Examining more closely the continuities and discontinuities between Paul's thought and the Jewish apocalyptic tradition will almost certainly result in a more precise account of how his apocalyptic eschatology is transformed in the light of the revelation of Jesus Christ.[19]

15. See de Boer *God's Apocalypse*, 207; Keck, "Paul and Apocalyptic," 86.
16. See Goff, "God's Wisdom," 175–76.
17. E.g., Wright, *Paul and the Faithfulness of God*, 1059.
18. See Macaskill, "Eschatology," 248–49.
19. I will offer my own suggestion in ch. 5 below. See also Davies, "Why Paul Doesn't

The "Two Tracks"

Questions have also been raised about another dichotomy said to exist in the Jewish sources, namely de Boer's "two tracks" analysis of "cosmological" and "forensic apocalyptic eschatology." In this connection, some have gone so far as to suggest that the analysis itself owes more to the Bultmann-Käsemann debate than it does to exegesis of the primary sources,[20] a charge that de Boer has since denied. That he finds the theological contours of the anthropological/cosmological debates between Bultmann and Käsemann helpful in his analysis does not, he insists, invalidate his findings, which are based upon (and should be judged in relation to) analysis of the apocalyptic literature.[21] In any case, whatever theological lenses are used, the important question upon which all agree is whether de Boer's proposal is analytically useful and exegetical faithful to the apocalypses and to Paul, and it is here that dialogue across the disciplines may prove fruitful. To give one example, Matthew Goff has recently noted, with approval, de Boer's recognition that the two "tracks" may be found intertwined in any given work, such as some of the texts found among the Dead Sea Scrolls.[22] Goff suggests, however, that de Boer has not fully perceived the significance of this insight for his analysis, particularly because it relies heavily on older definitions of apocalypticism (for example those of Vielhauer and Käsemann) that precede the discovery and analysis of the scrolls. Others have offered a similar critique, and it could equally be addressed to a number of apocalyptic readers of Paul, from Beker onwards.

Despite having been subjected to significant revision through the efforts of Second Temple Judaism scholars in recent decades, the essential tenets of these definitions persist in Pauline scholarship. This problem has perhaps been exacerbated by the tendency of some Pauline scholars to deploy de Boer's "two tracks" analysis in a strictly antithetical relationship rather than the more heuristic usage he seems to have originally intended. Whether or not it fairly represents his intention, or the early use of his ideas by Martyn, de Boer's most recent statements on the matter clarify that he is not supportive of such a dichotomous analysis, and here there is

---

Mention the Age to Come," 199–208.

20. Wright, *Interpreters* 159, 167; Frey, "Demythologising," 508–9.
21. De Boer, *God's Apocalypse*, 37.
22. Goff cites the *Treatise on the Two Spirits* (1QS 3:13—4:26) as a particularly clear example of the blending of "forensic" and "cosmological" themes. Goff, "Mystery," 176.

some cause for optimism. In particular, his most recent work sometimes deploys the metaphor of "patterns" of apocalyptic eschatology rather than "tracks."[23] This could prove a most helpful shift in language, since "patterns" can be more naturally overlaid in complex relationships. In his most recent restatements of his views, de Boer has been quite clear that the two apocalyptic "patterns" are not strictly dichotomous: the forensic pattern represents a "weakened form" of the cosmological one, and the latter can (and regularly does) contain elements of the former.[24] When it comes to Paul, this more nuanced articulation of his thesis should help to prevent overly simplistic and dichotomous analyses of the forensic and cosmological elements of, say, the letter to the Romans. Paul, de Boer has insisted, does not simply choose one or the other apocalyptic pattern, but christologically adapts elements from both.[25] As such, the challenge presented by de Boer's analysis is *how* we should articulate a nuanced and theologically coherent "both-and" rather than a simplistic "either-or." Since this takes us into soteriological matters, some possibilities for meeting this challenge will be discussed further in section 4.5 below.

4.2 The Apocalyptic Paul and Karl Barth

If it is true that the Apocalyptic Paul is somewhat lacking in cross-disciplinary conversation with Second Temple Judaism scholarship, the same cannot be said with respect to systematic theology. As the previous section of this book demonstrated, this is a characteristic concern of the movement. It may come as a surprise, then, to find that systematic theologians have also voiced concerns at some of what they have heard from the Apocalyptic Paul. That there should be pushback is, in itself, no surprise for any theological project, and no movement can spend its time responding to challenges on every front. However, given the regular and explicit claims that this is a reading of Paul building on the work of Karl Barth, any critiques from Barthian specialists will be particularly important to note. This is not the place to offer detailed engagement with the numerous ways Barth scholars have engaged with the variety of proposals gathered under the Apocalyptic Paul umbrella. But again, some "conversation starters" may be valuable, and I offer below a brief account of two of these. As we will see, there seems to

23. De Boer, *God's Apocalypse*, 10, 37, 210–11.
24. De Boer, *God's Apocalypse*, 37.
25. De Boer, *God's Apocalypse*, 211–12.

be a general concern among Barth scholarship that while the commitments of the Apocalyptic Paul might faithfully reflect the polemics of Barth's early work, they generally do not incorporate some of the nuances found in his later thought.

Bruce McCormack: Cosmological and Forensic Apocalyptic in Barth and the Apocalyptic Paul

One Barth scholar who has developed this line of enquiry is Bruce McCormack, who describes the Apocalyptic Paul's warm reception of Barth's commentary on Romans as something of a "minority opinion which is gaining strength" in Anglophone New Testament scholarship.[26] McCormack observes a considerable overlap between the apocalyptic reading of Paul (generally represented by Martyn and de Boer, though he notes the genealogical relationship to Beker and Käsemann) and his own work on Barth, and in particular the historical development of Barth's thought. To put it briefly, McCormack suggests the Apocalyptic Paul offers a reading of Paul that demonstrates clear affinities with the early Barth, especially in its focus on revelation/apocalypse and a soteriology characterized by military metaphors. In a more detailed engagement with de Boer, McCormack particularly interrogates the "two tracks" thesis as a reading of Barth and Paul. His conclusion is that while de Boer's "cosmological apocalyptic eschatology" may be a helpful category for understanding the thought of the early Barth, it proves less useful for reading Paul.[27]

According to McCormack, in the early years Barth's thought became more consistently apocalyptic leading up to and culminating in the 1922 *Romans* commentary, which represents the "full bloom" of his "cosmological apocalyptic" theology.[28] The work of Martyn and de Boer powerfully expresses the thematic emphases of this early work. But in so doing, McCormack argues, it has also repeated one of Barth's weaknesses, namely that this "cosmological" emphasis alone cannot account for the relationship of divine and human activity in Christian soteriology. Barth later recognized this weakness in his earlier work and provided a more nuanced account, shifting his emphasis back toward "forensic" categories.[29] In McCormack's

---

26. McCormack, "Longing," 144.
27. McCormack, "Longing," 146.
28. McCormack, "Longing," 136, 143.
29. E.g., in *CD* IV/1.

analysis, one of the weaknesses of the Apocalyptic Paul (at least as represented by Martyn and de Boer) is a failure to appreciate how Barth's more mature work modified his earlier "cosmological apocalyptic" account of Paul's thought by placing it in a judicial/forensic soteriological framework.[30]

In McCormack's reading of him, Barth's later soteriology is by no means indicative of a pendulum swing toward penal imagery, but in pressing deeper for a martial and ontological soteriology, it does not leave the courtroom behind. On the contrary, McCormack views apocalyptic theology in the later Barth as a "supplement" to forensic categories, an important modification of Reformation soteriology.[31] Thus, McCormack argues, the later Barth actually has more in common with de Boer's "forensic apocalyptic eschatology" than the "cosmological" track. Furthermore, he goes on to suggest that in developing this more forensic emphasis, the later Barth becomes a better reader of Paul, in whose letters the forensic is always foundational for the cosmological.[32] The theological ontology needed to deploy Barth's apocalyptic theology was developed, in his more mature account, in a forensic frame of reference, and shouldn't be divorced from it.[33] McCormack diagnoses this problem in some accounts of Pauline apocalyptic theology.

McCormack's assessment is that Barth's early cosmological apocalyptic reading of Romans suffered from an internal structural weakness inherited and repeated by Martyn and de Boer in their reception of his thought. "At this stage of his development," he argues,

> Barth has no doctrine of the incarnation, no account of the ontological constitution of the Redeemer. In the absence of it, the rich battery of images employed in cosmological apocalyptic—whether his or that found in the "Martyn school"—dissolves into so much rhetorical flourish.[34]

Whether or not one accepts McCormack's conclusions, his analysis of the issue should make us cautious of any would-be Barthian reading that brackets out or rejects the possibility of forensic soteriological categories

---

30. McCormack, "Can We Still Speak," 163.
31. McCormack, "Can We Still Speak," 180.
32. McCormack, "Longing," 146–48.
33. A fuller argument along similar lines can also be found in Smythe, "Karl Barth in Conversation." In Smythe's view, the later forensic framework of *CD* IV/1 is just as "apocalyptic," and avoids the problems usually associated with forensic views of justification.
34. McCormack, "Longing," 148n45.

in Paul's letters. Both the "forensic" and the "cosmological" are part of Pauline, and Barthian, apocalyptic theology. As noted above, this "both-and" is very much in line with de Boer's original intention and his more recent clarifications of the two apocalyptic "patterns." It is interesting to observe, however, that in de Boer's analysis the relationship between "forensic" and "cosmological" in Romans is the reverse of McCormack's reading of Barth.[35] For McCormack's Paul, the forensic is the foundation of the cosmological;[36] for de Boer, the cosmological overtakes and circumscribes the forensic. In either analysis, it should be clear that what we are *not* dealing with is merely the presence of alien forensic theology in Paul's letters, though sometimes this seems to be what is claimed. But this material need not (or should not) be explained as a rhetorical strategy, the voice of Paul's opponents not Paul himself, a charge McCormack brings against de Boer's reading of Galatians,[37] though (*mutatis mutandis*) it might also, and more effectively, be directed at Campbell on Romans.[38] For all his critical evaluation of the "Martyn school," McCormack certainly does not wish to reject an apocalyptic reading of Paul. The important question, again, is to ask precisely how these two Pauline soteriological patterns relate and cohere, and since this is a question that clearly has synergy with similar discussions taking place within Barthian theology, it represents a clear opportunity for continued dialogue between theologians and Paulinists.

Two brief examples from the contemporary Apocalyptic Paul scholarship will suffice to illustrate that such dialogue is already bearing fruit. First, one scholar who notes McCormack's challenge is Philip Ziegler, who appears to accept the critique that the Apocalyptic Paul has been somewhat superficially reliant on the early Barth without adequately nuancing this with his later thought. While also directing attention to Nathan Kerr as another who has developed an apocalyptic theology addressing these early-Barthian weaknesses, Ziegler's own work represents attempts to offer a fuller, more nuanced, account.[39] In his discussions of Pauline apocalyptic soteriology, Ziegler sounds very much like McCormack in speaking of the importance of "a forensic emphasis on saving divine judgement," which

---

35. See the discussion in de Boer, "Karl Barth, Theological Exegesis, and the Apocalyptic Interpretation of Paul," 11–37.
36. McCormack, "Longing," 146.
37. McCormack, "Can We Still Speak," 171.
38. This is a matter that will be given further attention in section 4.5 below.
39. Ziegler, *Militant Grace*, 100.

demands a "crucial cosmological supplement." As such, even where Ziegler (with de Boer) reverses McCormack's dogmatic ordering of the cosmological and forensic elements, it is clear that the goal is their integration.[40]

Second, in respect of McCormack's specific challenge concerning the question of divine and human activity, and the christological deficit thereby represented, the work of Susan Eastman may prove helpful. Eastman's account of Pauline apocalyptic thought, pressing beyond Martyn's *invasion* language to the language and logic of *incarnation*,[41] may well address McCormack's structural theological concerns while also providing a more explicit connection to a two-natures christological framework, with implications for how we construe apocalyptic soteriology. One might even say that, in these respects, Eastman's and Ziegler's proposals represent a "maturing" of the Apocalyptic Paul movement analogous to Barth's own theological development.

Robert Jenson: Canon, "Invasion," and the Coordinates of History

Mention of Martyn's category of *invasion* leads us to another systematic theologian who has responded critically to the Apocalyptic Paul on Barthian grounds. As is appropriate for a *Festschrift* essay, Robert Jenson's contribution to Davis and Harink's 2012 edited volume is more specifically an essay about Martyn, rather than Barth, but it does offer a somewhat Barthian appraisal of the appropriation of Martyn's proposals in systematic theology. Jenson begins by noting how systematic theologians have grown frustrated with the apparent theological naivety of many New Testament scholars. Martyn, he insists, is not one of them, and Jenson celebrates his work as a decisively theological project. Nevertheless, he presses two questions about Martyn's apocalyptic reading of Paul and its implications for the task of Christian dogmatics.

First, Jenson takes issue with Martyn's category of *invasion*. For a start, he argues, the category will find itself challenged systematically by the doctrine of creation. How can we speak of divine invasion, Jenson asks, if God is already present and ruling his world? He goes on to suggest that construing the apocalypse of Jesus Christ as a divine invasion is a commitment that

---

40. Ziegler, *Militant Grace*, 22–24. Again, see 4.5 below.

41. Again, see Eastman, "Apocalypse and Incarnation," 166. See also the implications of this in *Recovering*, 15–16, 185.

can only be maintained if Paul is treated as a "canon . . . within the canon."[42] It is not a framework that reflects the whole witness of Scripture and so, from a systematic theological perspective, cannot be made the basis of a doctrine of revelation (or indeed of any doctrine). Dogmatics cannot be purely Pauline, but must account for the whole canonical witness.[43] Surely, Jenson insists, any definition of apocalyptic thought must have something to do with the mode of prophecy labeled with that term, and found in the relevant Jewish texts.[44] If this is granted, then the notion of a "plot" for history must be included in apocalyptic thinking, along with language of principalities and powers, and so on. In this regard, Martyn's apocalyptic account of Paul has much to commend it, but for Jenson the centrality attached to the motif of divine *invasion* is inappropriate and not something we find in apocalyptic prophecy. If Martyn is right about Paul, he concludes, then Paul is "an eccentric . . . in that part of the biblical witness to which he is said most to relate."[45]

Second, and related to this, Jenson challenges Martyn's deployment of the geometric language of *vertical* and *horizontal*, language borrowed from Barth with important implications for an account of revelation and history. Jenson asks whether it is appropriate to conceive of history and salvation in such perpendicular terms and concludes that this discourse amounts to little more than "Platonism stripped to its geometry."[46] It is far better, Jenson argues, to think of revelation embracing history, rather than standing in incommensurable relation to it. As such, accounts of salvation history have more to offer than the coordinates of *vertical* and *horizontal*. Again, at this point Jenson's critique, like that of McCormack, appears to reflect the contrast between Barth's earlier and later thought. Whereas the Barth of the *Römerbrief* famously described the relationship between revelation and history as like that of a tangent and a circle (that is, they touch without really touching[47]) in his later work Barth changed his mind (or at least thoroughly nuanced his presentation) and spoke of the real intersection of the vertical

---

42. Jenson, "Dogmatic/Systematic Appropriation," 159.

43. Grant Macaskill offered a similar critique in a paper at the 2019 session of the SBL "Pauline Theology" group, reviewing Douglas Campbell's *Pauline Dogmatics*. In the book's two-word title, Macaskill argued, the adjective contradicts the noun.

44. One expects to see this critique from scholars of Second Temple Judaism. It is significant also to hear it from a systematic theologian.

45. Jenson, "Dogmatic/Systematic Appropriation," 160.

46. Jenson, "Dogmatic/Systematic Appropriation," 160.

47. Barth, *Romans*, 30.

and the horizontal: revelation not merely meeting history at a point but entering and assuming it. In the *Church Dogmatics,* Barth warned his readers against the polemical overemphasis on transcendence represented by his Romans commentary, which, while necessary as an "antiseptic" against the prevailing immanentism of the time, did not ultimately do justice to the doctrine of the incarnation.[48] While challenging the geometric metaphors, Jenson still sounds more like this later Barth in his account of revelation and (salvation) history, framed not in antithesis but relation.

This is not to say, however, that all accounts of salvation history are the same, and it is vitally important that the nature of this relation be addressed with precision. As Jenson sees it there are two options, which are the opposite of each other. The first is a more immanentist theology of salvation history that contains revelation within secular, "ordinary history." But rejecting this in the name of "punctiliar" invasion doesn't mean rejecting all linear accounts of salvation history, for there is also a second version of salvation history (one arguably embraced by the later Barth) which reverses this order: history within and *as a predicate of* revelation. Jenson suggests that the truth is this way around and throws the possibility out for discussion.

Again, it appears that the Apocalyptic Paul may have a problematic tendency to read Barth with only one "side" of a dialectic in view. In its zeal, with the early Barth, to reject natural theology and thus any immanentist version of salvation history, perhaps the more nuanced accounts of history Barth later developed have been obscured, and with them a version of salvation history that reverses this logical order, such as Jenson proposes. Likewise, in pushing back against the Apocalyptic Paul, those defending the importance of linear covenant/salvation history for Paul's thought may be insufficiently appreciative of this nuance and have inadvertently defended the wrong "form" of salvation history. We have, I think, a problem of talking at cross-purposes, at least in part. A helpful step forward here is again found in the work of Ziegler and Kerr, discussed above. Both have noted the weaknesses of Barth's earlier accounts of history and have instead drawn attention to his later insistence that "revelation is not a predicate of

---

48. Barth, *CD* I/2 §14, 50. See also *CD* IV/1 §62, 643–45. This use of the vertical and horizontal is not entirely absent, however, from his early work. See, e.g., *Calvin*, 73. We recall also Käsemann's similarly medical description of the doctrine of justification as a necessary immunization against the disease that was the progressive evolutionary account of history under German national socialism (see 16–17 above and Käsemann, *Perspectives,* 63–64).

history, but history is a predicate of revelation."[49] In this way they are able to develop a more subtle account of the relationship between revelation and history that remains apocalyptic in mode but appropriately addresses Jenson's critique of geometric metaphors and the language of "invasion."

4.3 Paul's Apocalyptic Epistemology: Revelation and Wisdom

Having considered the broader methodological matter of these two interdisciplinary conversations with the Apocalyptic Paul, we turn now to responses from Pauline scholars, arranged according to three theological themes: epistemology, eschatology, and soteriology. When it comes to the question of the epistemological emphasis in the Apocalyptic Paul, the conversation so far has been characterized by two different but related contrasts. The apocalyptic epistemological antithesis in Martyn's work was between "wisdom" and "revelation," whereas for Keck and Campbell the focus has been on Paul as an *ex post facto* thinker: the important contrast was between "prospective" and "retrospective" epistemologies. These antitheses, of course, have not gone unchallenged from various quarters. Though I will note some of the important insights arising from the study of the Jewish apocalyptic tradition, here and in the following two sections I will focus on the most important constructive criticisms within the guild of Pauline scholarship, and offer suggestions of ways forward from within the Apocalyptic Paul movement.

The Compatibility of Wisdom and Apocalypse

In respect of the antithesis between wisdom and revelation in Pauline apocalyptic epistemology, there have been some insightful developments. As we saw above, Martyn's account of Paul's epistemology, inextricably connected to his apocalyptic eschatology, centers on the new "way of knowing" characterized by divine invasion at the junction of the ages. The result of this framing of the issue is that Martyn is not satisfied with the language of "unveiling mysteries," since that inadequately captures the disjunctive nature of this divine invasion and its epistemological implications. If that is

---

49. Barth *CD* I/1: 143-62 and *CD* I/2: 58, cited and discussed by Kerr, *Christ History and Apocalyptic*, 73-79 and Ziegler, *Militant Grace*, 15, 24.

true of the revelation of mysteries, it is truer still of the category of wisdom, with its characteristic human reflection on this present world. Paul, in Martyn's view, can no longer argue on the basis of an "undisturbed" cosmos; because of the priority of divine invasion in Christ, Paul's logic is that of *announcement* rather than *argument*. In Martyn's view, taken up by Bowens and others, the apocalypse of Jesus Christ is an epistemological (and eschatological) earthquake that drives a chasm between these two ways of knowing. In a similar way, Douglas Campbell's trenchant critique of epistemological "foundationalism" also represents an emphatic rejection of any way of knowing oriented toward rational reflection on the world (citing Rom 1:19–20 as an example of a logic Paul rejects). Campbell here discerns a grievous theological error, the specter of "natural theology" so vigorously opposed by Barth. In his view, the two modes of epistemology represented by apocalypse and wisdom are, therefore, radically dichotomous.[50]

There is a broad consensus in Second Temple Jewish studies, however, that the epistemologies of wisdom and apocalyptic are not quite so radically incompatible. For one thing, there is a discernible historical connection between the two streams of thought, reflected by the presence of both epistemological convictions working together in the Jewish apocalyptic corpus, frustrating attempts to define a strict theological and generic incompatibility.[51] One scholar who is uniquely placed to speak on this matter is Grant Macaskill, having made contributions both to scholarship on Second Temple Jewish apocalyptic literature and to Pauline studies. Macaskill's doctoral dissertation examined the co-mingling of sapiential and apocalyptic elements in the Jewish literature and the Gospel of Matthew.[52] He has more recently pressed these "generic compatibility" insights further, investigating how wisdom and apocalypse might function coherently in a Christian dogmatic account of epistemology that takes with equal seriousness the canonical witness of both traditions. In short, what does it mean to speak, in Christian theology, of "revealed wisdom"?

Macaskill's response to this question takes with utmost seriousness the epistemological effects of the Christ event. Of course, in the light of

50. Campbell, *Deliverance*, 203.

51. There have been many discussions of this issue, largely springing from the SBL "Wisdom and Apocalypticism" group, but one influential essay is Collins, "Generic Compatibility." See also Goff, "Wisdom," 65 and DiTommaso, "Apocalypses and Apocalypticism (II)."

52. Macaskill, "Wisdom and Apocalyptic." Revised and published as Macaskill, *Revealed Wisdom*.

the revelation of Jesus, the first Christians could no longer approach the sapiential traditions of the Hebrew Scriptures in the same way. Martyn's instincts are correct at this point: the cosmos was disturbed, and with it human reasoning. What Macaskill suggests, however, is that the appropriate way to develop this insight while continuing to value the sapiential material in the Christian canon is that this material finds a new place within an epistemological framework that is christologically governed. Reflection on the natural world, a characteristic feature of the wisdom tradition, is not thereby flatly rejected or placed in stark opposition to the apocalypse of Jesus Christ. Since creation finds its origin and bearings in him, as Col 1 attests, a christologically governed reflection on the world will seek wisdom in the correspondence of creation to Christ. At this point Macaskill critiques Campbell's reading of Paul as an example of a problematic canonical deficiency in current attempts to trace a Christian apocalyptic epistemology.[53] The sapiential material of Proverbs and Ecclesiastes (and, for that matter, Rom 1) must be allowed to play its part in shaping an account of epistemology that appropriately integrates wisdom and apocalypse.

Among apocalyptic Pauline scholars, this is an integrative insight which would, I think, broadly be endorsed by Susan Eastman and Alexandra Brown, who have both acknowledged that wisdom and apocalyptic are sometimes found in concert in the Jewish apocalypses. Eastman is clearly conversant with the arguments from scholars of the Jewish texts linking wisdom and apocalypticism, citing Collins in particular, and notes Paul's affinities with these interwoven traditions.[54] For her part, Brown has argued that these two epistemological streams are, in fact, "quite clearly joined"[55] in Paul's own epistemology in his first letter to Corinth.[56] Crucially, for Brown (as for Macaskill), this is not to say that human wisdom remains unaffected by divine apocalypse, and as such she examines the nature of Paul's christological reworking of wisdom. The apocalyptic event of the life, death, and resurrection of Jesus Christ, she has argued, effects perceptual transformation such that human wisdom, while epistemologically valid, nevertheless cannot remain unchanged. In taking forward our analysis of Paul's apocalyptic epistemology, it seems that Brown's nuanced category of

---

53. See, e.g., Macaskill, *Intellectual Humility* 129–31. The question of canon was discussed from both intertextual and dogmatic perspectives in sections 4.1 and 4.2 above.

54. Eastman, *Recovering*, 65n6.

55. Brown, *Cross*, 32. For the connections with the apocalyptic literature see 45–64.

56. Brown, *Cross*, 30.

"apocalyptic wisdom"⁵⁷ or Macaskill's "revealed wisdom," christologically modified and governed, offers potential for integrating the two modes of knowing. I will take up this question in more detail in the next chapter, in relation to Brown's reading of 1 Cor 2.

Retrospective Epistemology

The second epistemological theme to consider here is the matter of the decisively *retrospective* nature of Pauline apocalyptic epistemology. As the summary above made clear, this is a central concern of Douglas Campbell's apocalyptic reading of Paul, though it can also be seen clearly in Martyn and Keck. None have been quite as forthright as Campbell, however, in considering this emphatically retrospective epistemology a matter of supreme importance for any account of Pauline theology, and indeed for the task of the Christian theologian today. There can be no other "starting point" from which Christian reasoning proceeds than the apocalypse of Jesus Christ. Anything else is to be rejected as the "deadly methodological heresy" of theological foundationalism.⁵⁸ There are, however, some important nuances that should be observed. For example, as we saw earlier, in Keck's account of Paul's *ex post facto* logic Jesus's resurrection is an epistemological starting point, to be sure, but not in an "absolute" sense. It is the starting point in the sense that Paul reasoned backwards from the resurrection *to rethink his inherited theology*. As Keck puts it, Paul did not only think "new and different thoughts," but "old thoughts differently."⁵⁹ This is an insight with important implications for history and eschatology. Our current focus is epistemology, and a more detailed consideration of Paul's apocalyptic eschatology will come in the next section, but since the two theological themes do not separate cleanly from each other, some comments on eschatology will be inevitable. Evaluating the impact of this retrospective epistemological commitment in Pauline scholarship is no easy task, since such methodological commitments often remain implicit or unexplored, and of course there remain many challenges at every turn, but the signs are that it seems to have met with a degree of broad acceptance.

---

57. Brown, *Cross*, 30, 103.
58. Campbell, "Apocalyptic Epistemology," 78.
59. Keck, *Romans*, 34–35.

Unsettled Questions for the Apocalyptic Paul

One Pauline scholar whose work is quite clearly characterized by a retrospective epistemology is Richard Hays.[60] While agreeing that Paul's thought has an "apocalyptic DNA,"[61] Hays has joined other Pauline scholars in critiquing the Apocalyptic Paul for espousing a false dichotomy between apocalyptic and salvation history. Hays has argued that a retrospective epistemology provides the key to solving this problem, maintaining a commitment to Paul's apocalyptic theology without jettisoning an emphasis on narrative continuity. He argues that Paul deploys an apocalyptic epistemology that works backwards, hermeneutically transforming salvation history and thereby re-reading, and not repudiating, the narrative continuity of Israel's story.[62] This continuity, Hays insists, is not progressive foundationalism, since it is found as we "read backwards."

There is an enormous mutual influence evident in the work of Hays and N. T. Wright, whose reading of Paul is regularly offered as a foil to this apocalyptic retrospective epistemology, most explicitly in the work of Campbell and Harink. Though both Wright and Hays are famously committed to a narrative hermeneutic, and to offering robust accounts of narrative continuity in their readings of Paul, their epistemological starting points have historically been significantly different. In one account, Wright's account of Paul's retrospective epistemology has been described as an "inverted progression" of Hays.[63] Both deploy this retrospective conviction in ways that go beyond a unidirectional reading of Paul's logic, but whereas Hays begins with the "solution" and reads backwards to the "plight," for Wright the movement is from "plight" to "solution." Wright's approach is actually more subtle than that, as we will soon see, but at this point his reading of Paul appears decidedly "prospective," and has thus met with the strongest of anti-foundationalist critiques from scholars such as Campbell and Harink.

The title of Wright's first major book on Paul, *The Climax of the Covenant*, indicates the importance that his Pauline theology has placed on the prospective narrative trajectory of God's covenant with Israel, reaching its climax in Christ. But things are not quite as straightforward as that surface level reading of Wright's epistemology might suggest. In the light of that

---

60. In relation to the Gospels, see Hays, *Reading Backwards*; *Echoes of Scripture in the Gospels*.

61. Hays, "Apocalyptic *Poiēsis*" 203.

62. Hays, "Apocalyptic *Poiēsis*" 204.

63. Blackwell et al., *Apocalyptic Imagination*, 11n23.

christological climax, Wright argues, Paul "reworks" or "reimagines" the foundational categories of Jewish thought, including its forward-moving narrative. However, Wright denies that his views represent an endorsement of the "epistemological foundationalism" about which Campbell is so deeply concerned. Wright agrees with Martyn that the apocalypse of Jesus Christ reveals the nature of the plight to which the gospel is the solution. He maintains, however, that this should not be understood in a manner radically discontinuous with Second Temple Jewish descriptions of the "problem" prior to Christ.[64] Wright has repeatedly insisted that he is not thereby advocating a "steady progress" version of salvation history. Paul's plight is not simply retained from his prior convictions, but neither is it created *ex nihilo* in response to an unanticipated solution: it is, in Wright's words, a "plight revised."[65] Thus framed, there seem to be some important similarities here with Keck's framing of Pauline epistemology. Perhaps the distance between Wright and the Apocalyptic Paul is not as great as the caricatures of both views might make it seem, and some epistemological common ground might yet be found?

That is perhaps an overly optimistic suggestion, though it is tantalizing to reflect on the prospect in the light of Wright's more recent work on theological epistemology, found in his 2018 Gifford Lectures.[66] Without rejecting his commitment to the covenantal narrative trajectory of Paul's theology, in this more recent account of Paul's theological epistemology, Wright appears to have taken a more explicitly retrospective approach, bringing him (arguably) much closer to Hays. In his most recent formulations, Wright draws out more fully some of the trajectories of his earlier thought to argue that in Christian theology there is a renewed mode of knowledge that is consequent to the resurrection. So far, so Martynesque, and at this point Wright is quite content to label this an "apocalyptic epistemology"[67] and recognizes that (suitably qualified) it has much in common with the argument encapsulated in Martyn's essay on "epistemology at the turn of the

---

64. See Wright, *Paul and the Faithfulness of God*, 757.
65. Wright, *Paul and the Faithfulness of God*, 752–64.
66. Published as Wright, *History and Eschatology*.
67. Wright, *Paul and the Faithfulness of God*, 1310; Wright, *Interpreters*, 218.

ages."[68] For Wright, the resurrection is the epistemological starting point, and the direction is retrospective: we "start with Easter and look back."[69]

It is worth unpacking Wright's views on Christian epistemology a little further. "The resurrection of Jesus of Nazareth," Wright says, "offers itself as the centre of a new kind of ontology, inviting a new kind of epistemology."[70] For Wright, this new ontology, this new world, happens within the old, thus making sense of, transforming, and retrospectively validating it.[71] As such, and only as such, we may speak of *natural theology*. The same is true, Wright argues, of salvation history, a narrative of promise that is both validated and radically modified by the resurrection. The forward movement of this long and winding Jewish story toward its goal is only seen as such when looking backward from the events of Easter.

At this point we are beginning to discuss the theme of eschatology, which will be covered in the next section, but suffice it to say for now that accusations that Wright's account of Pauline epistemology is straightforwardly prospective or foundationalist will require some rethinking, since what he has described appears quite clearly to be a demonstrably retrospective account of history. Campbell and others often challenge Wright precisely on the question of epistemological starting points, arguing that Wright's project is fundamentally flawed in its deployment of a prospective, foundationalist epistemology.[72] This critique should now be weighed carefully against Wright's insistence that theological epistemology starts with the resurrection of Jesus and works backward.

To return to the issue of wisdom and apocalypse, in places Wright argues explicitly against what he sees as a decidedly Marcionite account of apocalyptic epistemology that "cancels out 'ordinary' modes of knowledge."[73] This, he argues, capitulates to a false dichotomy in ontology

---

68. See Wright, *Paul and the Faithfulness of God*, 1356n7. Though regularly taking issue with wider aspects of Martyn's work, Wright regularly cites this essay with approval when it comes to the question of Paul's epistemology.

69. Wright, *History and Eschatology*, 191; and see also 213–14. Wright's earlier discussions of the resurrection, in which he engages in more prospective arguments, must now at least be balanced (if not circumscribed) by this more recent retrospective articulation.

70. Wright, *History and Eschatology*, 198.

71. Wright, *History and Eschatology*, 200.

72. I am thinking here particularly of Campbell's critique of Wright, e.g., in Campbell, *Pauline Dogmatics*, 697, 717. For an expansive critique along these lines see Adams, *Reality of God*.

73. Wright, *History and Eschatology*, 189.

and epistemology. For Wright, just as the new creation does not cancel out the old but renews it, revelation does not cancel but takes such "ordinary knowledge" to a new level, offering a "fresh perspective" or "dimension of meaning."[74] Might this approach find a degree of common ground with the epistemological transformation suggested in Brown's analysis of Pauline "apocalyptic wisdom" or Macaskill's "revealed wisdom"? There is no doubt still some debate to be had, but the conversation over Paul's apocalyptic epistemology could well make some progress at this point.[75] A number of questions come to mind here. Interrogating exactly *how* revelation transforms wisdom, one might ask whether Wright's language of a "new level," "fresh perspective," or "rejuvenated history" is sufficient to the task of expressing the radical nature of the epistemological transformation described.[76] Wright has a particular fondness for "re-" prefixes in describing the "freshly revealed" or "reworked" or "reimagined" character of Pauline theology (to borrow the chapter titles of part 3 of *Paul and the Faithfulness of God*). In the light of the above discussion of his theological epistemology, one might ask how much theological work these prefixes are doing in his account, and whether the language and metaphors of "rejuvenation" are sufficient for this new ontology and new way of knowing. A related matter is, of course, the perennial question of the ordering of the Pauline "plight" and "solution." While there is still some work to be done in exploring their respective accounts in this regard, Hays's retrospective reading of Christian epistemology seems to have been largely welcomed by Wright. But do they continue to construe plight and solution in inverted/opposite ways, as some have suggested?[77] These questions should resonate with some of the essential concerns of Keck, Brown, and Campbell, discussed above.

---

74. Wright, *History and Eschatology*, 189.

75. Richard Hays, chairing a public debate at Duke Divinity School in November 2014, suggested the epistemological centrality of Christ as a genuine point of convergence between Wright and the Apocalyptic Paul (represented at the event by Campbell and Eastman), with apparent general approval. It was a rare moment of agreement in that discussion but is no less significant for that. See the recording at https://youtu.be/mNzcwo6opqg (from 44:00 onward).

76. Wright, *History and Eschatology*, 212.

77. Again, see Blackwell et al., *Apocalyptic Imagination*, 11n23.

4.4 Paul's Apocalyptic Eschatology: Continuity and Discontinuity

The Problem of (Salvation) History

As we have noted, the question of apocalyptic epistemology is always inextricably connected to that of eschatology, and particularly the question of how we might construe apocalyptic theology and salvation history. Given the close association between the term "apocalyptic" and eschatological concerns, and the particularly generative force of Käsemann's challenge to progressive evolutionary accounts of *Heilsgeschichte*, it is hardly surprising that this has, from the beginning, been perhaps the most discussed issue in the debate over Paul's apocalyptic thought. It is important, therefore, that we attend to this question with care, and in particular interrogate the different senses in which the matter of (salvation) history is conceived by various figures. The challenges have sometimes been strongly worded on both sides. For example, there have been trenchant critiques of Martyn and his followers from one of the Apocalyptic Paul movement's most vocal critics, N. T. Wright. For Wright, salvation history is integral to Paul's own thought in Galatians and not, as Martyn argued, a category used by his opponents.[78] The rejection of salvation history that Wright sees inherent in Martyn's "invasion" language, and the subsequent development of this theme in contemporary scholarship, represents nothing less than a form of supersessionism, which (as he often puts it) "sweeps the history of Israel off the table."[79] There have been responses in kind, with Wright's account of the continuity of history in Paul described as one that amounts to a Hegelian, progressive view of history, and it is his account that really constitutes supersessionism.[80]

Clearly, the stakes are high. A good place to start, then, is by clearing away misreadings and caricatures. In the first place, Wright has repeatedly rebutted the characterization of his account of salvation history as a "smooth progressive development." A careful reading of his relevant arguments indicates that this is a misunderstanding at best (and at worst, a straw man).[81] One example will suffice to make the point. In his critique

---

78. See Martyn, *Issues*, 165, 169; *Galatians*, 336–52.

79. For an example of Wright's use of this phrase in polemics against the Apocalyptic Paul, see, e.g., *Paul and the Faithfulness of God*, 611–12, 1262.

80. Campbell, *Pauline Dogmatics*, 697, 699.

81. Wright names it as such in *Interpreters*, 163.

of salvation-historical interpretations, Douglas Harink cites Wright as a representative who advocates strongly for a view of salvation history in which God is "quietly and steadily working his purposes out as year succeeded to year" through the "long unwinding of Israel's and the world's story."[82] Reading these quotations in the fuller context of Wright's argument, however, it seems that Harink may have misunderstood. For one thing, at this point Wright is quite clearly describing not his own views but a version of salvation history rejected by the apocalyptic reading of Paul. Wright presents this "steady fulfilment" as an extreme alternative to the "irruptive" apocalyptic account, with the intention of denying both. Neither of these represents Wright's own position, as he makes clear a couple of pages after the quoted material.

> We cannot expound Paul's covenant theology in such a way as to make it a smooth, steady progress of historical fulfilment; but nor can we propose a kind of "apocalyptic" view in which nothing that happened before Jesus is of any value even as preparation. In the messianic events of Jesus's death and resurrection Paul believes *both* that the covenant promises were at last fulfilled *and* that this constituted a massive and dramatic irruption into the processes of world history unlike anything before or since. . . . Unless we hold on to both parts of this truth we are missing something absolutely central to Paul.[83]

Others have also noted this problem. For example, while not defending every aspect of Wright's account of history or his challenge to the apocalyptic school, Macaskill has noted that Wright is often unfairly mischaracterized in this regard.[84] Wright has since restated his views and has sought to correct this misunderstanding.[85] In one recent account he is explicit that his view is that the "long, dark and winding narrative of Israel's story with God" that has reached its climax in Christ is "anything but a smooth, steady progress or 'development'!"[86]

---

82. See Harink, "Partakers," 85, quoting Wright, *Fresh Perspective*, 9, 50–51, 134.

83. Wright, *Fresh Perspective*, 54.

84. Macaskill, *Intellectual Humility*, 118.

85. See also his clear response in Wright, "New Perspective on Käsemann," 253–54 (reprinted in *Interpreting Paul*, 12). See also, e.g., *Paul and the Faithfulness of God* 1479n11.

86. Wright, *History and Eschatology*, 200. See also Wright, "Sudden Fulfilment."

Unsettled Questions for the Apocalyptic Paul

But what of Wright's characterization of the Apocalyptic Paul as constituting a blanket rejection of the value of history before Jesus? Wright has offered versions of this critique in a number of places, but his most recent discussion of the problem can serve as an example. He describes the contemporary use of apocalyptic in Paul "in a specialised sense associated with J. Louis Martyn and his followers, denoting divine invasion 'vertically from above' *and allowing no room for earlier stories of the world in general or Israel in particular.*"[87] The charge here is implicitly (and sometimes explicitly) one of Marcionism.[88]

Unsurprisingly, this too is a charge that is denied.[89] Just as there are problems with the characterization of Wright as advocating a "smooth progression" of history, Wright's frequent charge that the Apocalyptic Paul seeks to "sweep off the table" the narrative of Israel's history seems also to be something of a misunderstanding. The Apocalyptic Paul school is, in various ways, committed to giving an account of the story of Israel, *appropriately framed*. Campbell, so often the prime suspect in Wright's critique, has recently expressed this commitment in terms that may seem surprising: "Paul narrates the pre-messianic history of Israel as a smoothly continuous and coherent story, *now that the figure to which everything has slowly been building has been revealed.*"[90] The italicized portion is of supreme theological importance, of course, because it captures Campbell's insistence on a retrospective epistemology, as discussed above. Nevertheless, what we certainly do not have here is a straightforward rejection of the story of Israel. If anything, Campbell's construal of history is *more* continuous than Wright's at this point.

It is important to understand here that Campbell frames the question of continuity and discontinuity by appealing to two modes of telling stories which he labels "*telic*" and "*epiphanic.*"[91] The former is a forward-moving narrative steadily working toward a goal, which Campbell considers a dangerous error that undermines the revelation of Jesus. The latter, however, is a retrospective telling of a story, which he affirms. Campbell's commitment to a retrospective epistemology leads him to tell the overarching story of

---

87. Wright, *History and Eschatology,* 133 (emphasis mine). See also similar charges on 222, 237.
88. E.g., Wright, *Interpreters,* 211n69.
89. See the repudiation of this in Campbell, "Apocalyptic Epistemology," 83.
90. Campbell, *Pauline Dogmatics,* 700 (emphasis original).
91. Campbell, *Pauline Dogmatics,* 77–78.

Israel leading up to the arrival of Jesus, so long as this is done *backwards*.⁹²
One may still tell the story of Israel with its *telos* in mind, but only in retrospect, and in the light of the revelation of Jesus. It seems that much the same point has recently been made by Wright, who has argued for the retrospective validation of the Jewish narrative, the proper goal of which is discerned only in the light of the dawn of the new creation.⁹³ No doubt there are still important questions to pursue, but perhaps the two approaches to giving a theological account of the history of Israel, at least in their most recent expressions, are not as far apart as is sometimes assumed. In any case, we should probably drop the accusations that one "side" is advocating a steady Hegelian (and therefore supersessionist) historical scheme while the other is quasi-Marcionite (and therefore supersessionist) in its denial of the story of Israel. There are, it seems, more nuanced positions involved in both accounts of salvation history.

The Problem of Continuity and Discontinuity

Part of the challenge here, no doubt, is one of rhetorical overstatement, sometimes straying into caricature. Setting this rhetoric aside, however, there is a more substantive theological problem generated by a presentation of the matter in such starkly, and I would suggest falsely, dichotomous terms as an antithesis between an irruptive (apocalyptic) discontinuity and an immanent, progressive (salvation-historical) continuity. Such a strict dichotomy was traced by Keck and others, but these are not the only two options available for a theology of history, as we saw earlier in Robert Jenson's arguments.

A careful reading of Martyn's apocalyptic account of history in Paul also reveals more nuance that is sometimes appreciated. He sharply contrasted the "punctiliar" and the "linear," to be sure, but in addressing the question of continuity and discontinuity, Martyn argued that Paul's apocalyptic thought can be helpfully framed by observing a crucial distinction between "theological continuity" and "anthropological discontinuity."⁹⁴ What is more, scholarship since Martyn has sought to press this further in accounting for both continuity and discontinuity in Pauline apocalyptic theology. For example, while she finds Martyn's approach helpful, Susan

---

92. He likens this to a "memoir" as opposed to a "quest."
93. See Wright, *History and Eschatology*, 204, 237.
94. In Martyn, "Events in Galatia," 176.

Eastman had challenged his proposal for remaining insufficiently nuanced, and for lacking a robust account of the gospel's intersection with, and power to create, human history. In Eastman's view, Martyn's sharp distinctions are problematized by the divine creation of human history and the concomitant intersection of divine and human action.[95] This is an important insight that may well open up numerous areas of constructive discussion with both McCormack and Wright in their critiques of Martyn. For Eastman, a more nuanced account of the relationship between apocalyptic and salvation history is found in the work of John Barclay, to whom we now turn.[96]

Barclay agrees with Martyn's identification of the apocalyptic theology of Galatians, but warns against too one-sided a reading, noting that this apocalyptic discontinuity is qualified by being placed side-by-side with a number of passages that affirm purposeful salvation historical continuity. "Galatians," he argues, "combines apocalyptic motifs with a salvation historical outlook."[97] He notes in this connection that, to some extent, a similar combination is characteristic of the Jewish apocalyptic tradition, citing as evidence the book of Daniel and texts from Qumran, as well as noting with apparent approval Beker's articulation of this theological combination. Of course, much depends on a careful definition of these key terms, and a proper theological framework in which they might cohere. His already important book *Paul and the Gift* has developed this early insight further and suggests the category of *promise* as a helpful framework in which to combine apocalyptic and salvation history. The "radical caesura" of the Christ event is related to the continuous narrative trajectory of the divine plan articulated in the promise of God, given first to Abraham.[98] For Barclay, any continuity in Paul's theology lies in the history of God's promise and not at the level of human history, with which the Christ event remains radically discontinuous. Here Barclay critiques Wright's way of construing the history of Israel as "preparation" if this is meant as an account of this human

---

95. See Eastman, *Recovering*, 15–16, 185. As in the Barthian soteriological discussion of 4.2, Eastman's challenge to Martyn at this point has intriguing echoes of the more mature Barth's reflections on his early work. To this we will return in ch. 5.

96. Eastman cites with approval the same argument in Barclay (*Obeying*, 96–105) that Martyn had rejected as "impossible" (Martyn, *Galatians*, 347n184; cf. Eastman, *Recovering*, 15–16 n36).

97. Barclay, *Obeying*, 104. One might also usefully consult Longenecker, *Triumph*, whose reading of Galatians also seeks to integrate the apocalyptic and salvation-historical themes. See, e.g., the summary on 176–77.

98. Barclay, *Gift*, 411.

level of history. Better, he suggests, to speak of this as "not preparation but pre-announcement."⁹⁹ On the other hand, while Barclay's approach to the problem has obvious similarities with Martyn's categories of "theological continuity" and "anthropological discontinuity," he views Martyn's strong emphasis on the punctiliar nature of the Christ-event as true only in respect of its relationship to human history, not to the continuity of the divine promise.¹⁰⁰ Barclay's framing of the matter may well move us forward towards a more nuanced articulation of both continuity and discontinuity in Paul's eschatology. Paul's gospel is punctiliar and discontinuous in respect of human history, while also being linear and continuous in respect of the divine plan and promise. Barclay's approach thus constitutes a challenge to construals of salvation history that straightforwardly locate continuity on the human level, but without thereby denying the reality of the covenant promise and the continuity of salvation history located at the divine level.

Another attempt to take this discussion forward along similar lines has come from Grant Macaskill, who has suggested that the debate over the Apocalyptic Paul, specifically on the question of continuity and discontinuity, has reached an impasse in large part due to the inherent limitations of the historical-critical methods usually deployed by New Testament scholarship.¹⁰¹ Though praising the theological commitments of scholars on both sides of the debate, a principle reason for their apparently irreconcilable positions in the continuity/discontinuity debate is, he suggests, an insufficient attention to the doctrinal location of that question. The debate, Macaskill argues, is in truth about something more foundational: the question of divine agency in relation to history. Macaskill has suggested the doctrine of *providence* as a theological framework that offers precisely the right resources with which the question of continuity and discontinuity in Paul's apocalyptic thought might be more fruitfully interrogated. By viewing the question in a theologically responsible way through the doctrine of providence, both apocalyptic discontinuity (represented by Martyn) and salvation-historical continuity (represented by Wright) might be coherently located, exposing potential weaknesses while also affirming the value of the key insights made on both sides of the conversation. Macaskill's intention

---

99. Barclay, *Gift*, 412n50. Barclay had earlier spoken of "historical progressions that *prepare the way* for the apocalyptic event" in the Jewish apocalyptic tradition (*Obeying*, 104 [emphasis mine]). This shift in vocabulary from "preparation" to "pre-announcement" represents a development in Barclay's thinking at this point.

100. See Barclay, *Gift*, 414n56, and *Obeying*, 99–100. See also "The Day is at Hand."

101. I am here drawing on the argument of Macaskill, "Providence."

in placing the debate within this theologically robust account of history is to frame the claims made in such a way that resists both the overly punctiliar tendencies of one side of the debate and the naturalistic view of history potentially latent in the other.[102] Since it is a doctrine that is derivative of the doctrine of God, providence has to do with divine self-disclosure. It is a doctrine that captures the theologically disjunctive aspects of Pauline thought without allowing such "invasion" language to result in a depiction of God as absent from the history of the cosmos. But it also requires us to speak of "salvation history," crucially framed not as a history "from below" but as God's activity *in* history, and thus in a way that resists the problem of naturalization. This, Macaskill argues, results in an "apocalyptic" reading of history that might allow us to move beyond the current Pauline stalemate with a greater degree of coherence and precision.

Whether or not they prove decisive, Barclay and Macaskill's proposals represent the sort of challenges to falsely dichotomous eschatological frameworks that have been offered and indications of what it might look like to frame a theologically responsible solution that holds together apocalyptic discontinuity and salvation-historical continuity in Pauline apocalyptic eschatology. Approaching the Apocalyptic Paul debate within a theological framework such as those of Barclay and Macaskill, perhaps we can interrogate with more precision what it is that is being asserted when apocalyptic discontinuity or salvation-historical continuity are emphasized. When it comes to talking about "history," perhaps there is some talking at cross-purposes that these more precise analyses might clarify. In the following chapter, I will add to these proposals one of my own, in dialogue with the apocalyptic literature and Karl Barth.

4.5 Paul's Apocalyptic Soteriology: Captivity and Complicity

So far in this second part of the book, we have been exploring some major critiques of the Apocalyptic Paul and suggesting constructive proposals for correcting false dichotomies. We now close with a third dichotomy which can be traced in recent work on Paul's apocalyptic soteriology, namely the antithesis between "cosmological" and "forensic" patterns of apocalyptic soteriology. In the background (and sometimes quite plainly in the foreground) this contrastive instinct is, as we have seen, a reflection of the

---

102. See also the exploration of this in Macaskill, *Intellectual Humility*, 112–13.

Bultmann-Käsemann debate. Bultmann observed a contradiction running through the New Testament between the "cosmic" and the "existential," which surfaces particularly when accounting for sin and salvation. For Bultmann, Sin as a cosmically determined human fate contradicts sin as human decision and consequent guilt.[103] Bultmann's approach to this contradiction was to explain the cosmic through the existential. Käsemann, however, thought that Bultmann's approach evaporated Paul's cosmological vision into individual anthropology.[104] He therefore pressed the question in the opposite direction, circumscribing the anthropological question of human guilt and decision by the cosmological question of divine sovereignty. Sinful acts of individuals are merely a manifestation of the cosmic enslavement to the power of death. As many have observed, the contours of this debate continue to shape the discussion of soteriology in the Apocalyptic Paul. At times this seems to have given the discussion a more antithetical framework than is helpful. De Boer's "two tracks" analysis, heuristically contrasting cosmological and forensic patterns in apocalyptic eschatology in a manner analogous to Käsemann and Bultmann, has been developed into something more like a strict antithesis in some approaches to Pauline soteriology. In places de Boer's own expression of the thesis seems to lean in that dichotomous direction, and he describes them in one place as "competing explanations" for the human plight.[105]

One example was seen above in the work of Campbell, whose work sharply contrasts the "forensic" soteriology of what he calls "Justification Theory" with his reading of Paul's cosmological-apocalyptic gospel. But again, it need not be the case that the two soteriological paradigms are handled so dichotomously. As we have seen, examination of the apocalyptic texts themselves have shown that the two soteriological paradigms regularly overlap and intersect, as de Boer was careful to observe.[106] Furthermore, systematic theologians have rejected an overly sharp dichotomy between the two soteriological paradigms in accounts of Barth's mature work. The question, of course, is whether the same can be said of Paul.

---

103. Bultmann, *New Testament and Mythology*, 11.

104. Käsemann, *Romans*, 150.

105. See de Boer *God's Apocalypse*, 209–11, apparently casting them as something like two poles, before settling on a Pauline account in which Paul adapts both by placing forensic categories within a cosmological pattern.

106. De Boer, *Defeat of Death*, 85.

For the most part, the survey of scholarship in this volume shows that the most common approach to this question is to offer some kind of integrated account of the two soteriological patterns in Paul's thought, though Campbell appears to be something of an exception. As we saw above, Campbell's analysis of Romans explains the presence of "forensic" material (especially in Rom 1:18—3:20) as a form of *prosōpopoeia*, a rhetorical "speech in character" or "parody." The forensic soteriological language represents not Paul's view but that of a legalistic "Teacher" who opposes him. As we saw earlier, de Boer has also offered a similar account of the rhetorical function of "forensic" elements in Rom 2:5–8, elements which are said to be only present in Paul's letter for reasons of argument with those who espouse a "forensic" soteriology.[107] Given de Boer's position that forensic elements are regularly found in the cosmological pattern of apocalyptic, it is not clear why the rhetorical proposals he and Campbell reach with Romans, or the similar one de Boer and Martyn have suggested for Galatians, are necessary.[108] As we have seen, strict antithesis between these two soteriological tracks was never the intention in suggesting the framework in the first place.

As noted earlier, Campbell's proposal has proven particularly controversial and has met with some strong challenges from both classicists[109] and Pauline scholars.[110] Among the various challenges to a strict antithesis between forensic and cosmological soteriologies, two of the more pointed responses have come from John Barclay and Simon Gathercole. In Barclay's assessment, Campbell's analysis that the two patterns of soteriology represent profoundly antithetical conceptions of God is flawed.[111] He attributes this problem to Campbell's extreme and somewhat idiosyncratic account of grace, and the account of the antithesis of divine and human agency that accompanies it. On the basis of this, Campbell contrasts his "apocalyptic" reading of soteriology with the decidedly "forensic" language of

---

107. De Boer, *Defeat of Death*, 183, and "Paul and Apocalyptic Eschatology" 365. See section 2.1 above.

108. Here de Boer largely follows Martyn (e.g., *Galatians*, 89–90). See, e.g., "Paul and Jewish Apocalyptic," 185. This argument has been restated for both Galatians and Romans (de Boer, *God's Apocalypse*, 136–37).

109. E.g., Griffith-Jones, "Beyond Reasonable Hope." The shift from formal category of *prosōpopoeia* to a looser Socratic parody was Campbell's response to this criticism.

110. In addition to the responses of Barclay and Gathercole described here, see also Macaskill, "Review," 158–59.

111. See, esp. Barclay, *Gift*, 171–73.

justification and judgment found in Rom 1–4. While Barclay is unconvinced on textual grounds by Campbell's rhetorical explanations of such language in Romans,[112] the heart of his critique concerns the underlying account of grace and divine/human agency.

Simon Gathercole has offered a broader response to the question through a discussion of the question of "Sin" and "sins" in Paul, again with a focus on the letter to the Romans, where this vocabulary clusters. While not denying the cosmological reading of Sin as a power, Gathercole has challenged approaches along these lines which result in downplaying or even sidelining the forensic language of "sins" as human transgressions of God's will. At the heart of this, Gathercole surmises, is a recent tendency in Pauline scholarship to prioritize cosmological categories over forensic ones. Gathercole names Stendahl, Schweitzer, and Sanders as playing their part, but offers a particular focus on the Apocalyptic Paul. Here Gathercole sees a problematic emphasis on the category of Sin as cosmological power that results in an unwarranted neglect of sin as human transgression. In this connection, Gathercole engages at length with Martyn (though the idea was of course de Boer's) as an eloquent defender of the thesis that cosmological and forensic apocalyptic eschatology are "two opposite systems,"[113] which are then described in strictly antithetical terms, an antithesis that Gathercole rejects. In reply, he advocates for a soteriology that integrates both patterns with equal importance in Paul's thought.

Let us pause here and take stock of this soteriological critique. We have seen that, first, a strict dichotomy between cosmological and forensic soteriological patterns is not considered characteristic of apocalyptic thought in Second Temple Judaism. Second, within systematic theology it is generally not considered an appropriate framework for describing Barth's mature thought. Third, such antithetical approaches are avoided by most within the Apocalyptic Paul movement and strongly challenged by those outside it. There seems to be little reason, therefore, to insist on readings of Paul that hold the forensic and cosmological patterns of soteriology apart.

However, we have already noted that de Boer's analysis is actually more subtle than the simplistic either-or which might be inferred from his rhetorical explanations of forensic themes in Romans and Galatians. In his most recent work, de Boer tackles the question addressed by Gathercole,

---

112. Barclay, *Gift*, 462n29.
113. Gathercole, "Sins in Paul," 147.

the issue of Sin and soteriology in Romans.[114] Here de Boer quite clearly argues for the importance of some kind of integration of the two tracks and seeks to develop a coherent account of this integration. De Boer specifically rejects as misplaced Gathercole's critique that the Apocalyptic Paul movement's emphasis on Sin as a power entails the rejection of the category of sin as human transgression. The former, even if strongly emphasized in an apocalyptic account of Paul, always also implies the latter.[115] On the question of whether human beings are victims of the power of Sin or accountable agents of sinning, de Boer's assessment is that "Paul's answer seems ultimately to be both-and rather than either-or."[116] At this point de Boer is happy to accept that the formulation of his earlier cosmological emphasis may need to be nuanced (and perhaps such nuance will involve abandoning language of "competing explanations" and the metaphor of "tracks" in favor of something less antithetical).[117] But certainly, there seems to be a broad, though not unanimous, consensus that the aim is an integrative account of both patterns in Pauline thought. In the words of the later Barth, what we need here is the integration of "the justification *and* deliverance of sinful man."[118] One example of this, as we saw above, is Keck's reading of Romans, accounting for the presence of both soteriological paradigms and explaining their coherence situationally. Paul reaches for the appropriate language for the particular aspect of the human condition being addressed at that point in his argument.[119]

Of course, this answer only gets us to the start of another question. How, then, might the "cosmological" and "forensic" apocalyptic patterns of soteriology be coherently integrated in Pauline theology? As de Boer puts it, when it comes to Paul's account of human sinning, "is the rule of Sin the result of their trespasses or are their trespasses the result of Sin's hegemony?"[120] Here, I suggest, there are also signs of an emerging agreement, and a number of recent contributions are taking the discussion forward in interesting ways. A potentially helpful category that has been

---

114. See de Boer, *God's Apocalypse*, 73–89, also published in Gupta and Goodrich, *Sin and its Remedy*, 14–32.

115. De Boer, *God's Apocalypse*, 76n19.

116. De Boer, *God's Apocalypse*, 82.

117. De Boer, *God's Apocalypse*, 82n38.

118. Barth, *CD* III/3 §50, 362 (emphasis mine).

119. See the discussion of Keck in 2.2 above.

120. De Boer, *God's Apocalypse*, 82.

suggested by various Pauline scholars is the notion of *complicity*, which allows the affirmation of both the reality of human responsibility and the enslaving cosmic power of Sin.

De Boer's recent discussion of the problem of describing the "both-and," accounting for the integration of sin as human transgression and Sin as cosmological power, also locates his solution in the notion of complicity. Human beings can be called to account for their sins inasmuch as they have acted complicity with the reign of Sin.[121] At this point, he cites the constructive contribution of Susan Eastman, whose work (as we saw earlier) has offered particular contributions to the Apocalyptic Paul conversation in the area of anthropology and human agency.[122] Taking her cue from Käsemann, Eastman offers an analysis of Paul's view of the person, particularly as developed in the structure and overlapping narratives of Rom 1–8,[123] as *both* culpable sinner *and* slave to the cosmic power of Sin. "Human actors," Eastman argues "are both captive and complicit."[124] Her participatory account of Paul's anthropology thus contributes to an analysis of his apocalyptic soteriology that integrates both forensic forgiveness and cosmological deliverance.

A similar line of thought has recently been developed by Philip Ziegler, for whom the notion of complicity is instructive for Pauline soteriology in an "apocalyptic key."[125] Martyn's emphasis on a "cosmological" apocalyptic soteriology captures well, Ziegler argues, the approach of the early Barth. However, as we saw earlier through McCormack's analysis, Ziegler notes that Barth's more mature work recognized a weakness in this earlier account and corrects it by integrating the "cosmological" emphasis with a more clearly "forensic" account of salvation. Martyn's account is therefore weakened by its over-emphasis on Barth's earlier, more sharply dichotomous, explication of Pauline soteriology.[126] Ziegler's own proposal, developed in dialogue with Käsemann, is that Paul's apocalyptic theology integrates human captivity to and complicity with Sin, to which the gospel

---

121. De Boer, *God's Apocalypse*, 85.

122. The early development of this was noted with approval by Martyn in some of his last contributions to the discussion. See Martyn, "Afterword," 163.

123. Eastman, "Apocalypse and Incarnation," 173-74; see also Eastman, "Double Participation," 99.

124. Eastman, *Person*, 111, see also "Apocalypse and Incarnation," 170.

125. Ziegler, "Christ Must Reign"; "Bound Over," 94.

126. See Ziegler, *Militant Grace*, 22, cf. Ziegler, "Some Remarks," 206.

offers both liberation and forgiveness as "two aspects of the one rectifying moment of God's sovereign grace."[127] Moreover, in Ziegler's reading of Paul, this integrative solution is more than a simple (and potentially paradoxical) affirmation of "both-and." It requires the proper coherent ordering of the two patterns. An emphasis on the controlling cosmological apocalyptic pattern of divine liberation from the power of Sin by no means negates the importance of human guilt, nor does it efface other soteriological motifs, but rather constitutes the necessary and more fundamental category within which they can be coherently integrated.

A third recent investigation of Pauline hamartiology that offers a framework for the integration of the two soteriological categories is that of Matthew Croasmun. In his monograph *The Emergence of Sin: The Cosmic Tyrant in Romans*, Croasmun presses beyond "Bultmannian reduction" and "Käsemannian dualism" not through resolving in favor of one or the other, nor through offering a middle way, but through an account of Paul's apparent "personification" of s/Sin in Romans that integrates both the cosmological and forensic themes of his apocalyptic soteriology, "because both extremes recognize important features of the Pauline text."[128] Sin, for Croasmun, is *at once* a matter of human individual culpability, a feature of human social structures, and a cosmic tyrant. What prevents this threefold assertion from being mere paradox is Croasmun's use of the concept of "emergence," an interdisciplinary discourse that allows various ontologies to be deployed simultaneously at different levels of analysis. Applied to Pauline hamartiology, this approach offers the possibility of speaking of s/Sin as at once a cosmic and forensic phenomenon, thereby resolving the Bultmann-Käsemann debate without taking either side. Whether or not Croasmun's work has offered an enduring solution to this problem remains to be seen, but it is certainly a sign that integrative solutions may yet be found. It seems to me that there are suggestive similarities between this kind of "multi-level approach" and the divine/human levels of Barclay's proposal in respect of the eschatological problem of continuity and discontinuity, discussed in the previous section.

Lastly, Alexandra Brown has recently taken up Gathercole's challenge to Martyn's cosmic-apocalyptic account of Sin in his reading of Paul and has been sympathetic to the critique that an emphasis on this "cosmological" narrative can lead to the neglect of human agency and sin as

---

127. Ziegler, *Militant Grace*, 61. See also 29 and "Bound Over," 93–94.
128. Croasmun, *Emergence*, 13.

transgression.¹²⁹ Brown agrees with Gathercole that the two soteriological patterns are compatible and should be framed as such. Attending to the narrative of 1 Corinthians, Brown offers an account of how "Sin" and "sins" (the two are quite equally distributed across the letter) might logically cohere. For Brown (building on Gaventa, Eastman, and Croasmun) this coherence lies in an account of Pauline soteriology that places "sins" as human acts of transgression *within* an apocalyptic/cosmic frame of Sin as a corrupting cosmic power. The account of sin and its remedy found in 1 Corinthians thus reaches its most foundational truth in Paul's framing of the letter with the divine invasive act of chapter 1 and the martial and cosmic claim of 15:54–56: "Death has been swallowed up in victory. Where, O Death is your victory? Where, O Death, is your sting? The sting of Death is Sin, and the power of Sin is the Law." The chapters that form the bulk of the letter, in which human actions and transgressions in the present age ("sins," plural) are discussed, are thus literarily and logically framed by this cosmic account of the power of Sin (singular) and the power of God. In Brown's view, this is an apocalyptic soteriological framework that does not diminish the importance of human acts of "sinning." It is an inseparable soteriological "both-and" expressed in the narrative of 1 Corinthians and further developed by Paul, with greater structural coherence, in Romans. As in Gaventa's and Eastman's readings of Rom 5–8, as well as Bowens's reading of 2 Corinthians, Brown's reading of 1 Corinthians sees Sin as a cosmic power that blinds, enslaves, poisons, and corrupts human agency. Unlike others described here, Brown does not explicitly deploy the category of "complicity" and leaves somewhat undeveloped the question of how human guilt factors in her account, but nevertheless her goal throughout is to give an account of Paul's apocalyptic soteriology that emphasizes his apocalyptic/cosmological soteriology while avoiding the neglect of human agency. In short, appropriately understood and related, substitutionary and liberative/apocalyptic remedies for sin are not incompatible.¹³⁰

These are just four brief examples of how this problem is being approached, and no doubt many questions remain. For example, in our accounts of Paul's integrated cosmological and forensic soteriology, what is the logical order of these two themes/narratives? Does the cosmological pattern fundamentally underpin or frame the forensic pattern (Ziegler, Brown) or circumscribe and overtake it (de Boer)? Is it the other way

---

129. Brown, "Battlefield."
130. Brown, "Battlefield," 76.

around (as in McCormack's reading of the later Barth)?[131] Or are the two somehow of equal importance (Gathercole) or simultaneously true at different levels of analysis (Croasmun)? Does the category of "complicity" to enslaving powers solve this problem, or does it imply an insufficiently robust account of human responsibility and guilt?

If those were not enough questions to keep us going, we might also ask whether Paul even attempted a coherent account, or whether this is a question that did not ultimately interest him.[132] For that matter, when it comes to describing the "dark side" of Pauline soteriology, the doctrine of sin and evil, should we even expect coherence, or is that itself a theologically problematic endeavor? For example, in his account of Paul and the origin of evil, Campbell is one of many who appeal ultimately to Barth's argument that sin amounts to "nothingness" (*das Nichtige*).[133] Evil, by its nature, lacks coherence. If it were coherent, it would be ordered, which would mean that it was not wholly evil. While this may work nicely as a solution for the "problem" of the (in)coherence of a dual pattern of sins/Sin and its origin, it is not clear how we might deploy this kind of thinking when trying to speak coherently of an integrated dual narrative for God's saving "solution." After all, as Ziegler (who also turns to Barth's argument at this point) has put it, how we approach the doctrine of sin affects both "our grasp of that from which we are redeemed and the manner of our redemption."[134]

---

131. See section 4.2.

132. As Gathercole suggests in "Sins in Paul," 157.

133. In Campbell, *Pauline Dogmatics*, ch. 6, esp. 118–19n8. Barth's (in)famous *Das Nichtige* argument is found in *CD* III/3 §50.

134. Ziegler, "Bound Over," 100.

CHAPTER 5

Paul's Apocalyptic Theology in Interdisciplinary Perspective

IN THE PREVIOUS CHAPTER I indicated some of the main areas of critique that have been voiced in relation to the Apocalyptic Paul and outlined some recent proposals taking the conversation further. In this final chapter, I want to offer some constructive contributions of my own, to develop some of these critiques and to propose readings of aspects of Paul's apocalyptic theology that address them. I have attempted throughout this chapter to meet the challenge, issued throughout this book, of curating a three-way interdisciplinary conversation between recent scholarship on the apocalyptic literature, proposals from the Apocalyptic Paul, and systematic theology.

The first section examines the theme of the "two ages" and considers the use of this apocalyptic trope across the Pauline epistles. In particular, the surprising absence of the phrase "age to come" provides a starting point for developing the question of Paul's relationship to Jewish apocalyptic thought, in which a "two ages" scheme is sometimes assumed to be ubiquitous, an assumption which has been challenged by recent scholarship. Consideration is then given to the evidence from Paul's letters and the interpretation of this evidence by the Apocalyptic Paul. I then propose my own interpretation of the Pauline evidence, in dialogue with the theology of Karl Barth and with Ann Jervis, whose recent work on Paul's view of time has asked important questions of the Apocalyptic Paul.

Subsequent sections of this chapter follow roughly the same three-part structure but focus more sharply on a couple of specific texts and themes, as case studies in interdisciplinary interpretation. I start with 1 Cor 2, and examine what this passage can tell us about Paul's apocalyptic epistemology. As we have seen, recent work by specialists in apocalyptic literature has examined the interplay between wisdom and revelation in that corpus, and I begin by summarizing some of that work. These insights are then brought into dialogue with the Apocalyptic Paul, in particular the work of Alexandra Brown on 1 Corinthians, and recent systematic theology in the Barthian tradition.

The third and final section looks at the interplay between cosmology and eschatology, focusing on the famous allegory of Sarah and Hagar in Gal 4. The motif of "cities as women" is found in numerous places in Jewish and Christian apocalyptic literature, and the section begins with some consideration of this material. It then moves on to examine how the passage has been interpreted in the Apocalyptic Paul, with a particular focus on Martyn and de Boer's commentaries on Galatians. I then propose a fresh reading, in dialogue with John Barclay, again interacting with insights from Barth's *Church Dogmatics*.

These investigations of Pauline texts are, by necessity, brief and suggestive. In part this reflects the huge challenge of becoming conversant with three major (sub)disciplines, a challenge to which I have only partly risen. My intention, however, is not to offer the definitive synthesis but rather to indicate the kind of interdisciplinary approach that might address some of the issues and questions raised in the previous chapter, and in this way to take the conversation forward constructively.

5.1 Paul and the "Age to Come"

The "Two Ages" in Recent Jewish Apocalyptic Scholarship

As we have seen throughout this book, there is a long history of apocalyptic interpretations of Paul focused on his modified Jewish apocalyptic eschatology, in which the notion of the "two ages" has been a central feature, taken to be a (if not *the*) fundamental characteristic of Jewish apocalyptic thought,[1] often relying on analyses of that literature developed by Vielhauer, Hanson, and Russell.[2] This, however, is found much more widely than one school of Pauline interpretation. Indeed, it is almost an axiom of New Testament studies that some version of an "inaugurated" two-age framework

---

1. De Boer, *Defeat of Death*, 7. See further Agamben, *Time That Remains*, 62.
2. See, e.g., de Boer, *Paul Theologian of God's Apocalypse* 4, and the works cited therein.

shapes Paul's eschatology. It is a standard feature of dictionary definitions[3] and introductory textbooks, usually accompanied by timeline diagrams[4] and catchphrases such as "now and not yet," or "eschatological tension." Moreover, this kind of "inaugurated" modification of the Jewish apocalyptic doctrine of the "two ages" is often considered a Christian innovation. Leander Keck, we recall, argued that Paul's christological adaptation of the "two ages" eschatology creates "an irreducible tension between the 'already' and 'not yet' which is generally absent from apocalyptic theology."[5] Keck is by no means alone in this, and his is not the most dramatic assessment of this Pauline "innovation." Oscar Cullmann described the tension created by the overlap of the ages "the *new element* in the New Testament"[6] and "the silent presupposition that lies behind all that it says."[7] N. T. Wright focuses attention on the Pauline nature of this novelty, arguing that the inauguration of the age to come is "Paul's specific contribution" and "foundational to [his] entire worldview."[8] Again, James Dunn, though recognizing that similar eschatological hopes are present elsewhere, insists that "an eschatology split in this way between such a decisive 'already' and yet still a 'not yet' was a new departure" and "the distinctive feature of Paul's theology."[9]

In the previous chapter, however, it was suggested that such interpretations are evidence of an oversimplifying tendency in the handling of Jewish apocalyptic eschatology in Pauline scholarship, which too often reduces this literature to "background" for Christian theological innovation. It is the view of some that such accounts of Pauline eschatology are evidence of a worrying trend of presenting the Jewish apocalyptic tradition in overly simplistic dichotomies in order to cast Paul's theology as the solution.[10] One of the clearest examples of this phenomenon is the way in which the eschatological notion of "two ages" is used in Pauline scholarship, and a

---

3. "The NT borrowed the doctrine of the two aeons from Jewish apocalyptic, in which we find the same expressions from the 1st century B. C. onwards." Sasse, "Αἰών, Αἰώνιος," 206.

4. A classic example is James Dunn's linear diagrams in *Theology of Paul the Apostle*, 464.

5. Keck, "Paul and Apocalyptic Theology" in *Christ's First Theologian*, 86.

6. Cullmann, *Salvation in History*, 172.

7. Cullmann, *Christ and Time*, 145–46.

8. Wright, *Paul and the Faithfulness of God*, 476–67; 562.

9. Dunn, *Theology of Paul the Apostle*, 465.

10. See, for example, Goff, "Mystery of God's Wisdom," 175–76 and Boccaccini, *Paul's Three Paths*, 16–23. I will engage with Goff's essay in the next section.

regular critique of the Apocalyptic Paul among specialists in the Jewish apocalyptic literature is the way in which this corpus has been construed, as both oversimplified and anachronistic.

In respect of oversimplification, studies of the apocalyptic literature have shown that the corpus has a range of approaches to the questions of time and eschatology, including the notion of two ages, yes, but also frameworks such as the periodization of history, cyclical patterns of time, and the relationship between *Urzeit* and *Endzeit*. Some texts also show evidence of combining multiple frameworks.[11] This diversity is not always recognized or appreciated by Paul specialists, who sometimes seem to default to an assumed "two age" scheme. For example, despite the clear importance of the periodization of history in the eschatology of the book of Daniel, when Keck reads it in relation to Paul's apocalyptic theology, he nevertheless insists that "the theme of two aeons was fundamental whether the phrasing itself appears or not."[12] Although the blessing in Dan 2:20 uses the phrase "from age to age" (Heb. מִן־עָלְמָא וְעַד־עָלְמָא; LXX εἰς τὸν αἰῶνα), the context there clearly indicates an emphasis on times and seasons rather than an eschatological dualism. Far more prevalent is the periodized eschatology found in Daniel's visions of the four beasts in chapter 7, the "seventy weeks" of chapter 9, and the statue in chapters 10 and 11.

As to the charge of anachronism, it has been suggested by scholars of the Jewish apocalyptic literature that the "two ages" motif is hardly developed at all in the texts of the Second Temple period and is more likely a later rabbinic pattern, projected back onto earlier texts. This is important to note. One can certainly see clear evidence of an eschatological dualism in a wide variety of later texts (such as the Shepherd of Hermas, the Testament of Job, the Epistle of Barnabas and 2 Clement[13]) but the evidence from the Second Temple Jewish apocalypses themselves is not quite so clear-cut. Nevertheless, texts such as 1 En. 71:15 and 4 Ezra 7:50 give sufficient warrant, in my view, to continue to include the idea in discussions of apocalyptic eschatology. The point stands, however, and we should certainly avoid treating the doctrine of "two ages" as an unambiguous indicator of Jewish apocalyptic thought.

11. For a useful overview, see G. Macaskill, "Eschatology" in Gurtner, *T&T Clark Encyclopedia of Second Temple Judaism*, 248–49.

12. Keck, *Christ's First Theologian*, 80.

13. E.g., mSanh. 10.1-4; Herm. 24.1-7 (combined here with a historical periodization eschatology); 53.1-8; T. Job 4:6; Ep. Barnabas 15:8, (again a combined scheme); 2 Clem 6:3-5.

Commentary on Paul's letters is not entirely ignorant of this insight.[14] Martyn, for example, recognizes that the Hebrew phrases הָעוֹלָם הַזֶּה and הָעוֹלָם הַבָּא are not found before 70 CE.[15] The questions, of course, are the degree to which this more diverse appreciation of apocalyptic eschatology has been appreciated in Pauline scholarship, and whether apocalyptic interpretations of Paul in particular are guilty of assuming an overly simplistic eschatology of two ages. "Apocalyptic eschatology" is a far more variegated and complex phenomenon than is sometimes suggested; in any given text there are various ways in which realized and future elements may be interrelated.[16]

In respect of the broader question of Pauline theological innovation, Loren Stuckenbruck has argued that "inaugurated eschatology" itself is not a unique feature of Christian thought, but is an eschatological framework found earlier in the Jewish apocalyptic tradition that predates Paul.[17] Stuckenbruck has argued that these texts demonstrate eschatological arrangements of past and future which are analogous to Pauline "inaugurated eschatology," as well as, importantly, the role of the present in apocalyptic thought. For example, in some texts, divine victory over evil was not only a future hope for the *Endzeit* but something that had already happened definitively in the *Urzeit* (for example in the Flood) and therefore this serves to assure God's people in the present of his already-but-not-yet triumph.[18] While he does not deny that early Christian thought may represent a genuinely new departure in some respects, there is more continuity here than is usually assumed. Clearly, greater care is needed in how we articulate any Pauline innovation in dialogue with the Jewish apocalyptic tradition, particularly when it comes to eschatology. I will shortly offer my own suggestion, resourced by Christian theology, for what that might look like. First, though, we turn to a fresh appraisal of the evidence from Paul's letters, and begin with this (perhaps surprising) fact: the phrase "age to come," so prevalent in discussions of Paul's eschatology, never occurs unambiguously in his writings.

---

14. E.g., Martyn, *Galatians*, 98; cf. also Wright, *Paul and the Faithfulness of God*, 1059.

15. See also Sasse, "Αἰών, Αἰώνιος," 206.

16. Macaskill, "Eschatology," 248–49.

17. Stuckenbruck, "Overlapping Ages," 309–26 and Stuckenbruck, "Posturing 'Apocalyptic' in Pauline Theology," 240–56. See also Macaskill, "Eschatology," 249.

18. Stuckenbruck, "Overlapping Ages," 323–24.

The "Age to Come" in the Apocalyptic Paul (but not in Paul?)

The expression ὁ αἰὼν οὗτος, "this age" or "the present age" and its equivalents, occurs regularly in Paul,[19] often accompanied by the near-synonymous phrase ὁ κόσμος οὗτος, "this world." The longer phrase τοῦ αἰῶνος τοῦ ἐνεστῶτος πονηροῦ, "the present evil age," appears in Gal 1:4, and Martyn rightly highlights this in his apocalyptic interpretation as "the first of numerous apocalyptic expressions in the letter."[20] Another variation is found in the pastoral epistles, which prefer the phrase ὁ νῦν αἰών, literally "the now age."[21] English translations sometimes obscure these nuances or shift inconsistently between "world" and "age."[22]

But what about its corollary, "the age to come"? Here the evidence is a lot thinner than one might assume, and what we do have is ambiguous at best. The closest we come to the phrase in the undisputed letters is 2 Cor 9:9, and the expression εἰς τὸν αἰῶνα. This, however, comes as part of a quotation from Ps 111 and is usually understood as an eternity formula, translated "forever." This translation decision is supported by the textual variant εἰς τὸν αἰῶνα τοῦ αἰῶνος, which brings the quotation in line with the LXX.[23] Paul regularly uses the plural "ages" in such contexts, such as the stock benediction phrase εἰς τοὺς αἰῶνας [τῶν αἰώνων],[24] but this is clearly a Hebraic formula (rendering עוֹלָמִים) and is, I think, also best understood as a circumlocution for the notion of "eternity" rather than evidence of a dualistic scheme. In 1 Tim 6:19 we find the phrase εἰς τὸ μέλλον, which the NRSV translates rather blandly as "for the future," but with some justification since the word αἰών is absent.

Casting the net slightly wider, we do find the phrase in Eph 1:21, but again there are problems with this piece of evidence. Leaving aside questions of Pauline authorship, an appeal to this verse for evidence of an

19. See Rom 12:2; 1 Cor 1:20; 2:6–8; 3:18; 2 Cor 4:4.
20. Martyn, *Galatians*, 97.
21. 1 Tim 6:17; 2 Tim 4:10; Titus 2:12.
22. For example, the NRSV translates both ὁ αἰὼν οὗτος in 1 Corinthians and ὁ νῦν αἰών in the pastoral epistles with the same English phrase "the present age," obscuring the subtle difference. In Rom 12:2 ὁ αἰὼν οὗτος is translated "this *world*" (though with a footnote) and in 2 Corinthians, ὁ θεὸς τοῦ αἰῶνος τούτου is rendered "the god of this *world*."
23. Found in F, G, K, and several minuscules.
24. Rom 1:25; 9:5; 11:36; 16:27; 2 Cor 11:31; Gal 1:5; Phil 4:20; 1 Tim 1:17; 2 Tim 4:18, and Eph 3:21, with the slight modification εἰς πάσας τὰς γενεὰς τοῦ αἰῶνος τῶν αἰώνων.

eschatological dualism of two ages will have to account for the way Ephesians uses this language. In that letter, the "ages" indicate a plurality of *past* (3:9) or *future* ages (2:7), not a present/future dualism. This idea of multiple past "ages" is also found in Col 1:26 and 1 Cor 2:7–10, where it is related to the distinctly apocalyptic theme of the revelation of mysteries (on which see below). If anything, these passages are evidence of a Pauline apocalyptic eschatology of the periodization of history, rather than a two-age dualism.

There is one significant piece of evidence in favor of a Pauline "two ages" eschatology which requires a more thorough discussion, 1 Cor 10:11, where we read the phrase εἰς οὓς τὰ τέλη τῶν αἰώνων κατήντηκεν, "on whom the ends of the ages have come" (NRSV) or, as we shall see, "have met." Alexandra Brown reads this as an indication that Paul "presupposes the two ages," while being "apocalyptically innovative" in his adaptation of that Jewish apocalyptic framework.[25] Martinus de Boer tentatively suggests that this expression "may be an allusion" to eschatological dualism, understanding the phrase as indicating "the end of the old age and the beginning of the new."[26] This sort of reading has a long pedigree in apocalyptic interpretation of Paul, going back at least to Johannes Weiss, for whom the plural "ages" may be understood geometrically as the meeting point, in Paul's generation, of the end of one line and the beginning of the other.[27] However, it is by no means a niche interpretation limited to the Apocalyptic Paul, but is found quite widely in Pauline scholarship.[28] For example, it appears in N. T. Wright's reading of Paul. Though he is not fully committed to the point, Wright reads 1 Cor 10:11 as a possible indication that Paul "sees the end of the 'present age' meeting up with, and overlapping with, the leading edge of the 'age to come' . . . converging in the single event of Jesus the Messiah."[29] This is one place where Wright is in general agreement with the Apocalyptic Paul.

Wright and de Boer's apparent hesitancy to be dogmatic on this point is appropriate, since reading 1 Cor 10:11 as evidence of a Pauline apocalyptic dualism requires some creative theological work with the meaning

---

25. Brown, *Cross*, 124.

26. De Boer, *Paul, Theologian of God's Apocalypse*, 5.

27. Weiss, *Der Erste Korintherbrief*, 254. Weiss goes on to cite 4 Ezra 6:7–10 in support of this proposal (a passage I discussed in relation to eschatology in the Apocalyptic Paul in Davies, *Paul Among the Apocalypses*, 90–92).

28. See also, for example, Agamben, *Time That Remains*, 73; Hays, *Echoes of Scripture in the Letters of Paul*, 168–69.

29. Wright, *Paul and the Faithfulness of God*, 552.

of τὰ τέλη. For my part, I am not sure that the word τέλος can be stretched to mean "beginning" in this way on lexical grounds, a point which Wright concedes, and I also wonder if it is theologically coherent to think of eternity having a "leading edge." But here I have introduced the theological theme of "eternity," to which we will shortly return.

By all accounts, 1 Cor 10:11 is a complicated piece of syntax, but it is perhaps better to read the phrase as an intensifying plural, or even further evidence that Paul is here working with an eschatology of historical periodization (in line with 2:7–10, noted above), reading the "ages" as phases of history which have now come to their appointed "ends."[30] Such a reading becomes more compelling if we surrender the idea that a "two ages" framework is an apocalyptic *sine qua non*, and recognize the diverse and interwoven ways in which Paul and his apocalyptic contemporaries deployed their eschatological frameworks. Indeed, given that the surrounding context in the letter concerns pivotal events in Israel's salvation history, if Paul wanted to introduce an eschatological dualism at this point one might expect to see clearer signals. Whether or not this is a convincing reading, what is clear from this brief survey of the evidence is that the argument for an eschatological dualism of "two ages" in Paul is less than compelling.

It should be noted at this point that I am not the only one to observe this pattern in Paul's eschatological language. De Boer himself notes that the "age to come" only occurs in Ephesians,[31] though it is not clear that this observation has been followed through in relation to his commitment to eschatological dualism in Paul. Sustained attention is presently being given to this question in relation to Paul's theology of time by Ann Jervis, who has explored the Pauline evidence, making similar observations, and has also called into question whether Paul indeed thought in terms of "two ages."[32] I will engage more closely with her work in the constructive proposals that follow.

---

30. This is the other option Wright suggests. See again Wright, *Paul and the Faithfulness of God,* 552 and Hays, *Echoes of Scripture in the Letters of Paul,* 168–69.

31. De Boer, *Paul, Theologian of God's Apocalypse,* 5.

32. Jervis's monograph on time in Paul is still forthcoming, but some discussion can be found in Jervis, "Promise and Purpose in Romans 9.1–13," 9–11. There are numerous points of contact between that essay and the present discussion, though also some important differences in our theological interpretations of Paul. I remain grateful to Ann for the ongoing conversation we have had on this topic, and eagerly anticipate her forthcoming volume.

Once the reader is attuned to the lack of the phrase "age to come" in Paul, it begins to appear even more conspicuous by its absence. In places, it almost seems like Paul is actively avoiding the phrase where it might be more natural to use it. For example, in 1 Cor 1:20 and 2:6–8, the "wisdom of this age" (σοφία τοῦ αἰῶνος τούτου) is contrasted not with the "wisdom of the age to come," as one might expect, but with "God's wisdom" (θεοῦ σοφία). Again, in Gal 4:25–26, Paul contrasts the "present Jerusalem" (ἡ νῦν Ἰερουσαλήμ) not with the "future Jerusalem" or the "Jerusalem to come" but, somewhat awkwardly, with the "Jerusalem above" (ἡ ἄνω Ἰερουσαλήμ). In the discussions below I will examine these two passages as case studies in Pauline apocalyptic thought and explore the connections they suggest between Paul's epistemology, eschatology, and cosmology.

Elsewhere, Paul has a range of alternative ideas and phrases with which he contrasts the "present age," including "new creation" and the "kingdom of God."[33] Again, if we assume the necessity of a "two age" dualism for Paul's apocalyptic thought, then there is a strong reason to parse such phrases as circumlocutions for the "age to come," as indeed Martyn and others have sometimes done. "To speak of the present age," Martyn argues, "is obviously to imply that there is another age (or something like another age)" and this is evidence of Paul's "assumption of eschatological dualism."[34] We see a similar interpretation in de Boer, no doubt owing to the importance he attaches to eschatological dualism in his paradigm for apocalyptic thought. For him, such phrases in Paul are "surely other ways of speaking about the age or world to come."[35] But, as we have seen, a dualistic framework of "two ages," though important among various apocalyptic eschatological themes, is neither necessary nor sufficient as a defining characteristic of apocalyptic thought, in Paul or elsewhere.

Of course, the absence of a phrase does not prove the absence of an idea. It may well be that we need to posit, as Martyn suggests, "*something like* another age," in order to make theological sense of Paul's eschatology, but given the ambiguity (absence, even) of positive evidence for the notion of the "age to come" in Paul's writings, this should be approached with care. I will shortly turn to that task and offer what I hope is a theologically sensitive suggestion for how we might describe this "something like another

---

33. "New creation": 2 Cor 5:17; Gal 6:15. "Kingdom of God": Rom 14:17; 1 Cor 4:20; 6:9, 10; 15:24, 50; Gal 5:21; 1 Thess 2:12.

34. Martyn, *Galatians*, 98.

35. De Boer, *Paul, Theologian of God's Apocalypse*, 5–6. See also 207n34.

age" in Paul's thought. This will involve moving beyond the limitations of word study and will bring these discussions of Jewish apocalyptic literature and Pauline scholarship into dialogue with the theology of Karl Barth, particularly his account of time and eternity.[36] Barth has been chosen as the primary interlocutor due to his influence on the Apocalyptic Paul, discussed in the previous chapter. Along with his own writings, however, we will also engage with some recent secondary literature on his thought, bringing these voices into a three-cornered conversation with contemporary scholarship on the apocalypses and on Paul. Before that begins, however, we must briefly consider some interpretative proposals for the absence of the phrase "age to come" in Paul's letters.

One possibility, proposed by Keck and de Boer, is that Paul avoids the phrase because it is theologically obsolete.[37] In the light of the resurrection, Paul realizes that the "age to come" is now no longer "to come" but is present. At first this seems an elegant and compelling explanation, but careful investigation of the wider New Testament evidence reveals that it is by no means clear-cut that the "eschatological inauguration" of the Christ-event by itself has resulted in the theological obsolescence of the phrase "age to come." We find the phrase occurring in the context of the resurrection and the present "inaugurated" Christian experience in Eph 1:21 (οὐ μόνον ἐν τῷ αἰῶνι τούτῳ ἀλλὰ καὶ ἐν τῷ μέλλοντι, "not only in this age but also in the age to come"), and Heb 6:5 (μέλλοντος αἰῶνος, "age to come"), without any sense that it is obsolete. This casts some doubt, at least, on this apparently simple explanation.

There is another explanation we might consider. Given that, as we saw above, "eschatological inauguration" is not unique to Paul, his eschatology may well be essentially continuous with his Jewish apocalyptic contemporaries. Again, this is a position with much to commend it. In my view, however, despite the value of the emphasis on Paul's continuity with his Jewish tradition, we must still reckon with the radical discontinuities implied by Paul's theological claims about Jesus, and their implications for his eschatology. Though granting that the idea of "inauguration" is not something unique to Paul, this does not mean that that all claims to Pauline innovation are invalid or easily dismissed as apologetic defenses of "Paul's genius."[38]

---

36. Specifically, as found in *CD* I/2 §14 and *CD* II/1 §31.3.

37. See Keck, *Christ's First Theologian*, 93, 106; de Boer, *Paul, Theologian of God's Apocalypse*, 5–6, 9, 207.

38. David Congdon has challenged descriptions of Paul's inaugurated eschatology as

Despite the insights of these two interpretative options, there is, I think, a need to develop a more thorough theological account of Paul's avoidance of the language of the "age to come."

Before we move beyond the vestibule of lexical study, there is one more eschatological phrase which has not yet been discussed: ζωὴ αἰώνιος, imperfectly rendered "eternal life," which is found quite regularly in the Pauline corpus.[39] In using this phrase, Paul appears to be making use of the language of a future αἰών. The pattern of his usage, however, is noteworthy: Paul consistently uses it adjectivally, qualifying the noun ζωὴ, and not as a substantive. His use of the language of the "age" is consistent in designating a quality or mode of life as αἰώνιος. This consistent adjectival usage, I suggest, reflects Paul's theological concerns. As I hope to show below, it is not the temporal advance of a timeline that best describes Paul's distinctive eschatology, but an emphasis on the *qualitative* distinction between the two "ages." For this task, the language of the "present age" versus an "age to come" is insufficient, since it implies that what the Christ event has effected can be adequately described as an arrangement (or "inaugurated" re-arrangement) of linear time. For Paul, I suggest, the eschatological transformation effected by the resurrection of Jesus and the giving of the Spirit is insufficiently represented by such schemes; it is not merely "the presence of the future."[40] What his pattern of language suggests is that the "present age" has been embraced by "God's kind of time." To be sure, there is an important element of futurity here, but this is not merely a question of eschatological tension or extension. Paul's language appears rather to emphasize the infinite *qualitative* distinction between our kind of time and God's, and the radical realization of the fellowship between those "times" effected by the Christ-event.

---

an apologetic move. The combination of present and future eschatology into an "already but not yet" scheme is, he claims, one of several "simplistic dismissals of the problem posed by early apocalyptic eschatology" invented in the mid-twentieth century by conservative scholars, offering "an easy way out," which has since become "immensely attractive for obvious reasons" (*Rudolf Bultmann*, 10–11). Congdon cites Ladd and Wright for popularizing this position. Wright has responded (in "Hope Deferred?," 57), arguing that inaugurated eschatology is not an invented apologetic move, nor is it a second-generation phenomenon, but is there in the earliest Pauline writings, and an innovative part of his thought (64).

39. Rom 2:7, 5:21, 6:22–23; Gal 6:8; 1 Tim 1:16, 6:12; Titus 1:2, 3:7.

40. The title of G. E. Ladd's famous book on inaugurated eschatology, *The Presence of the Future: The Eschatology of Biblical Realism* (Eerdmans, 1974).

Paul's "Two Age" Eschatology in Apocalyptic and Interdisciplinary Perspective

At this point we are well-placed to bring this question of Paul and the "age to come" into an interdisciplinary conversation. We begin with one scholar who has recently investigated Paul's conception of time, Ann Jervis.[41] A driving conviction of her enquiry is that Pauline studies has reached something of an impasse regarding the question of salvation history and apocalyptic theology. I will take up this question in more detail below, but for now it is important to note that a better understanding of Paul's view of time is certainly needed if any progress is to be made, for different approaches to this idea are arguably at the heart of the current stalemate. Jervis puts the question in the form of an alternative: is Paul's view of time linear, progressing in stages (as salvation historical interpretations would largely assume)[42] or does he operate with a framework of "two ages," with the "present age" invaded by the "age to come" (as argued by the Apocalyptic Paul movement)? As we have already seen, the evidence of both the Jewish apocalyptic literature and the Pauline letters suggests that the situation is far more complex than a simple choice between these two options. For one thing, it is certainly not the case that a "two ages" eschatology constitutes the only apocalyptic option.[43] Pauline theology, like other contemporary apocalyptic frameworks, sometimes works with a periodization of history, and is even able to combine different temporal schemes in its apocalyptic eschatology.

In the face of the impasse created by these two options, Jervis takes the discussion in another direction. Rather than the more linear approaches to time (whether salvation history or the "two ages")[44] she suggests that "Paul thinks of the promise/s chiefly in the context not of the human linear

---

41. As noted above, Jervis's major work on this topic is forthcoming, but a good summary of her thought so far is found in "Promise and Purpose."

42. Jervis's exemplar here is N. T. Wright, and his description of the Christ-event as a "new chapter" in the great story (Jervis, "Promise and Purpose," 2).

43. As Jervis appears to imply when she says of this second view that it "adapted Jewish apocalyptic eschatology in the light of Christ" (Jervis, "Promise and Purpose," 2).

44. It is important to note, as Jervis also does, that the "two ages" is not simply a linear framework in the Apocalyptic Paul. Martinus de Boer, as we have seen, understands the "ages" both temporally and spatially. Nevertheless, a linear logic very often characterizes the use made of this framework (as seen above).

experience of time, but rather in the context of the life of God—God's time."⁴⁵ Her working hypothesis, which she investigates in relation to the question of the promise in Rom 9, is that "Paul conceived of time in a manner other than the linear progression that a promise-fulfilment format assumes."⁴⁶ To be sure, from the human point of view God's promises move from past to present in a linear fashion; but the proper theological location for the category of "promise," Jervis suggests, is not human temporality but the life of God.⁴⁷

Jervis's emphasis on the distinction between human time and the life/time of God is theologically sophisticated and has a lot of potential to offer a way through the impasse between salvation historical and apocalyptic readings of Paul. Her contrast of Paul's view of time with all linear schemes, and her emphasis on "God's time," is similar to the suggestion I made earlier, that Paul operates with an "infinite qualitative distinction" between God's time and ours. The phrase is, of course, something of an abstraction. It comes to us, via Kierkegaard, from Barth's famous prefaces to his commentary on Romans,⁴⁸ which make much of the qualitative distinction between time and eternity. Jervis, however, takes issue with Barth at this point: "unlike one of his most famous interpreters," she argues, citing Barth's Romans commentary, "Paul does not juxtapose eternity and time, that is, put them in opposition. In fact, while Paul refers to eternity in several places, as we shall see, he does so in a way that indicates he thought there was a relationship between eternity and the human experience of time—and so, I will suggest, that both are temporal modes."⁴⁹ Jervis's primary argument is that Paul's view of time does not involve a conception of time and eternity as being one of "temporality" versus "timelessness," modes of being fundamentally at odds with one another or juxtaposed in his thought. Rather, when Paul speaks of eternity he has in mind a *temporal* mode of existence, proper to God, "that embraces (while transcending) the human linear temporal mode."⁵⁰ At this point it is interesting to note, as Jervis herself does, that this emphasis on "God's time" has far more in common with Barth's

---

45. Jervis, "Promise and Purpose," 4.
46. Jervis, "Promise and Purpose," 8.
47. Jervis, "Promise and Purpose," 12.
48. Specifically, the second preface to his *Romans*, 10.
49. Jervis, "Promise and Purpose," 16.
50. Jervis, "Promise and Purpose," 23.

later thought than his earlier commentary on Romans. We will shortly turn to that later Barthian analysis in relation to Paul's apocalyptic eschatology.

Jervis's interpretation certainly offers a challenge to salvation-historical readings of Paul's eschatology (though again we must be wary of caricatures of such positions, as we saw in the previous chapter), and has much in common with the Apocalyptic Paul's emphasis on the "two ages," as she recognizes. However, there is valuable nuance in her contribution, not least in the way in which her argument challenges the view, often found in the Apocalyptic Paul, that "the relationship between the new creation and human history is oppositional—the new creation invades."[51] In Jervis's reading of Paul, the concept of "eternity" is understood very differently, with the result that there is a "porous" relationship between "God's time" and human history. In what follows, I want to offer some further thoughts on the way in which Barth's later discussions of God and time might contribute still further to this important nuancing of the issue.

First, however, I want to suggest that there is much to commend the idea of an "infinite qualitative distinction" between our time and God's time as an analytical tool for exploring Jewish apocalyptic thought. For example, it is a helpful analytical tool for the sort of thing we see in 2 En. 65, where we read the following account of creaturely time:

> And the LORD set everything forth for the sake of man, and he created the whole of creation for his sake. And he divided it into times: And from time he established years; and from the years he settled months; and from the months he settled days; and from the days he settled 7; and in those he settled the hours; and the hours he measured exactly, so that a person might think about time, and so that he might count the years and the months and the days and the hours and the perturbations and the beginnings and the endings, and that he might keep count of his own life from the beginning unto death, and think of his sins, and so that he might write his own achievement, both evil and good.[52]

Here we see God's creation and ordering of the "kind of time" assigned to creatures: time that can be counted and measured, time which comes with "beginnings and endings" as a reminder to humanity of their mortal and moral limitations. When all of this "countable time" has come to its end,

---

51. Jervis, "Promise and Purpose," 26.
52. 2 En 65.3–4 (trans. Charlesworth).

there will be a final judgment and the ushering in of the eternal "great age," which the passage goes on to describe:

> And then all time will perish, and afterward there will be neither years nor months nor days nor hours. They will be dissipated, and after that they will not be reckoned. But they will constitute a single age. And all the righteous, who escape from the LORD's great judgment, will be collected together into the great age. And the great age will come about for the righteous, and it will be eternal.[53]

In Enoch's vision of the final judgment, all creaturely and countable time is dissolved into a singularity with "neither years nor months nor days nor hours." This "great age" is time in infinite qualitative distinction to creaturely time, for it is the kind of "eternal" time proper to God and offered in eschatological reward to the righteous. The qualitative difference between this kind of time and all the measured times of human history is such that the latter are effectively considered as one age, gathered together and contrasted with the "great age." We observe, moreover, that 2 En. 65 combines the eschatological periodization of the counted "times" of history with an eschatological dualism of two ages, reminding us again of the layered complexities of apocalyptic eschatology. What is of particular interest here, however, is the distinction being made between the kind of time proper to creatures and the kind of time/life proper to God. For this, the notion of an infinite qualitative distinction can be a helpful theological tool, not only for analysis of Paul's thought but for that of apocalyptic eschatology more broadly.

Much depends on how the notion of "eternity" is filled out. I want to suggest that if we are to use the notion of an infinite qualitative distinction in a Christian theological analysis of Paul's apocalyptic eschatology, it is important that this idea is framed in "thoroughly trinitarian terms."[54] The limitations of geometric abstractions were noted in the previous chapter in relation to Robert Jenson's critiques of the Apocalyptic Paul. Instead of relying too heavily on such abstractions (whether that is the geometrical

---

53. 2 En 65:7–8 (trans. Charlesworth).

54. George Hunsinger, "*Mysterium Trinitatis*: Karl Barth's Conception of Eternity," 189. I fully accept that at this point some readers may wish to reject the premise of reading Paul theologically and "Christianly," and that is fine. Hopefully this discussion will offer sufficient stimulus for nuanced and constructive discussion on Paul's apocalyptic thought, even if some colleagues do not share my convictions or conclusions. One area in which that discussion might develop is in giving an account of the role of the Christ-event in Paul's apocalyptic thought, an event that is (as I hope to show) fundamental to his logic and his particularly deployment/development of his Jewish apocalyptic heritage.

metaphors of vertical and horizontal, mathematical points, or the abstraction of an infinite qualitative distinction), we should work with the logic of the Christ-event itself. Philippians 2 notwithstanding, Paul's letters do not place a strong emphasis on the doctrine of the incarnation, focusing instead on the cross, the resurrection, and the giving of the Spirit. However, its logic is vital for an appreciation of his distinctive eschatology.[55]

Here we turn to Barth, but not to his more polemical methodological work in the Romans commentary, rather to the more mature reflection of the *Church Dogmatics*, and in particular volume II/1, where the importance of Christology for his theology of time is explored in depth. By some accounts, Barth's trinitarian reformulation of the question of time and eternity represents a remarkably unprecedented contribution in Christian theology.[56] Barth's persistent christological approach is clear here: in attempting to understand the question of God and time, we must begin not with geometry but Christology. As he had previously put it in his first volume, "there can be nothing but abstraction here unless we are really ready, in an honest investigation of truth, to start where the New Testament itself starts."[57] For Barth, we should not begin with an abstract construal of eternity as non-temporality since that is, at best, a peripheral notion in the Scriptures.[58] Though he was himself certainly not allergic to geometric metaphors in discussing the question of time and eternity, he was also wary of how these abstractions can limit our ability to express the kind of time proper to God since they fail to capture the triune God's possession of *life*.[59] Again, we note that there are significant points of connection here between Barth's and Jervis's readings of Paul, discussed above.

What is needed, then, is an approach to Paul's apocalyptic eschatology that does not deal in abstractions but reckons with the "mode of time unique to the Trinity."[60] For Paul, the revelation of Jesus Christ meant that our time and God's time have met. Though the qualitative difference between these "kinds of time" is infinite, in Christ they are joined, and are now (as Barth puts it) "not in metaphysical antithesis but indissoluble

---

55. See Eastman, "Apocalypse and Incarnation," 165.
56. Hunsinger, "Mysterium Trinitatis," 189–90.
57. Barth, CD I/2, 57–58.
58. Barth, CD II/1 610.
59. Barth, CD II/1 611. On 639–40, Barth recognizes the limitations of "the point or the line, the surface or the space" and indeed of all geometric and abstract talk of eternity that does not speak of this living God and leads, however involuntarily, to secularization.
60. Hunsinger, "Mysterium Trinitatis," 199.

relation."[61] The nature of this relation is the proper concern not of spatio-temporal metaphysics but of Christology, and it is here that the question of Paul's apocalyptic theology, and in particular his use of the "two ages" motif, should be located.

There are at least three implications of this, which can be explored fruitfully in continued dialogue with Barth's analysis.[62] First, in Paul's understanding of God's action in Christ, the divine life had genuinely touched time, and assumed it without obliterating it. To say that God became human is therefore to say that in Jesus Christ the creator of time becomes temporal: "'The Word became flesh' also means 'the Word became time.'"[63] Christ has a past and a future, and as such the chronology of past and future still matter to Paul. It is thus still appropriate, and not only as the creaturely mode of existence, to speak in linear chronological terms, and *in this sense* even of *Heilsgeschichte*.[64] Though Paul seems to have considered the phrase "age to come" inadequate to that theological task, he did not reject all linear chronological logic in favor of a punctiliar invasive moment or a mathematical point. Barth considered this truth to be of supreme importance, that, in Christ, God has temporality. Without it, the Christian message dissolves into "the comfortless content of some human monologue" and "inarticulate mumbling."[65] In Paul's apocalyptic eschatology, unlike that of 2 En. 65, countable human time is not merely a created and soon-to-be-dissolved concession to the creature so that we may know our finitude but is a mode of existence that has been taken up by God himself in the Christ-event. This, I suggest, is the christological heart of Paul's distinctive reworking of apocalyptic eschatology. There remains a sense in which the militaristic language of "invasion," regularly deployed by the Apocalyptic Paul, remains useful, especially when it is used in respect of the effect of the Christ-event in relation to the anti-God powers of this age.[66] In respect of a theology of time as a whole, however, it is more appropriate to speak of

---

61. Barth, *Theology of John Calvin*, 73.

62. Especially as found in Barth, *CD* II/1, §31.

63. Barth, *CD* I/2, 50; see also *CD* II/1, 616–17.

64. The two possible senses of "salvation history" are explored by Jenson, "Dogmatic," 161.

65. Barth, *CD* II/1, 620.

66. On which see the work of Lisa Bowens, esp. *An Apostle in Battle*.

the "real fellowship" between God's life and human history.[67] This is not so much *invasion* as *embrace*.[68]

The second implication of framing Paul's apocalyptic eschatology in explicitly christological terms is in relation to the way his encounter with Christ relates to his understanding of history. The Damascus Road revelation of Jesus to Paul (or rather "in" him, as he says in Gal 1:16) was not a straightforward developmental stage or event Paul then indexed to an unchanged and generally accepted philosophy of history. But neither was it a fresh start *ex nihilo*. Prior to his encounter with the risen Christ, Paul already understood the Scriptures of Israel as a witness to (and, as we will see below, an expectation of) God's self-revelation. It was not that he began with a secular account of "mere" human history, which only took theological shape after Damascus Road. His account of history, therefore, was already a distinctly *theological* one.

Of course, as he looked back on this theological account of history from the perspective of the Christ-event, a profound and retrospective transformation took place. Paul saw with new eyes the nature of that which the Old Testament expected, and his understanding of time and history could not remain the same. The Christ-event revealed that the one God of Israel, to whom the Scriptures bore witness, had in Jesus decisively entered human history, creating fellowship between our time and his.[69] This revelation did not leave time unchanged, but time itself was transformed by the embrace of God's life in Christ. The familiar eschatological language of "two ages" approximated such a transformation in Paul's understanding of history but remained ultimately insufficient. Time was not the constant into which Paul now had to fit the revelation of Jesus; it was the other way around. In Paul's apocalyptically transformed understanding of time and history, the self-revelation of God in Jesus was now the constant, and Paul's view of time had to change to fit this newly revealed reality.[70]

The third and final implication of this approach concerns the question of "eschatological dualism." Although the evidence shows that Paul does not unambiguously deploy a "two ages" framework, there remains a sense in which it is still appropriate to use such familiar apocalyptic language. We

---

67. Barth, *CD* II/1, 616.

68. See, e.g., Barth, *CD* II/1 623: time's extension is "in eternity like a child is in the arms of its mother."

69. "God's time for us" (*Gottes Zeit für uns*) as Barth puts it.

70. See Barth *CD* I/2, 57 and *CD* II/1, 617.

can still speak, I think, of the Pauline "now" and the "not yet," provided we do so in a highly qualified sense. In speaking in this way, we are not simply indicating a temporal *tension* created by an advanced horizontal timeline. To be sure, this "horizontal" description expresses part of the truth, but only in respect of the creaturely mode of experience. Yet, even there, Paul indicates that there has been substantial transformation through union with Christ, in whom human time has been joined to the divine life. This christological insight is, I suggest, what drives Paul's preference to use his alternatives to the phrase "age to come," such as "eternal life" or "new creation." It is not a coincidence that we regularly find such phrases on Paul's lips in contexts where he is speaking about union with Christ.[71] As such, when speaking of the "now and not yet" in Paul's eschatology, what is being indicated is the presence of God's kind of time to ours, and the union of our life with his in Christ. Again, without completely suppressing the militant nature of God's act in Christ, we must also affirm that this may also be characterized as peaceful coexistence.[72]

For Barth, the God who possesses all ages has marked out their ends and beginnings in history, without being limited by them.[73] Linear-temporal words such as "ends" and "beginnings" make sense only within a creaturely mode of existence, and the language of the "two ages" is appropriate to the extent that this is the eschatological frame of reference. In Paul's christologically transformed apocalyptic eschatology, however, it is no longer possible to speak straightforwardly of an "age to come," since he interprets the Christ-event as not merely the advance foretaste of another piece of such marked-out linear time, but the gift of God's kind of time to ours.

5.2 Wisdom and Revelation in 1 Corinthians 2

We now turn, as all apocalyptic readings of Paul must, from eschatology to epistemology. In the last chapter I suggested that there was a need for a christologically-modified account of "revealed wisdom" for making sense of the epistemology of Paul's apocalyptic thought. This can usefully be developed in relation to 1 Cor 2, a text where we find an unusually dense cluster of epistemological terminology. According to Brown, this passage

---

71. E.g., "new creation" in 2 Cor 5:17 and Rom 6:4, "eternal life" in Rom 5:21; 6:22–23; and 1 Tim 1:16.

72. Barth, *CD* II/1, 612.

73. Barth, *CD* II/1, 610.

displays "by far the greatest concentration of such language anywhere in the Pauline corpus."⁷⁴ Most relevantly for the present discussion, the epistemological language of wisdom, revelation, and "mystery" is placed in an apocalyptic eschatological framework, indicated by Paul's frequent use of the expression "this age." The phrase is introduced in 1:20, and then repeated in verse 6 (twice), verse 7 (in the plural), and verse 8. In 3:18 and 8:13, it again appears in relation to epistemology, culminating in Paul's comments on the "ends of the ages" in 10:11, which we have just discussed.

Despite all this, 1 Cor 2 is, as noted above, a passage where the "age to come" is conspicuous by its absence. What results is a particularly intriguing asymmetrical apocalyptic contrast, with the "wisdom of this age" (σοφία τοῦ αἰῶνος τούτου, v. 6) placed in antithesis not with its more natural opposite, the "wisdom of the age to come," but with "God's wisdom" (θεοῦ σοφία, v. 7). This is just one of the many intriguing apocalyptic contrasts in the passage, and by no means represents the totality of what should be discussed under the heading of epistemology,⁷⁵ but it is perhaps helpful to isolate this juxtaposition, and to use it to ask about the relationship between wisdom and revelation in Paul's apocalyptic thought.

Revealed Wisdom in Jewish Apocalyptic Thought

We begin, as before, by placing this passage in the context of Paul's Jewish apocalyptic contemporaries, and by doing so in the light of the advances in our understanding of that tradition made in recent years. In chapter 4, we noted that one of the areas of development in recent scholarship on the Jewish apocalyptic literature is an increased (and increasingly nuanced) emphasis on other themes besides eschatology. The notion of "revealed wisdom," and the resulting challenge to previously assumed boundaries between the sapiential and apocalyptic traditions, is one such theme.

This is by no means a new area of discussion, of course. The debate about the relationship between "wisdom" and "apocalyptic" has run for

74. See Brown, *Cross*, 107.

75. In particular, there is a close connection between the noetic/epistemic aspects of epistemology and the moral/ethical ones. First Corinthians is a great example of their intrinsic combination, since it is a letter that deals heavily in ethics and morality, expositions of which are rooted in Paul's particular approach to wisdom and revelation. Revealed wisdom involves both epistemic and moral goods. I am grateful to Grant Macaskill for alerting me to this, and to the tendency in discussing epistemology to disconnect them. Alexandra Brown, with whom I will shortly interact, has given sustained attention to the ethical aspects of Paul's epistemology.

decades (at least going back to the work of Gerhard von Rad in the 1970s) and has been particularly focused on form-critical and genre questions such as social contexts, genetic literary relationships, and generic compatibility. It is nothing novel, therefore, to insist that the idea of a "pure" distinction between the two genres/traditions is modern artifice, resulting from an unhelpful reification of scholarly abstractions.[76] Though one does still encounter it as an assumption in scholarly discourse, it is now firmly established in the field of Second Temple Judaism that the two genres (and the traditions they reflect) intersect.[77] Put another way, any given text can be seen to participate in multiple genres, conceived as textual "constellations" rather than bounded sets, and such textual participation in both wisdom and apocalyptic is commonly found.[78] For example, though there are some important epistemological differences, 1 En. 42 sounds very much like the opening chapters of Proverbs in its invocation of the figure of Lady Wisdom:

> Wisdom could not find a place in which she could dwell;
> but a place was found (for her) in the heavens.
> Then Wisdom went out to dwell with the children of the people,
> but she found no dwelling place.
> (So) Wisdom returned to her place
> and she settled permanently among the angels.
> Then Iniquity went out of her rooms,
> and found whom she did not expect.
> And she dwelt with them,
> like rain in a desert,
> like dew on a thirsty land.[79]

---

76. This is one of the conclusions of Collins, "Wisdom, Apocalypticism, and Generic Compatibility," 385–404, which is a useful introduction to the contours of the genre discussion.

77. For evidence of this, one need only note the existence of the well-established SBL Group on *Wisdom and Apocalypticism*, which has challenged artificial boundaries and has brought together these once-separated sub-fields to interrogate the nature of this relationship. An excellent collection of the group's work from 1994–2002 can be found in Wright and Wills, *Conflicted Boundaries in Wisdom and Apocalypticism*, and the state of the discussion is helpfully discussed in the editors' introduction and opening essay by George Nickelsburg ("Wisdom and Apocalypticism in Early Judaism: Some Points for Discussion," 17–37).

78. For a discussion of this phenomenon in relation to "wisdom literature" see Will Kynes, *Obituary for "Wisdom Literature,"* ch 4. In relation to the apocalyptic literature, see Najman, *Losing the Temple and Recovering the Future*, esp. 21–23.

79. Trans. Charlesworth.

There have been some significant contributions in this area in the last few years. A recent volume edited by Loren Stuckenbruck and Benjamin Reynolds has further highlighted the importance of epistemology in apocalyptic literature and has brought this discussion into more extensive conversation with the New Testament, including, significantly for the present discussion, several essays on the Pauline epistles.[80] A driving conviction of the volume is that the disclosure of mysteries is a theme no less important to apocalyptic thought than eschatology, and the current imbalanced emphasis on temporal matters in earlier scholarship on apocalyptic thought (upon which much contemporary New Testament scholarship depends) needs to be corrected.[81] One crucial aspect of this correction is careful attention to the way in which the epistemological themes of wisdom and revealed wisdom are developed in the apocalyptic tradition, and how this is picked up in the New Testament.[82] To this end, the volume gathers eighteen essays by specialists in apocalypticism on almost every book of the New Testament, with each contributor addressing "the question of whether a revelatory understanding of the Jewish apocalyptic tradition sheds any light on understanding the shaping of New Testament thought."[83]

The essay on the Corinthian letters is provided by Matthew Goff, who has given sustained attention over the last decade to the epistemology of Second Temple Jewish writings. His discussion, which focuses on the question of revealed wisdom, is very helpful for placing the discussion of Paul's apocalyptic epistemology in the context of contemporary Jewish apocalypticism. Goff begins by lamenting a tendency in Pauline scholarship, noted at various points in the present discussion, to emphasize the differences between Paul and Jewish apocalypticism rather than what they have in common, and at times to portray that tradition as beset by "false dichotomies that Paul transcends."[84] By contrast, Goff places his focus on reading the Corinthian correspondence not as evidence of Paul's radical departure from the Jewish apocalyptic tradition but his continuity with it. One of the most significant indications of this continuity is, for Goff, Paul's

---

80. Stuckenbruck and Reynolds, *Jewish Apocalyptic Tradition and the Shaping of New Testament Thought*.

81. See the introduction to that volume, 6–7.

82. Another is the question of "revealed cosmology" (Stuckenbruck and Reynolds, *Jewish Apocalyptic Tradition*, 8).

83. Stuckenbruck and Reynolds, *Jewish Apocalyptic Tradition*, 9.

84. Goff, "Mystery of God's Wisdom," 176.

deployment of the epistemological themes of revelation and wisdom in the opening chapters of his first epistle to Corinth. Another is the frequent references to "mystery" in these early chapters (as well as the *inclusio* formed by 2:1 and 15:51), which are suggestive of "the theological horizon against which the rest of the letter should be understood."[85] This horizon is, Goff argues, best described in relation to contemporary Jewish apocalypticism.

Goff's argument is not only that Paul speaks of revealed mysteries in ways that are similar to the Jewish apocalypses, but that his apocalyptic epistemology places such revelation in combination, not antithesis, with wisdom. This, he argues, has considerable continuity with the interweaving of the apocalyptic and sapiential traditions found in Second Temple Judaism, and he demonstrates this with a particular focus on a text to which he has given considerable attention, *4QInstruction*.[86] Here, revealed wisdom comes especially in the form of a "mystery that is to be" (רז נהיה), a motif that participates in both the apocalyptic and sapiential traditions while also connecting epistemology to eschatology. In the pedagogical ethos of the text, this revelation leads to an appeal to reflection, which in turn leads to understanding. The epistemology and pedagogical ethos of *4QInstruction*, Goff has argued, reflect a complex participation in both wisdom and apocalyptic traditions: "While many of 4QInstruction's teachings are devoted to the worldly and practical success of its addressee in a manner reminiscent of Proverbs, the epistemology of the composition reflects an apocalyptic worldview."[87] The result is "a form of education that combines elements from the sapiential and apocalyptic traditions."[88] In Goff's view, this merging of revelation and reflection finds a parallel in Paul's epistemology in 1 Corinthians, which also draws upon and combines both the apocalyptic and sapiential traditions.[89]

1 Corinthians 2 in the Apocalyptic Paul

The insights of the last few decades of work on this topic in Second Temple Judaism scholarship are particularly relevant to the discussion of

---

85. Goff, "Mystery of God's Wisdom," 179.

86. See, Goff, *Worldly and Heavenly Wisdom of 4QInstruction*; Goff, "Wisdom, Apocalypticism, and the Pedagogical Ethos of 4QInstruction," 57–67.

87. Goff, "Pedagogical Ethos," 64.

88. Goff, "Pedagogical Ethos," 66.

89. Goff, "Mystery of God's Wisdom," 180.

epistemology in Paul's apocalyptic thought, especially when it comes to the question of how the apostle understands the relationship between revelation and wisdom. Because of its emphasis on revelation, reflecting a Barthian antipathy to natural theology, we might expect the Apocalyptic Paul to develop a starkly dualistic challenge to the category of wisdom, perhaps offering "revelation" as the antithesis to "natural" human knowing, and indeed that is sometimes what one hears between the lines of the movement's critiques. The reality, however, is more complex than that.

Perhaps the most useful interlocutor here is Alexandra Brown, who makes a similar observation about the complex interaction of apocalyptic and sapiential traditions in Paul's theology. In chapter 2 we traced the contours of Brown's argument on this matter, and so we need not repeat that summary here. However, some additional comments on her handling of 1 Cor 2 will be useful, for it is here that Paul makes perhaps his most intriguing epistemological arguments, arguments that Brown explores in relation to Paul's Jewish apocalyptic and sapiential contemporaries. As we saw earlier, for Brown there is no simple dichotomy in Paul's thinking, but an integration of both the wisdom and apocalyptic traditions. This is no truer than in the opening section of Paul's first letter to Corinth, which "reflects his knowledge of Hellenistic Jewish wisdom traditions popular in his day no less than it reflects his apocalyptic heritage. These two streams of tradition, wisdom and apocalyptic, are at some points in concert and at others in conflict, a fact Paul exploits for the articulation of his own apocalyptic wisdom of the cross."[90] In all this Paul is largely in continuity with the Jewish apocalyptic tradition.

In what way, then, is Paul's distinctive articulation of revealed wisdom to be described? Given its opening paraenetic tenor, it is fruitful to compare Paul's epistemology with the position he seeks to correct in Corinth. In Brown's view, Paul's epistemology clearly joins wisdom and revelation, a basic position with which his Corinthian audience would agree. The source of their differences, she suggests, lies in the way in which this epistemological combination functions, a difference that turns upon their respective understandings of Christology.

Despite this emphasis on the joining of wisdom and revelation, contrastive dualities are by no means absent from the opening chapters of the letter. Here, Brown's analysis shows its indebtedness to Martyn (particularly his description of "apocalyptic antinomies") in tracing a series of

---

90. Brown, *Cross*, 30.

"antithetical patterns" in the opening two chapters of 1 Corinthians.[91] Paul's description of the gospel, his paraenetic appeal, and his autobiographical statements in 1:18—2:4 all seem to set up an epistemological contrast between "wisdom" and the "foolishness" of the cross. However, in the opening verse of this autobiographical passage, Brown observes an "unexpected and destabilizing opposition" in Paul's contrast between "folly" and "power."[92] In this asymmetrical juxtaposition, an important epistemological and soteriological point is made: the opposite of folly is not wisdom, as the Corinthians likely supposed, but *power*. This contrast is repeated in 2:5, where "wisdom" is more explicitly named as "human wisdom," and "power" the "power of God." This is the apocalyptic dichotomy Paul deploys in his challenge to the Corinthian position.[93]

However, as the next paragraph begins, Paul appears to contradict himself: "yet among the mature we do speak wisdom . . ." The immediate qualification to this statement explains why this is not contradictory and does so in clearly apocalyptic terms: the "wisdom" which Paul speaks is "not a wisdom of this age or of the rulers of this age, who are doomed to perish." Here, Paul's epistemology intersects with his apocalyptic eschatology, as he speaks twice of "this age" (though not the "age to come," as we have seen). The apocalyptic epistemological contrast, then, is not between "wisdom" and "folly," or between "wisdom" and "revelation" (understood in a straightforward manner), but between two kinds of wisdom with eschatological coordinates. The first is a "human wisdom," characteristic of "this age" and its rulers. Its opposite, as we have seen, is the "power of God," which, as 2:7 goes on to explain, is "God's wisdom, secret and hidden (ἐν μυστηρίῳ τὴν ἀποκεκρυμμένην, literally "hidden in mystery"), which God decreed before the ages for our glory." Thus, the human wisdom of the present age (wisdom "according to the flesh," 1:26, cf. 2 Cor 5:16) is contrasted with the category of "revealed wisdom," lined up with the power of God, a power hidden in mystery before the ages and now revealed in the message of the cross.

In the first part of this chapter our focus was on the eschatological contrast in Paul's apocalyptic theology between the present age and the

---

91. There are various "pairs of opposites" explored in Brown's arguments. For summaries see Brown, *Cross*, 76, 101.

92. Brown, *Cross*, 75.

93. For an analysis of the relationship between divine power and Paul's apocalyptic epistemology in the second letter to Corinth, see Bowens, *Apostle in Battle*, discussed earlier.

kind of time proper to God. Here our attention is on the concomitant epistemology, which is a fundamental contrast between "human wisdom" and "apocalyptic wisdom."[94] The remainder of 1 Cor 2 expounds this "apocalyptic wisdom" in relation to the Spirit, who is the agent of revelation, concluding in verse 16 with the tantalizing declaration that although none may know the mind of God, this revelation has been given to those who have "the mind of Christ." This "enigmatic" but profound christological statement is, for Brown, the "capstone of Paul's argument" and "a definitive statement of his apocalyptic epistemology."[95]

Despite its clear importance for understanding Paul's christologically transformed apocalyptic epistemology, it is a statement that has received relatively little attention in commentary, which Brown notes with regret.[96] She offers her own attention to the significance of the phrase with respect to anthropology (the transformed noetic disposition of the person in Christ) and ethics (the creation of new social relationships in Christ, a theme Brown's closing chapter develops in detail). More can be said, however, about the way in which Paul's apocalyptic epistemology is shaped by his Christology, and how attention to the christological pattern of human knowing might help us articulate what it is that is distinctive about Paul's thought in relation to his Jewish apocalyptic context. To that end, in what follows I will attempt to bring Brown's reading of 1 Cor 2 into a three-way conversation with Goff's work on revelation and wisdom in Second Temple Judaism, and with contemporary discussion of these same themes in Barth's theology.

1 Corinthians 2 in Apocalyptic and Interdisciplinary Perspective

As we have seen, Paul, like his Jewish apocalyptic contemporaries, rejects a simple dichotomy between wisdom and apocalypse but rather integrates them in his epistemology. What matters to Paul is wisdom decreed "before the ages," hidden but now revealed. We begin by noting again Goff's argument about Paul's continuity with the Jewish apocalyptic tradition. The point is well taken, and on the face of it, he and Brown appear to be in broad agreement on this basic idea. There is, of course, a clear difference in

---

94. Brown, *Cross*, 103.
95. Brown, *Cross*, 139; 108.
96. Brown, *Cross*, 140.

emphasis: while Goff underlines Paul's continuity with the Jewish apocalyptic tradition, Brown clearly places emphasis on his discontinuity.

> Both Paul and his hearers are indebted to Jewish and Greek traditions . . . But Paul's experience has made him acutely sensitive to the interpretation of those traditions, especially when he thinks a particular interpretation compromises the gospel . . . the apocalyptic theology of his Jewish heritage is still usable for Paul, although it is now reassessed in the light of what to him is the decisive apocalyptic event—the life, death, and resurrection of Jesus Christ.[97]

Goff has objected to the characterization of the Jewish apocalyptic tradition as Paul's "heritage,"[98] on the grounds that this implies a reduction of that tradition to lifeless "background" rather than a living tradition in which he participated. Again, the question is whether Brown is using the term in quite that way. My sense is that she, and others in the Apocalyptic Paul movement, would agree with Goff that there was no static Jewish apocalyptic tradition *against* which Paul can be read, but in speaking of his "heritage," the intention is to describe him *within* that living and vibrant tradition. Much, then, depends on careful definitions and (as ever) a good scholarly conversation about how such terms shape the question of continuity and discontinuity in the Apocalyptic Paul.[99] I wonder, then, if much of the perceived difference here is more a matter of rhetorical emphasis and/or over-correction in which of these two poles are emphasized, rather than a genuine disagreement. For my part, I agree that it is important to understand the continuity of Paul's thought with his Jewish apocalyptic contemporaries, but I do not think it necessary to set up as alternatives, as Goff seems to do, Paul's "radical transformation of Jewish apocalypticism" and his "considerable continuity with it."[100] Rather, Paul's radical transformation can be understood as occurring squarely *within* that living apocalyptic tradition, which is, after all, by no means a stable and homogenous one. The idea of revelation that radically transforms one's understanding of the nature of reality is, after all, at the heart of apocalypticism.

---

97. Brown, *Cross*, 31.

98. Goff, "Mystery of God's Wisdom," 186, though he does not cite Brown specifically.

99. At the time of writing, preparations are underway for just such a conversation, hosted by the *Enoch Seminar*, with the title "Was Paul an Apocalyptic Jew? A Case in Jewish Diversity in the Second Temple Period."

100. Goff, "Mystery of God's Wisdom," 192.

The crucial task, rather, is to enquire about the precise nature of this apocalyptic transformation in Paul's thought. While charting his continuity with the vibrant Jewish apocalyptic tradition within which he seems to think, we must also attend carefully to the ways in which his thinking is discontinuous. Without such precision, the continuity/discontinuity debate is in danger of becoming something of a distraction which diverts attention from the actual shape and content of Paul's apocalyptic thought.

In this connection we turn to Grant Macaskill, another scholar who has explored the question of "revealed wisdom" in *4QInstruction* and the New Testament,[101] and who has also made some considerable contributions to the discussion about the Apocalyptic Paul. In a recent study, Macaskill turned his attention to the theme of intellectual humility in the New Testament, and during his analysis he describes Paul's apocalyptic theology in the following epistemological terms:

> the apocalyptic character of Paul's theology, if acknowledged to be consistent with the wider New Testament, represents the human capacity to obtain knowledge and understanding as fundamentally or essentially limited. The requirement for revelation to take place *apart from* the routinely available knowledge that may be obtained by reflection on the created world demands an account of the human intellect and its scientific potential that recognizes its limitations, and recognizes further that these limitations can never be overcome by development or growth, but only by the revelatory agency of something outwith ourselves.[102]

Thus there is a great deal of continuity between Pauline epistemology and the understanding of human knowledge found in the Jewish apocalyptic tradition, with its recognition of human epistemic limitation and an insistence on external revelation. Once we attend to the precise nature of that revelation in Paul, however, we begin to see how his thought becomes distinct within the apocalyptic tradition. To put it bluntly, for Paul, "revealed wisdom" is thoroughly christological in both form and content. As a result, any articulation of Paul's apocalyptic epistemology, and his particular construal of the relationship between wisdom and revelation, will have to be informed by his Christology. This christological re-framing of apocalyptic

---

101. See Macaskill, "Wisdom and Apocalyptic in the Gospel of Matthew"; Macaskill, *Revealed Wisdom and Inaugurated Eschatology in Ancient Judaism and Early Christianity*.

102. Macaskill, *Humility*, 132. Chapter 4 of Macaskill's book, upon which this discussion draws, explores several aspects of the New Testament's apocalyptic epistemology, including some important discussion of Paul.

epistemology affects both the *object* and *subject* of knowledge, both of which have been transformed by the Christ-event.[103]

The first of these insights, that the *object* of knowledge has been transformed, remains relatively common ground with the Jewish apocalyptic tradition, though its christological effects are important. After his experience of the apocalypse of Jesus Christ, Paul retrospectively re-reads his life and the Scriptures, including the wisdom tradition, in a new christological light. This is to be expected if one takes seriously a commitment to revealed wisdom. Hitherto hidden mysteries are revealed, and for Paul this hidden mystery, God's revealed wisdom, and thus the content of his message, is Christ himself. Paul pushes this even further, however, in a direction that must not be overlooked: Christ is not merely the content of the message, or one more item on a "list of revealed things," but *is himself* God's revelation: Christ is, for Paul, "the power of God and the wisdom of God" (1:24; cf. 1:30). In this way the object of knowledge is Christ, the wisdom of God made flesh.

Second, Paul's understanding of the knowing *subject* has been disrupted by the Christ event. It is not simply that new knowledge has been revealed, but that the knowers themselves have been transformed through union with Christ, for without this transformation none can know the mind of God. For Paul, the new-creation reality brought about by the Christ-event meant that his own "identity," including his identity as a knowing subject, had been disrupted and was now understood christologically. His statement that "it is no longer I who live, but it is Christ who lives in me" (Gal 2:20) applied as much to the noetic aspects of his life as any other.[104] For Paul, the Christ-event has effected a redefinition of the knowing self-in-relation, the renewal of the "spiritual mind" in Christ, the human self now understood extrinsically. This extrinsic redefinition of the knowing subject is what Paul expresses in the closing words of 1 Cor 2: believers are those who are not merely the autonomous recipients of revelation, but those who have received Christ himself, have been united to him, and who therefore now have the "mind of Christ." It is only in union with Christ that the human mind may know the mind of God, for it is in him that the two are joined. Thus, for Paul, the logic of Christology determines the logic of human knowing, including the nature of the knower. "Hence," Macaskill

---

103. On which see Macaskill, *Humility*, 107–8.

104. Including the moral life, on which see Macaskill, *Living in Union with Christ*; and Eastman, *Paul and the Person*.

says, "we are dealing with a complex revelatory event that demands reflection on the activity of God—the distinctive operations of Father, Son and Spirit—in the redemptive work of revelation."[105] Or, as he later puts it, "God's wisdom operates within the economy of his relations with the world."[106]

Macaskill goes on to devote a whole chapter to the importance of the incarnation for Pauline epistemology, with particular reference to intellectual humility in Phil 2, where we find the clearest development of the logic of the incarnation for the question of the epistemic and ethical life.[107] However, in 1 Corinthians (and arguably elsewhere in Paul's writings) the primary christological category is not the incarnation but Jesus's death and resurrection. We have already explored the importance of the cross for human epistemic transformation through the work of Alexandra Brown, who has examined this in dialogue with Luther, for whom the opening chapters of 1 Corinthians were deeply formative. In Brown's fresh epistemological and ethical hearing of Luther's *theologia crucis*, knowledge of God comes only through the cross, which affects not only what is known but how one knows. This is the essence of what Brown calls Luther's "cross-based epistemology," the revelation of God's love at the cross that effects "a new existence, not just a new perception."[108] Paul's apocalyptic epistemology thus involves not only the revelation and reflection of a new reality, but its creation.[109] Moreover, as we have seen in the work of Lisa Bowens on 2 Corinthians, this epistemological new creation is something understood in cosmic and martial terms. Paul's apocalyptic epistemology is closely linked to his cosmology. The human mind is an arena of spiritual warfare: knowledge of God is contested by satanic forces, strongholds are set up against that knowledge, but are destroyed, not by warfare waged κατὰ σάρκα but by divine power that takes thoughts captive for Christ.[110]

There is much to commend in Macaskill's christological framing of Pauline apocalyptic epistemology, in Brown's and Bowens's readings, which, as we have seen, develop in various ways the important epistemological insights of J. Louis Martyn's work on the cross and human knowing

---

105. Macaskill, *Humility*, 107.
106. Macaskill, *Humility*, 167.
107. See Macaskill, *Humility*, chapter 5, esp. 146–63.
108. Brown, *Cross*, 152.
109. Brown, *Cross*, 159.
110. 2 Cor 10:1–6. See again Bowens, *Apostle in Battle*.

in 2 Cor 5:16.¹¹¹ In particular, both Macaskill and Brown share a commitment to "revealed wisdom" as the hallmark of an apocalyptic epistemology, articulating Paul's continuity with the Jewish apocalyptic tradition in that regard, while developing a distinctly christological approach to how that looks in Paul. I want to suggest, however, that the epistemological ground of Paul's message in 1 Corinthians is neither the incarnation nor the cross, but the resurrection. Although the crucifixion of Jesus features heavily in the letter's opening chapters, its climax is the prolonged exposition of the resurrection in chapter 15. Of course, the two should not be separated since the resurrection is the resurrection of the crucified one. Nevertheless, in what remains of this section, I will try to account for the significance of the resurrection of Jesus for Paul's distinctive apocalyptic epistemology, again in dialogue with Barth, and especially some recent discussions about his understanding of revelation and wisdom.

At this point, the reader may be skeptical. By many accounts, Barth is the ideal interlocutor if one wants to emphasize revelation but is far from the best choice when it comes to wisdom and human epistemic agency. As Martin Westerholm puts it, "[c]ritical treatments of Barth's work generally suppose that an account that so stresses revelation as the principle of theological inquiry cannot leave space for an adequate description or deployment of human reasoning."¹¹² Westerholm's study of Barth's theological rationality, however, suggests that such negative assessments of Barth are unwarranted, even in respect of his earlier writings. There is a growing consensus in Barth scholarship that his emphasis on divine sovereignty need not be read as antithetical to the significance of human agency, and Westerholm develops this insight in particular relation to human epistemic agency.

Though Westerholm focusses on Barth's early work,¹¹³ some comments from the first volume of the *Church Dogmatics* are a helpful starting point, for here Barth offers a sustained account of its relationship to

---

111. Once again, see also Martyn, "Epistemology at the Turn of The Ages."

112. Westerholm, *Ordering*, 4.

113. Especially, and of particular significance for the present discussion, Barth's 1924 commentary on 1 Corinthians 15, *Die Auferstehung der Toten* (ET: *The Resurrection of the Dead*). This focus on the early Barth is a significant aspect of Westerholm's argument. The logic of Barth's account of human epistemic agency is found, Westerholm argues, in the early 1920s, not just the *Church Dogmatics*. Westerholm sees a number of parallels between the logic at work in the early Barth's reflections on the resurrection and his later work on the Trinity in *CD* I/1 (see Westerholm, *Ordering*, 129n150).

revelation and the knowledge of God. There are, I think, several points of connection between Barth's first volume and the shape of Pauline apocalyptic epistemology suggested above. First, Barth would certainly agree that to speak of the revelation of God cannot be to speak of God as merely another predicate of knowledge, as another "revealed thing." Knowledge of God must not be defined as a sub-species of "a general concept of knowledge" but is *sui generis* and the absolute ground of knowledge.[114] That it is God's *self-revelation* is by no means incidental, for it means that "God's revelation has its reality and truth wholly and in every respect—both ontically and noetically—within itself."[115]

Barth would also affirm that the *object* of this knowledge requires a transformation of the knowing *subject* and the mode of knowledge. "Only God Himself," he says in commenting on 1 Cor 2:9–10, "can be the subject of the knowledge of God."[116] God makes himself known in revelation, but in doing so that knowledge does not become the "possession" of the human knower. Since God cannot be just one "knowable thing" among others, the fundamental epistemic location changes, and the knowing self becomes not an autonomous knower, but a self extrinsically located in God's own knowledge. This is, as Westerholm puts it, "the opposition between the 'logic and consequences' of the Cartesian *cogito, ergo sum,* and the logic of the principle that Barth presents as its Pauline counterpart: '*cogitor, ergo sum,*' I *am* known, therefore I am."[117] That this is a Pauline way of thinking about the knowledge of God—that is, God's knowledge of us—can be seen in another of 1 Corinthians' laconic epistemological expressions: εἰ δέ τις ἀγαπᾷ τὸν θεόν, οὗτος ἔγνωσται ὑπ' αὐτοῦ, "anyone who loves God is known *by* him" (8:3). This is a challenging text, but I read it as an indication that, for Paul, one of the implications of the gospel is that human epistemic (and therefore moral) agency is fundamentally "extrinsic," founded not upon any autonomous claim to possess knowledge of God (v. 2) but upon his knowledge of us. Human knowing is framed and radically altered by union with Christ, through whom all things are created and for whom all things exist (v. 6). When divorced from this christological (and therefore ecclesial)

---

114. Barth, *CD* I/1, 190.
115. Barth, *CD* I/1, 305.
116. Barth, *Resurrection of the Dead*, 25.
117. Westerholm, *Ordering*, 122, citing Barth, *Resurrection of the Dead*, 46.

framework, epistemic and moral agency can turn in upon itself and become idolatrous and corrupted, which seems to be the case in Corinth.[118]

The idea also appears in the transformation of the epistemic subject in Paul's self-correction in Gal 4:9: νῦν δὲ γνόντες θεόν, μᾶλλον δὲ γνωσθέντες ὑπὸ θεοῦ, "Now, however, that you have come to know God, or rather to be known by God . . ." In his commentary on Galatians, Martyn reaches similar conclusions here to those of Barth on 1 Corinthians. In Paul's apocalyptic theology, according to Martyn, the opposite of "not knowing God" is not, as one might expect, "knowing God" (which Martyn calls "religion") but rather "being known by God" (which is "the foundation of theology").[119] Thus Paul's self-correction encapsulates his epistemological argument. The basis of all thought about God is not our knowledge of him but his knowledge of us, established in the Christ-event, "not an image projected from the known into the unknown" but "the incursion of the unknown into the orb of what was presumed to be the known."[120]

As such, "normal" human reasoning is circumscribed, and reordered by the revelation of God in Christ, and by God's knowledge of humanity. Participation in this knowledge is still a kind of wisdom, but since the epistemic agency is extrinsic, it does not stand guilty of the charge of epistemological foundationalism (which, as we saw earlier, is Douglas Campbell's central concern) because it is "God's wisdom" (1 Cor 2:7), revealed but not thereby "given away" to creation.

To summarize our case study so far, this is what Paul's apocalyptic epistemology looks like, in its christological reshaping. It is certainly not a question of a simplistic dichotomy between revelation and wisdom, and in this regard, Paul stands in broad continuity with the Jewish apocalyptic tradition. However, Paul's epistemology radically transforms the apocalyptic motif of "revelation of hidden wisdom,"[121] since that which has been

---

118. On all this see Macaskill, *Living in Union with Christ*.

119. Martyn, *Galatians*, 412–13.

120. Martyn, *Galatians*, 413.

121. At least in 1 Corinthians. Despite the similarities (noted above) between Barth's exegesis of 1 Corinthians and Martyn's reading of Galatians, for Martyn, here there is a stark contrast between the two letters: "in Galatians, Paul's apocalyptic is not focused on God's unveiling something that was previously hidden, as though it had been eternally standing behind a curtain (contrast 1 Cor. 2:9–10). The genesis of Paul's apocalyptic—as we see it in Galatians—lies in the apostle's certainty that God had invaded the present evil age by sending Christ and his Spirit into it." (Martyn, *Galatians*, 99. I engaged with Martyn's concerns and the problems with the language of "invasion" here in Davies, *Paul Among the Apocalypses*, 142–43).

disclosed is not simply another "revealed thing" but is God's *self-revelation* in Christ. Here, then, the logic of the incarnation is vital, since the "knowing humanity" is Christ's humanity, and the "knowing mind" is the "mind of Christ." Theological epistemology and anthropology are inseparable and find their nexus in Christology. Likewise, the cross, as the decisive cosmic incursion, is crucial for disrupting the "wisdom of this age," overthrowing cosmic opposition to the knowledge of God, and effecting the epistemological dislocation and transformation of the knowing self, as we have seen in our discussion of the work of Brown and Bowens.

For Barth, however, it is the resurrection that forms the paradigm and foundation of Christian thought, not merely as an eschatological concern, but the ground of a new way of knowing. "For Barth, Christ's resurrection grounds the noetic standpoint that the believer takes up in faith; Christ's history presents the material points of reference that orient those who occupy this standpoint; and Christ's mode of presence shapes the formal orientation of Christian thought."[122] This cognitive transformation, for Barth, is Paul's main concern in writing to the church in Corinth, and thus 1 Cor 15 is not merely an eschatological addendum to the letter, or even its rhetorical climax, but its epistemological foundation.[123]

In this sense Barth's reading of that chapter has much in common with contemporary discussions of apocalyptic thought: the resurrection is not only about eschatology but epistemology. For example, in this passage discussing the phrase "last things," Barth (at least to my ears) sounds very much like the contemporary descriptions of Jewish apocalypticism, weaving motifs of *Urzeit* and *Endzeit*, of eschatology and epistemology, and therefore the revelation of the foundations of the cosmos.

> Last things, as such, are not *last* things, however great and significant they may be. He only speaks of *last* things who would speak of the *end* of all things, of their end understood plainly and fundamentally, of a reality so radically superior to all things, that the existence of all things would be utterly and entirely *based* upon it alone, and thus, in speaking of their end, he would in truth be speaking of nothing else than their beginning.... The end of history must be for him synonymous with the prehistory, the limits of time of which he speaks must be the limits of all and every time and thus necessarily the *origin* of time.[124]

122. Westerholm, *Ordering*, 127–28.
123. Westerholm, *Ordering*, 87.
124. Barth, *Resurrection of the Dead*, 104.

In Paul's apocalyptic thought, the resurrection is eschatological, a "last thing," in exactly this sense. It is the reality *from* which one reasons; it effects the transformation of the knowing subject as the "eschatological subject who is found in Christ" and is the ground of a new way of knowing.[125] Through union with the resurrected Christ, the believer occupies the noetic standpoint of the resurrection. The transformed knower is a new creation who has the mind of Christ, no longer knowing according to the flesh but according to the power of God revealed in the resurrection, which overthrows any stronghold set up against the knowledge of God. This apocalyptic power of God is, however, also the wisdom of God. Since this is the ordering of thought to reflect reality, and the human ethical and rational reflection on that reality, it is properly called "wisdom." But since this "reality" is the new-creative "reality of the resurrection" revealed in Christ,[126] it is *apocalyptic* wisdom in a christological mode. Paul's apocalyptic epistemology corresponds to a revealed theological ontology.[127] The object and the ground of that reflection is the new creation revealed in the resurrection of Christ. This standpoint alone, Westerholm argues, "permits reason to fulfill its proper task in resolving the problem of truth."[128] This is rationality that remains human while being grounded in and re-oriented by the self-revelation of God in the Christ-event, in his incarnation, death, resurrection, and (this side of his return) his presence with humanity in the mode of promise.

At this point, our discussion of Paul's apocalyptic epistemology has become a discussion of his eschatology (the two are bound to intersect), and here in particular we must raise the question of continuity and discontinuity, a question to which we now turn in our last case-study.

---

125. Westerholm, *Ordering*, 123 and *passim*.

126. Barth, *Resurrection of the Dead*, 211–12.

127. See Barth's discussion of the "reality of revelation" in CD 1/2 §13. As noted in the previous chapter, it seems to me that there is much here that is similar to N. T. Wright's recent Gifford lectures, in which Wright gives an account of the resurrection as the ground of "a new kind of ontology, inviting a new kind of epistemology" (*History and Eschatology*, 198), which is decidedly apocalyptic and retrospective. That said, Wright's description of this as "rejuvenation" (212) remains, I suggest, insufficient to this task. Despite their numerous disagreements, Wright and Campbell are, it seems to me, actually quite close together in their commitment to the resurrection as the foundation of a new ontology and epistemology (cf. 94–98 above, and,e.g., *Pauline Dogmatics*, 73, 700).

128. Westerholm, *Ordering*, 233.

5.3 Time and Space, Continuity and Discontinuity in Galatians 4

In this final section, we will consider one more text where Paul deploys apocalyptic imagery, the allegory of Hagar and Sarah in Gal 4:21—5:1. We noted this passage earlier, along with 1 Cor 2, as an example of Paul's apparent avoidance of the straightforwardly linear-temporal language of the "age to come." In what follows our attention will return to Paul's apocalyptic eschatology and will offer an interpretation of the passage in dialogue with Second Temple Jewish apocalypses and Karl Barth's understanding of (salvation) history. In the imagery of Gal 4, however, the temporal is closely related to the spatial, as Paul once again introduces an enigmatic and asymmetrical contrast between the "present Jerusalem" (v. 25) and the "Jerusalem above" (v. 26). As with 1 Cor 2, we will use this asymmetrical contrast as the springboard to a broader discussion of Paul's apocalyptic thought, here focused on eschatology and cosmology.

Something that is obscured in English translations of this passage is that Paul has made a subtle shift in the word "Jerusalem." Up until this point in Galatians he has used the grammatically neuter word Ἱεροσόλυμα (1:17–18; 2:1), but here in 4:25–26 he changes to the feminine Ἰερουσαλήμ. No doubt this is at least partly under the influence of LXX Isa 40–66, from which Paul quotes in 4:27, and which speaks of Jerusalem (Ἰερουσαλήμ) as a "mother," a "daughter," a "barren woman," a "grieving widow" and a "bride."[129] In addition to this connection, however, the shift to the feminine also reflects Paul's deployment of a widespread trope of Second Temple Jewish apocalyptic writing (itself a development of the Isaianic tradition[130]): the depiction of a city, particularly Jerusalem/Zion, as a woman.

Women as Cities in Jewish Apocalyptic Literature

The personification of cities as women is a widespread phenomenon in both Jewish and Christian apocalyptic literature, including within the New Testament itself. Notable, of course, is Revelation's famous contrast between the harlot Babylon in chapter 18 and Jerusalem the bride in chapter

---

129. Isa 50:1; 51:17–18; 52:1–2; 62:1–5, 11; 66:7–11.

130. It is "an apocalyptic reinterpretation of the Isaiah passage" (Hogan, "Mother Zion and Mother Earth in 2 Baruch and 4 Ezra," 208) see de Boer, *Galatians*, 297). One might also fruitfully consider the motif in Ezek 40–48.

21. The trope is also found in cosmological/eschatological contexts in the sister apocalypses 4 Ezra and 2 Baruch. It is in the fourth vision of the book of 4 Ezra (chapters 9–10, but especially 10:25–59) that the city-as-woman imagery is most developed. The meaning of the imagery is well summarized, however, by the briefer remarks of 7:26, indicating the eschatological and revelatory function of the image: "For behold, the time will come, when the signs which I have foretold to you will come; that the city which now is not seen shall appear, and the land which now is hidden shall be disclosed."[131] The deployment of the imagery in 2 Bar. 4:2–6, which also echoes Isa 40–66, is particularly noteworthy for our present purposes:

> Or do you perhaps think that this is the city about which I said: On the palms of my hands I have inscribed you? This building that is now built in your midst is not the one revealed with me, the one already prepared here when I intended to make Paradise. And I showed it to Adam before he sinned, but when he transgressed the commandment, it was taken away from him, as was also Paradise. And after these [things] I showed it to my servant Abraham, by night, between the halves of the sacrifices. And furthermore, I also showed it to Moses on Mount Sinai when I showed him the likeness of the tabernacle and of all its implements. And now, see, it is preserved with me, as is also Paradise.[132]

Here there is a much starker contrast between the earthly and heavenly Zion. The true holy city of which Isaiah spoke is not the one found on earth but the one preserved "eternally" with God, prepared at the time of creation and revealed at moments of covenant significance to Adam, Abraham, and Moses. It thus stands as a sign of continuity, having been kept throughout salvation history, hidden with God in order to be revealed (and again we note the positive importance of the categories of covenant and salvation history in apocalyptic thought). Michael Stone suggests a similar interpretation of the woman Zion in 4 Ezra 10, which he reads as a cosmological metaphor for the "environs of God," much like the temple or the *Merkavah*.[133] Regularly, the imagery is deployed in Jewish apocalyptic literature to speak of the "eternal" dwelling place and purposes of God, and thus of complex relationships between time and space, history and eternity.

---

131. Translation from Stone and Henze, *4 Ezra and 2 Baruch*.
132. Tr. Stone and Henze.
133. See Stone, "City in 4 Ezra," 402 and Hogan, "Mother Zion," 220.

"The unseen city," as Edith Humphrey notes in her important study of the motif, "often had bound up with it the idea of pre-existence."[134]

Others have noted the connections between these passages and Gal 4, and their differences. Karina Martin Hogan, for example, considers the use of "mother Zion" in 2 Baruch to be decidedly unlike Paul's in Galatians, which, she argues, sets up "an oppositional dualism"[135] between the two women/cities. Certainly, Paul uses this imagery to set up an oppositional contrast between the two women, which correspond to two cities, and their offspring. As noted above, however, in his application of the imagery to the two "Jerusalems" in verses 25–26, there is a peculiar asymmetry in the wording of Paul's contrast. Rather than juxtaposing the "now/present Jerusalem" (ἡ νῦν Ἰερουσαλήμ) with the "future Jerusalem" or the "Jerusalem to come," he contrasts it with the "Jerusalem above" (ἡ ἄνω Ἰερουσαλήμ). It is an asymmetrical image that is remarkably fruitful for an account of Paul's apocalyptic cosmology and eschatology, as we will see.

For now, however, it is helpful once again to remember the diversity of the apocalyptic corpus. Not all uses of the trope in the apocalypses have this same logic; there are other deployments of the "heavenly Jerusalem" image that hope for a more immanent transformation/restoration of the holy city on earth. But in at least one thread of the Jewish apocalyptic tradition, the imagery of a heavenly Jerusalem, often depicted as a woman/mother, invokes complex relationships of space and time (and non-linear understandings of the latter). It is this kind of apocalyptic spatio-temporal logic, I suggest, that characterizes Paul's asymmetrical contrast between the two Jerusalems in Gal 4.

Galatians 4 and the Apocalyptic Paul

In her focus on Paul's oppositional dualism, Hogan's analysis of this passage echoes that of J. Louis Martyn, for whom Gal 4:26 represents another Pauline "apocalyptic contrast."[136] Martyn, however, is by no means the only Pauline scholar to read the women-as-cities imagery in its Jewish apocalyptic context. Most commentators on this passage note, at the least, the

---

134. Humphrey, *Ladies*, 23, discussing the work of Stone on 4 Ezra. As noted earlier, Humphrey's work on maternal metaphors in apocalyptic literature is cited by Susan Eastman in *Recovering*, 19n44.

135. Hogan, "Mother Zion," 208.

136. Martyn, *Galatians*, 440.

importance of the "Jerusalem above" trope in the Jewish apocalyptic tradition.[137] For example, Hans Dieter Betz not only observes the connection between the imagery and the apocalypses, but also notes the diversity of the trope, which has "various types" ranging from immanent restoration to a pre-existent and eternally preserved heavenly Jerusalem.[138] Paul's deployment of this apocalyptic motif, in Betz's analysis, is of the latter variety. Moreover, his reading of the theological force of Paul's use of this apocalyptic trope shows that Martyn's is by no means the most starkly dualistic interpretation. For Betz, the Hagar/Sarah allegory encapsulates Paul's polemic intention "to create a dualistic polarity between 'Judaism' and 'Christianity.'"[139] In the light of the long Jewish tradition that lies behind Paul's imagery, I find it hard to agree with Betz's interpretation here. As with his epistemology, there may well be a polemical and dualistic polarity at work, but it is one operating *within Judaism,* not between "Judaism" and "Christianity." Paul is found here at his most Jewish, albeit in a distinctly apocalyptic mode.[140] As I hope to show, once the appropriate theological framework is recognized, the nature of Paul's exploration of covenant continuity and revelatory discontinuity becomes clearer and need not result in such supersessionist analyses.

For our present purposes, however, our focus is on the Apocalyptic Paul, and particularly the reading of Gal 4 offered by Martyn and de Boer. For Martyn, the imagery of the two women/cities evokes a "series of polar opposites,"[141] contrasting the logic of circumcision and the human power of the flesh in one column, and the divine promise in the power of the Spirit in the other. Viewed with the question of history in mind, this corresponds to a dichotomy between "the natural power of procreation" and the "power of God's promise."[142] The conclusion Martyn draws here is that the Jerusalem above is "not determined by a line of descent from any entity that is earthly and past."[143] It is Martyn's purpose to argue that the apocalyptic character

---

137. In addition to Betz, see, e.g., Dunn, *Galatians*, 253–54; Longenecker, *Galatians*, 214; Schreiner, *Galatians*, 303.

138. Betz, *Galatians*, 246.

139. Betz, *Galatians*, 246.

140. See Scott, "Comparison of Paul's Letter," 193–218 and now his book-length treatment in *Apocalyptic Letter to the Galatians.*

141. Martyn, *Galatians*, 432, cf. 438; 450.

142. Martyn, *Galatians*, 435–36.

143. Martyn, *Galatians*, 441.

of Paul's thought is evidenced by a "thoroughly punctiliar"[144] exegesis, fundamentally opposed to any linearity.

In thinking further with Martyn about this passage, it is interesting to return to the asymmetry of the Pauline contrast between the two Jerusalems. There is not, strictly speaking, a contrast of "polar opposites," as Martyn says,[145] or at least not an expected one. The polar opposite of the "present Jerusalem," one might reasonably assume, is the "future Jerusalem," not the "Jerusalem above." Martyn and others have noted this awkward asymmetry, and sometimes it is smoothed out in interpretation. Schreiner, for example, notes that this contrast has a "vertical" dimension, but moves on quickly to interpret the contrast as an expression of Paul's inaugurated eschatology, effectively re-reading the vertical as a horizontal.[146] Though Michael Cover's analysis is very different, in that he reads the imagery more with the Platonic tradition than Jewish apocalypticism, he still insists that the "above" of Paul's contrast "acquires an implicit temporal dimension."[147] For his part, Martyn maintains the necessary verticality in his interpretation, but he nevertheless still brings temporality into his reading, parsing "above" as "above and future."[148] De Boer comments on the awkward nature of the dualism and Paul's mixture of temporal and spatial categories, which he recognizes as "a common feature of apocalyptic thinking, since the age to come already exists in heaven above."[149] Once again this demonstrates that de Boer is working closely with the apocalyptic literature in his analysis of Paul's apocalyptic theology. However, the limited eschatological framework within which these texts are being read again surfaces in his reading of the Pauline asymmetry in 4:25–26, in which he ultimately emphasizes an assumed two-age eschatology in his interpretation, supplying the absent language of the "age to come" to make sense of Paul's thought: "the present Jerusalem [is] a reality of the old age . . . and the Jerusalem above a reality of the new age."[150] As we saw in the first part of this chapter, there are other

---

144. Martyn, *Galatians*, 444.

145. Martyn, *Galatians*, 439.

146. Schreiner, *Galatians*, 303.

147. Cover, "'Now and Above; Then and Now,'" 228.

148. Martyn, *Galatians*, 440.

149. De Boer, *Galatians*, 302, citing (on 301) Rev 3:12; 21:2, 10; 4 Ezra 7:26; 8:52; 10:27, 44–46; 13:35–36; 2 Bar 4:2–6; and Heb 12:22.

150. De Boer, *Galatians*, 301. We have already discussed the absence of the "age to come" in Paul. We should note, however, that de Boer's spatio-temporal reading of "age" here makes his analysis more nuanced than the simple linearity one might assume.

reasons to question the over-emphasis on a two-age eschatology in Paul's apocalyptic thought, and the assumption of a linear temporal framework.

We may still fruitfully interrogate, with Hogan, Martyn, and de Boer, the "apocalyptic antinomy" Paul develops here, but with perhaps a more deliberate attention to the temporal/spatial asymmetry of the contrast. In contrasting the "present Jerusalem" with the "Jerusalem above," Paul appears to have disjointed any horizontal eschatological line on which such an antinomy might neatly be placed. For the present purposes, despite the useful connections between the "heavenly Jerusalem" and Jewish eschatological hopes, it remains the case that Paul seems to go out of his way to avoid a symmetrical eschatological contrast between the present and the future. More can be said about how this asymmetrical contrast might inform a Pauline apocalyptic theology of history.

Galatians 4 in Apocalyptic and Interdisciplinary Perspective

The complex eschatology implied by Paul's asymmetrical language suggests that we need something more sophisticated than a linear analysis of time and (salvation) history, and a thus a more sophisticated approach to the question of continuity and discontinuity. A simple linear analysis will not suffice, and though the addition of an extra dimension is a welcome improvement, the often-invoked geometric abstractions of horizontal and vertical remain ultimately insufficient.[151]

What is clear from Paul's apocalyptic contrast in Gal 4 is that continuity is not to be located in any respect in relation to the "present Jerusalem." This polemic may, at first sight, appear as a radically discontinuous, even supersessionist, assessment of "Judaism" as a religion "according to the flesh." A lot depends on the nature of the theological framework within which he is read. If the only frame of reference is the line of earthly history, Paul's imagery may well be read as a stark rejection of the present Jerusalem and its "replacement," or as a pure irruptive vertical intersecting the doomed horizontal of salvation history. But the asymmetry of the Pauline contrast suggests that something more complex is going on here, and that a more nuanced relationship between continuity and discontinuity is at work in his theology of history.

In this connection, Martyn is helpful in his suggestion, noted in the previous chapter, of a Pauline framework of "anthropological discontinuity"

---

151. See again Jenson's critique, in 4.2 above.

and "theological continuity."[152] In Martyn's reading of the Galatians 4 allegory, "continuity is to be found only in *God* and in God's salvific deed, not in the creation of a historical linearity."[153] Too often, however, apocalyptic readings have emphasized only one side of this dialectic, the radical vertical irruption of divine activity into the horizontal of human history, without sufficient development of the nature of the theological continuity, and its intersection with human history. Certainly, in Paul's application of the allegory to his Galatian readers, there is a polemically discontinuous message in the personification of the "present Jerusalem" as Hagar, the slave woman, and the passage's closing ethical imperative and stark declaration: "drive out the slave and her child; for the child of the slave will not share the inheritance with the child of the free woman" (4:30). However, in 4:28–29 there is also an emphasis on salvation-historical continuity ("just as at that time . . . so it is now also"). Both words must be spoken at once.

In this endeavor, it is crucial that we to attend to the *location* of this continuity in Paul's deployment of the apocalyptic imagery. Covenant continuity is located not in the extension of human history, but in the "Jerusalem above," which is Sarah, and her child Isaac, born of the promise. It is with this child that the Galatian readers are to identify themselves, not as a polemical replacement of the covenant people, but as children of the free woman and co-heirs. The theological continuity of the people of God, both at "that time" and "also now," has never been located at the level of human history but was and is found in the divine word of promise which constitutes God's people. Something like Martyn's two-level analysis is helpful for understanding Paul's logic here, and without such a framework our interpretations are consigned to affirming some version of a supersessionist articulation of the people of God, or at best an appeal to paradox. But it is precisely in the awkward asymmetry of the Pauline contrast that we find the necessarily complex eschatological framework within which both continuity and discontinuity can be helpfully articulated. It is, moreover, an analysis comparable with at least some deployments of maternal imagery and the "Jerusalem above" in the Jewish apocalyptic literature, as we have seen. Here some nuance to Martyn's proposal is needed.

One such nuanced reading of Gal 4 has recently been suggested by John Barclay, whose approach to continuity and discontinuity in Galatians was noted in the previous chapter. For Barclay, Paul's deployment of the

152. Martyn, "Events in Galatia," 176.
153. Martyn, "Events in Galatia," 176.

"heavenly Jerusalem" image "jolts the reader beyond the horizon of human projections."[154] Here, Paul indicates his affinity with the Jewish apocalyptic tradition, and especially those like 4 Ezra 10, where, Barclay argues, "the city is most emphatically *God's* creation, not the development or completion of a human project on the historical plane."[155] Nevertheless, in Barclay's reading of Galatians these apocalyptic motifs are combined with salvation history; Paul's radical discontinuous antitheses are held together with continuity (and this combination, too, is something one finds in the Jewish apocalyptic tradition).[156] This is not to endorse a reading of the purposeful trajectory of human history as a developmental narrative, but rather as the history of divine promise. In terms of human history, the Christ-event represents discontinuity. In terms of God's promise, it is completion and fulfillment (thus Gal 4:4). As Barclay puts it, "the Christ-event completes a narrative line projected by the divine promise, but not a narrative progression in human history."[157] The difference between "projection" and "progression" here is essential, as is the two-level analysis within which both continuity and discontinuity can be affirmed. This analysis allows Barclay to challenge N. T. Wright's reading of salvation history as "preparation" for Christ,[158] and to affirm Martyn's emphasis on the radical caesura of the Christ-event, but without reducing this to a punctiliar singularity. It is discontinuous at the level of human history, but continuous at the level of divine promise.[159] For Barclay, the promise is not "preparation" but "pre-announcement."[160]

Barclay's discussion, much like that of Susan Eastman discussed in the previous chapter, offers a valuable development of Martyn's two-level analysis.[161] What makes this particularly helpful is that it takes us further than geometric abstractions or the irruptive language of "invasion," for the logic of the category of *promise* has both verticality and a necessary extension. It requires not only the interruptive word of promise but also its fulfillment in that which is promised. The word of promise is not an abstract punctiliar phenomenon, or a mere intersecting line across the arc

---

154. Barclay, *Gift*, 417n66.
155. Barclay, *Gift*, 302.
156. See Barclay, *Obeying the Truth*, 104, and the discussion in the previous chapter.
157. Barclay, *Gift*, 412.
158. Barclay, *Gift*, 412n50.
159. Barclay, *Gift*, 414, cf. 388–89.
160. Barclay, *Gift*, 412n50.
161. See Eastman's critique and development of Martyn in *Recovering*, 16.

of history; it is a category that involves extension, but of a very specific sort. A word of promise remains theologically continuous but does not thereby become reduced to a punctiliar singularity disconnected from human history. It touches the world in all its genuine historicity, in that it is a promise given to specific people. Here there is an important corrective to Martyn's paradigm. "Taken by itself," Eastman argues, "the language of anthropological discontinuity does not provide a way to talk about the intersection of the gospel with real, 'linear' human lives ... a sharp distinction between 'theological' and 'anthropological continuity' impedes any further description of the gospel's power to create a history."[162] In Paul's allegory of Hagar and Sarah, the two women are not mere ciphers for abstract phenomena, but real people who were addressed by the divine word of promise. Crucially, approaching the question of continuity and discontinuity within this logic of promise enables us to affirm with utmost seriousness the historicity of Sarah and Hagar, Isaac and Ishmael, not simply as actors on the stage of human history, bound up by the logic of cause-and-effect, but as recipients of the word of promise from "above." There is causality and extension in the salvation-historical narrative, but is it a "vertical" causality.

Having offered largely positive engagements with Martyn and Barclay, I now want to bring their readings into dialogue with Karl Barth, whose work on revelation and time/history in the *Church Dogmatics* is particularly salient at this point. In particular, a fruitful connection can be made, I think, between Barclay's reading of the logic of promise in Galatians 4 and Barth's category of "expectation" (*Erwartung*).[163] For Barth, the Old Testament, like the New, is the witness to revelation, located in God's self-relation to Israel in the covenant. It is this covenantal self-relation of God to his people that creates them as a nation, with a particular history. The character of this covenant in the Old Testament is, however, one of multiplicity. There are multiple covenants, with Noah, Abraham, Moses, and more. For Barth, each of these is, in its own way, *the* covenant, and yet none of them are *the* covenant. In each of these instances of God's self-relation the covenant is present in the mode of promise, which is for Barth the promise of Jesus Christ, who is God's covenant. As such, the character of revelation in the Old Testament is one of *expectation*, the witness (in all its concrete historicity) to God's presence as the coming one. Barth summarizes this as

---

162. Eastman, *Recovering*, 16.
163. Developed in Barth, *CD* I/2 §14.

follows, pursuing, as always, his christological interpretation of covenant history to its conclusions:

> This covenant attested in the Old Testament is God's revelation, because it is expectation of the revelation of Jesus Christ. It is expectation of the revelation of Jesus Christ once for all in its strict genuine historicity. As freely, as concretely, as uniquely as in the Old Testament *berith*, God in Jesus Christ becomes history, and with the same mercy and strictness man in Christ is adopted by God. To that extent, therefore, Jesus Christ is already the content and theme of this prehistory, of the Old Testament covenant.[164]

This is a rich passage, but for our present purposes, it is instructive to focus on Barth's development of the category of "expectation." The time of expectation, for Barth, is by no means an "autonomous time of preparation,"[165] since the event expected is one "altogether introduced by God, breaking into all other history from above."[166] So far, so congenial to the Apocalyptic Paul. But this is only one side of the dialectic, and Barth continues to develop the other. This "expectation" must not be reduced to an abstraction, since it expects something "actually within history, a real historical event . . . [Old Testament expectation] is no illusion, but the kind of expectation when the expected One has already knocked at the door and is already there, though still outside."[167]

In this way, Barth's development of the category of "expectation" enables the affirmation of both continuity and discontinuity while avoiding the twin dangers of immanentism and ahistoricism. There is continuity, provided the locus of this continuity is God and his covenant, and there is discontinuity, in that this remains a divine word breaking into history. "Expectation" is thus resistant to being framed as a pure vertical line, or as a punctiliar singularity, since it involves both the word of promise, spoken to the people of God throughout history, and its fulfillment. Expectation thus has genuine historicity and extension, but not of a simple horizontal or earthly kind. Its extension is the enduring presence of the covenant word of promise, and its fulfillment in Christ, to all (human) history. It still expresses the vertical nature of the "Jerusalem above," though without

---

164. Barth, *CD* I/2, 81–82.
165. Barth, *CD* I/2, 100.
166. Barth, *CD* I/2, 99.
167. Barth, *CD* I/2, 99–100.

reducing this to the punctiliar logic of "invasion," since it does not merely meet time at a point but enters and assumes it.[168]

It is perhaps significant for the ongoing conversation about the Apocalyptic Paul's reception of Barth to note once more the brief parenthetical comment Barth makes here, also noted earlier in relation to Robert Jenson's critique. At exactly this moment in his argument, Barth warns the reader about certain elements in his commentary on Romans, where he expressed "the idea of a revelation permanently transcending time, merely bounding time and determining it from without."[169] This, Barth says, was the result of his commentary's "antiseptic" task in the face of the prevailing dangers of the time. However, by his own admission, this construal of the relationship between revelation and history does not do justice to the doctrine of the incarnation. This warning, and the more mature work on this theme found in the *Church Dogmatics*, should perhaps receive more attention, and particularly the crucial conclusion Barth reaches, noted earlier by Kerr and Ziegler, that in entering and assuming time, "revelation is not a predicate of history, but history is a predicate of revelation."[170]

Barth's analysis clearly has much in common with Barclay's, but there are certain advantages. Barclay reads the word of promise as a "preannouncement" which constitutes "reverberations in history of the Christ event."[171] In Barth's "time of expectation," however, and its emphasis on both the presence and the coming of God, expected revelation is not "prerevelation" but actually *is* revelation,[172] participating in the time of the fulfillment of the promise in its own particular way. It thus affirms with seriousness the historicity of that word of revelation spoken in the covenant with Israel and throughout salvation-history while also affirming the radical discontinuity of the divine word. Barth's approach speaks doubly about the Old Testament. First, there is the promise and the covenant in the specific historical situation, God's presence through the ages (though more often hidden) with his people in their genuine historicity. Second, and at the same time, the word of promise also speaks of its fulfillment in the coming of God in Jesus Christ.

---

168. Barth, *CD* I/2, 50.

169. Barth, *CD* I/2, 50.

170. Barth, *CD* I/2, 58. cf. Barth *CD* I/1: 143–62. Again see Kerr, *Christ History and Apocalyptic*, 73–79 and Ziegler, *Militant Grace*, 15, 24.

171. Barclay, *Gift*, 412n50; 418.

172. Barth, *CD* I/2, 86; 100.

To return to where we started, and to put it in the language of 2 Baruch, the continuity of divine promise is "preserved with God," who prepared this word before creation and has spoken it to Adam, Abraham, and Moses in the covenant promises. If we must resort to geometry, the vertical touches the horizontal wherever we find this divine word of promise spoken, which is to say throughout all of salvation history, a history constituted and predicated by that word. But here again we see the limitation of such geometric metaphors, for they risk reducing the divine word to an abstraction and can obscure the nature of the covenant promise. As a word spoken *by* God, it maintains its discontinuity since it remains always a divine word that cannot be domesticated by human history. And as a word spoken *to* particular human lives (in all their concrete and contingent historicity), it maintains continuity without ever collapsing into human history. As with our discussion of wisdom and apocalyptic epistemology in the previous section, the word of promise is given without being given away.

In Gal 4, Paul's asymmetrical contrast between the "present Jerusalem" and the "Jerusalem above" is not the straightforward assertion of apocalyptic discontinuity against salvation-historical continuity but rather establishes the proper "vertical continuity," located in the divine promise, over against an enslaved "horizontal" of earthly history "according to the flesh." The "Jerusalem above" is an apocalyptic discontinuity in that it is the divine word of promise that breaks into human history from above. But it is not a punctiliar phenomenon since it has extension through salvation history in the word of promise, which has always been the proper locus for the perdurance of the people of God. Paul's polemic is against those who would abandon this and attempt to redefine God's people on the basis of earthly realities rather than the promises of God.

CONCLUSION

The Tone and Tasks of the Apocalyptic Paul

IN CHAPTERS 1–3 OF this book, I charted the history of scholarship on Paul's apocalyptic thought, and then the contemporary contours of the Apocalyptic Paul movement. Due to the constraints of such a rapid survey, there may be imprecisions and characterizations with which some may take issue, though that too is an important part of the conversation. No doubt there remain important omissions, though I have tried, within the constraints of these pages, to give as thorough and faithful an account as possible of the main voices in the Apocalyptic Paul conversation, including some of those newly emerging. I am under no illusions, however, that I have offered anything like a comprehensive account, and this volume should of course not be seen as any substitute for reading the literature first-hand. Nevertheless, it is my hope that the whistle-stop tour of a hundred years of Pauline scholarship offered in those chapters has achieved the more modest goal of providing what this book's title promised: a helpful retrospective on the Apocalyptic Paul.

Chapter 4 was more prospective, taking us beyond survey to outline the main live issues on the table, as I see them, and possibilities for the future of the conversation. Here, I tried to name genuine points of disagreement, while also describing and correcting unhelpful misunderstandings. The first two sections of the chapter examined the main interdisciplinary challenges faced by the Apocalyptic Paul. In my view, one of the causes for optimism here is that this is an account of Paul's thought that promises to transcend our usual disciplinary subdivisions, though this sometimes remains a promise unfulfilled.[1] Somewhat paradoxically, it is also

---

1. I am by no means the only one to have issued a call for such work across the disciplines of Pauline studies and systematic theology. Some substantial work has been

a conversation that threatens to swing the opposite direction, to become yet another silo of like-minded Protestant Anglophone Paulinists. As the conversation continues about Paul's apocalyptic theology, the choice and breadth of conversation partners will be of great importance. If there is to be any hope of consensus, or even constructive disagreement, it will take generous conversation between Paul specialists, systematic theologians, and scholars of apocalyptic literature both canonical and extra-canonical. Superficial or dated analyses of these related fields of enquiry will not be sufficient. Moreover, the character of this conversation must be carefully curated by all participants. Lines in the sand and caricatures of opposing views will only serve to reinforce our echo chambers rather than to foster wisdom. An important commitment that such conversation must make is to avoid partisan thinking and a view of the theological task as tribal warfare between rival "schools." What matters, of course, is not the Apocalyptic Paul but Paul, and his account of the gospel of Jesus Christ.

The kind of shared commitment to generous dialogue we will need is not, however, something that can be brought into existence by sermonic appeal. It will require the disciplined and sustained practice of intellectual humility as well as the careful pressing of theological disagreement. In chapter 4, I named some of the areas in which important critiques have been directed at the Apocalyptic Paul, in its account of Paul's epistemology, eschatology, and soteriology. I also hope to have indicated some of the potential for constructive conversation in these areas, as well as some of the important differences that remain. In particular, it is important that the Apocalyptic Paul is not handled as a homogenous mass, as if it were a monolithic "school" occupied with a mere repetition and exegetical application of J. Louis Martyn's talking points. Of course, his work was and remains programmatic, but there have been some developments of his key insights as well as disagreements with him, both within the Apocalyptic Paul and outside of it. There are, as a result, a number of important nuances that must be appreciated, and some key differences between Apocalyptic Paul scholars.

The handling of the apocalyptic literature is certainly one of those areas of difference. Many outside the Apocalyptic Paul movement (e.g., Wright and Stuckenbruck) have named this methodological concern as one of their principal objections to the group's endeavors. The picture, again,

---

done in recent years with reformed thought. See, e.g., Chester, *Reading Paul with the Reformers* and now Driel, *Rethinking Paul*.

is complex. On the one hand, Martinus de Boer has repeatedly affirmed the importance of this corpus for defining "apocalyptic eschatology," a commitment evidently shared by emerging scholars such as Lisa Bowens, whose work on Paul displays careful attention to the Second Temple Jewish apocalyptic literature. On the other, Douglas Campbell seems less invested in that enterprise. Clearly, though there is a general consensus regarding the importance of the apocalyptic literature, there is still scope for further discussion on this matter. Similarly, not all scholars are as explicit as Campbell in calling their project "Barthian," though the legacy of his Romans commentary remains an important feature of the discussion. Yet the validity of the claim that this is a reading of Paul in concert with Barth has itself been challenged by some Barth scholars (e.g., McCormack), and those who are trying to exploit the potential of an apocalyptic reading of Paul within systematic theology have taken such challenges on board, going with and beyond Barth in their contributions (e.g., Kerr and Ziegler). There are some intriguing developments in the area of Paul's epistemology, and some real possibilities for constructive conversation on the questions of the integration of wisdom and revelation (e.g., Brown and Macaskill), as well as an emerging consensus, of sorts, around the importance of a Pauline retrospective epistemology (e.g., Wright, Gaventa, and Campbell). In the area of eschatology some, such as Eastman, have challenged what they see as excessively dichotomous accounts of the place of salvation history in Martyn's description of Paul's apocalyptic thought, and have developed more nuanced alternatives. This should be a welcome development for those (such as Wright) who have considered the Apocalyptic Paul seriously deficient in precisely this area. Likewise, the strict soteriological antitheses, which some in the movement have deployed in their readings of Paul's apocalyptic theology, have been challenged both from "inside" and "outside" the movement. Nuanced accounts of an apocalyptic soteriology are emerging as a result, and new voices are entering the discussion, often crossing the traditional boundaries between the sub-disciplines of theological enquiry, with stimulating results.

Having thus outlined what I see as some key questions and developments, in the final chapter of this book I attempted to demonstrate the potential for taking this discussion of Paul's apocalyptic theology forward through dialogue across the disciplines. To that end, I offered there some contributions of my own, in the form of case studies in Paul's apocalyptic theology. At the heart of this discussion is the question of Paul's continuity "within" apocalyptic Judaism, and the role that his understanding of the Christ-event plays in his particular expression of apocalyptic thought. I began with a fresh examination of Paul's use of the apocalyptic trope of "two ages," before pressing some of the questions described in chapter 4 in relation to a couple of Pauline passages. First, Paul's apocalyptic epistemology was investigated in relation to 1 Cor 2, with a focus on the way in which revelation and wisdom interact. Second, his apocalyptic eschatology and cosmology were examined through a study of Gal 4, with specific attention to the question of continuity and discontinuity. In these interpretative case studies, I have tried to incorporate some of the insights of more recent scholarship in the Second Temple Jewish apocalyptic literature, and to bring these into dialogue with recent contributions to Pauline studies, especially from those who broadly identify themselves with the Apocalyptic Paul movement. In addition, the thought of Karl Barth (particularly as developed in his *Church Dogmatics*) has been brought to the table, along with some of his recent interpreters, to provide a second line of conversation and a theological framework for my interpretative proposals.

In closing, I want to offer something of summary of what I take to be the most important talking points of this conversation in relation to these two lines of discussion, the first of which is with the study of Second Temple Jewish apocalypticism. As noted above, the Apocalyptic Paul does, in the vast majority of cases, express a commitment to reading Paul in the context of the Second Temple Jewish apocalyptic tradition and its literature. Assertions of the contrary should, therefore, be revised. Of course, this commitment is variously articulated and understood, and the delivery on its promise is at times unfulfilled. Nevertheless, it is sufficiently shared among apocalyptic interpreters of Paul to call into question overly simplistic dismissals of the movement as hopelessly disconnected from Paul's historical and literary context. As such, the terms of the debate should be set neither as a contest over the term "apocalyptic" nor as an acquiescence to the terminological stalemate of "using the word in different ways." Rather, the more appropriate (and far more useful) question that should be asked is how we are to understand the relationship between Paul and the Jewish apocalyptic tradition, his continuity and discontinuity with(in) it. Once again, the complexity of this question will require constructive dialogue between these two guilds, avoiding superficial and dated second-hand analyses on either side.

Despite this commitment, however, there is a legitimate question concerning the Apocalyptic Paul's engagement with the most recent secondary scholarship on the apocalyptic literature. One of the more significant results of that scholarship that must be developed in an apocalyptic reading of Paul is the re-evaluation of the role of imminent eschatology, which should no longer be considered *the* defining feature of Jewish apocalyptic thought, as asserted by some older analyses. In Jewish and Pauline apocalyptic thought, eschatology remains an important theme, of course, but a fuller picture should be painted, incorporating apocalyptic epistemology, cosmology, soteriology, and anthropology. As we have seen, some recent contributions to the Apocalyptic Paul have investigated these themes in useful ways, suggesting that an increasingly fruitful dialogue is emerging.

The second line of conversation is with the guild of systematic theology. It is widely recognized that the Apocalyptic Paul is irreducibly theological in its posture, and the key to unlocking Paul's particular development of the Jewish apocalyptic tradition is to be found in his Christology. For some, particularly within Protestant theology, it is precisely the relentlessly christocentric and evangelical (in the sense of *evangelisch*) character of this reading of Paul that has made it so compelling, both as a reading of Paul's letters and as a theological account of the gospel for our time. For others, however, this christocentrism represents a significant problem: a tell-tale sign of a Christian apologetic agenda and thus an impediment to interdisciplinary dialogue. This need not be the case. A commitment to an irreducibly theological account of Paul can be maintained without casting off historical and literary connections, and indeed much can be said about Paul's apocalyptic thought without sharing such theological commitments. Likewise, there is validity in asking both historical and theological questions in the study of Second Temple Jewish apocalypticism. Thus, these important methodological differences notwithstanding, there is plenty of space for the constructive conversation for which this book has advocated. As Käsemann argued, the historical and the theological can and must be integrated.

In developing its theological account of Paul, the Apocalyptic Paul has made no secret of its indebtedness to Karl Barth, ever since Ernst Käsemann. That Barth should be the primary theological interlocutor is hardly surprising, given his signature commitment to revelation and his relentlessly christological approach to the theological task. What has become apparent, however, is that some Barth scholars have raised significant questions about the way in which his thought has been construed. To be sure, several elements of the Apocalyptic Paul echo theological emphases in Barth, such as his revelatory epistemology, his cosmological soteriology, and his "invasive" account of the relationship between the Christ-event and (salvation) history. Sometimes, however, these emphases have been developed, or at least expressed, in falsely antithetical ways, without sufficient attention to Barth's dialectical treatment of such themes and the christological shape they take, especially in his more mature thought. Further dialogue between these guilds, therefore, is important as that conversation develops. This line of discussion is already underway and has been bearing fruit for a decade or so, but there is certainly scope for more. Greater nuance and depth are emerging as systematic theological insights (and not only those of Barth) are brought to bear on Paul's apocalyptic theology of time and history, the nature of his retrospective epistemology, his understanding of revelation and wisdom, of theological anthropology, and of cosmological and forensic soteriology.

At the risk of adding yet more complexity to an already challenging three-sided conversation, I want to add a final thought concerning an all-too-common problem in Pauline studies: the tendency toward a sort of Pauline exceptionalism, and of treating Paul's letters as effectively a "canon within the canon." If (as I have argued) there is a need for the Apocalyptic Paul to be in constructive dialogue with scholars of the Jewish apocalyptic tradition, and with systematic theologians, then this conversation must also be extended to scholarship on apocalyptic thought elsewhere in the New Testament. The is a great deal of work in this area from which the Apocalyptic Paul could learn, not only on the book of Revelation but also on the gospels.[2] After all, the story of the Apocalyptic Paul, as I have surveyed it here, began not with Käsemann's work on Paul's doctrine of justification, but with Weiss's and Schweitzer's discussions of Jesus and the kingdom of God. As the Apocalyptic Paul moves forward, this broader canonical horizon may have much to offer.

Of course, no single scholar can hope to have mastered the complexity of these various fields, each of which has its own lively internal debates. In

---

2. In addition to the huge corpus of scholarship on the book of Revelation, one thinks of Joel Marcus's apocalyptic reading of the Gospel of Mark (esp. in Marcus, *Mark*), Grant Macaskill's work on Matthew (Macaskill, "Wisdom and Apocalyptic"), and (more recently) Benjamin E. Reynolds on John (Reynolds, *John Among the Apocalypses*). Again, there is also Reynolds and Stuckenbruck, *Jewish Apocalyptic Tradition*, which gathers essays on apocalyptic thought in the whole New Testament.

this book, I have attempted to become as conversant as possible with the Apocalyptic Paul, Second Temple Jewish studies, and Barthian systematic theology, and to draw some of these threads together, but such a project runs the very real risk of becoming "jack of all trades and master of none." Nevertheless, in a discussion where the problems of guild overspecialization and the "siloing" of disciplines have been regularly observed, this was, I believe, a risk worth taking. However, the task of clarifying the prospects for Pauline apocalyptic theology properly belongs not to a monograph but to a polyvocal scholarly conversation. I hope this volume serves as a stimulus for such interdisciplinary discussion, a demonstration of its potential, and some constructive contributions, as the conversation continues about the Apocalyptic Paul.

Bibliography

Adams, Samuel V. *The Reality of God and Historical Method: Apocalyptic Theology in Conversation with N. T. Wright.* Downer's Grove, IL: IVP Academic, 2015.

Agamben, Giorgio. *The Time That Remains: A Commentary on the Letter to the Romans.* Stanford: Stanford University Press, 2006.

Barclay, John M. G. "The Day is at Hand: Barth's Interpretation of Pauline Eschatology", paper delivered at the Annual Karl Barth Conference, *The Finality of the Gospel: Karl Barth and the Tasks of Eschatology*, Princeton Theological Seminary, June 19-19, 2019. [proceedings forthcoming as Ziegler, P. and Dugan, K. eds. *The Finality of the Gospel: Karl Barth and the Tasks of Eschatology* Leiden, Brill: 2022.]

———. *Paul and the Gift.* Grand Rapids: Eerdmans, 2013.

———. *Obeying the Truth: A Study of Paul's Ethics in Galatians.* Edinburgh: T. & T. Clark, 1988.

Barclay, John M. G., and Simon J. Gathercole, eds. *Divine and Human Agency in Paul and his Cultural Environment.* London: A. & C. Black, 2006.

Barth, Karl. *Church Dogmatics.* 4 vols. Edinburgh: T. & T. Clark, 1956–1975.

———. *The Epistle to the Romans.* Translated by E. Hoskyns. Oxford: Oxford University Press, 1933.

———. *The Resurrection of the Dead.* Translated by H. J. Stenning. Eugene, OR: Wipf & Stock, 2003.

———. *The Theology of John Calvin.* Translated by G. W. Bromiley. Grand Rapids: Eerdmans, 1995.

Beker, J. Christiaan. *Paul the Apostle: The Triumph of God in Life and Thought.* Philadelphia: Fortress, 1980.

———. *Paul's Apocalyptic Gospel: The Coming Triumph of God.* Philadelphia: Fortress, 1982.

Betz, Hans Dieter. *Galatians (Hermeneia).* Minneapolis: Augsburg Fortress, 1979.

Blackwell, Ben C., et al., eds. *Paul and the Apocalyptic Imagination.* Minneapolis: Fortress, 2016.

Boccaccini, Gabriele. *Paul's Three Paths to Salvation.* Grand Rapids: Eerdmans, 2020.

Bowens, Lisa M. *African American Readings of Paul: Reception, Resistance, and Transformation.* Grand Rapids: Eerdmans, 2020.

———. *An Apostle in Battle: Paul and Spiritual Warfare in 2 Corinthians 12:1-10.* Tübingen: Mohr Siebeck, 2017.

———. "Divine Desire: Paul's Apocalyptic God of Rescue" *Theology Today* 75 (2018) 9–21.

Bibliography

———. "Investigating the Apocalyptic Texture of Paul's Martial Imagery in 2 Corinthians 4–6." *Journal for the Study of the New Testament* 39 (2016) 3–15.

Brown, Alexandra R. *The Cross and Human Transformation: Paul's Apocalyptic Word in 1 Corinthians*. Minneapolis: Fortress, 2008.

———. "Letters from the Battlefield: Cosmic Sin and Captive Sinners in 1 Corinthians." In *Sin and its Remedy in Paul*, edited by Nijay K. Gupta and John K. Goodrich, 63–80. Eugene, OR: Cascade, 2020.

———. "Paul's Apocalyptic Cross and Philosophy: Reading 1 Corinthians with Giorgio Agamben and Alain Badiou." In *Apocalyptic and the Future of Theology: With and Beyond J. Louis Martyn*, edited by Joshua B. Davis and Douglas K. Harink, 96–117. Eugene, OR: Cascade, 2012.

———. Review of Davies, *Paul Among the Apocalypses*. *Catholic Biblical Quarterly* 80 (2018) 330–31.

Bultmann, Rudolf. *Jesus Christ and Mythology*. New York: Scribner, 1958.

———. *Kerygma and Myth*. New York: Harper & Row, 1961.

———. *New Testament and Mythology and Other Basic Writings*. Philadelphia: Fortress, 1984.

———. *Theology of the New Testament*. London: SCM, 1951.

Campbell, Douglas A. "Apocalyptic Epistemology: The *Sine Qua Non* of Valid Pauline Interpretation." In *Paul and the Apocalyptic Imagination*, edited by Ben C. Blackwell et al., 65–85. Minneapolis: Fortress, 2016.

———. "An Apocalyptic Rereading of 'Justification' in Paul: Or, an Overview of the Argument of Douglas Campbell's The Deliverance of God." *Expository Times* 123 (2012) 382–93.

———. "An Attempt to Be Understood: A Response to the Concerns of Matlock and Macaskill with The Deliverance of God." *JSNT* 34 (2011) 162–207.

———. *The Deliverance of God: An Apocalyptic Rereading of Justification in Paul*. Grand Rapids: Eerdmans, 2009.

———. *Pauline Dogmatics: The Triumph of God's Love*. Grand Rapids: Eerdmans, 2020.

———. *The Quest for Paul's Gospel: A Suggested Strategy*. London: Continuum, 2005.

Chester, Stephen, *Reading Paul with the Reformers: Reconciling Old and New Perspectives*. Grand Rapids: Eerdmans, 2017.

Collins, John J. *Apocalyptic Imagination: An Introduction to Jewish Apocalyptic Literature*. Grand Rapids: Eerdmans, 1998.

———. "Towards the Morphology of a Genre." *Semeia* 14 (1979) 1–20.

———. "Wisdom, Apocalypticism and Generic Compatibility." In *Seers, Sybils and Sages in Hellenistic-Roman Judaism*, 385–404. Leiden: Brill, 1993.

Congdon, David. "Is Bultmann a Heideggerian Theologian?" *Scottish Journal of Theology* 70 (2017) 19–38.

———. *Rudolf Bultmann: A Companion to His Theology*. Eugene, OR: Cascade, 2015.

Cover, Michael. "'Now and Above; Then and Now' (Gal 4:21–31): Platonizing and Apocalyptic Polarities in Paul's Eschatology." In *Galatians and Christian Theology: Justification, the Gospel, and Ethics in Paul's Letter*, edited by N. T. Wright et al., 220–29. Grand Rapids: Baker Academic, 2014.

Croasmun, Matthew. *The Emergence of Sin: The Cosmic Tyrant in Romans*. Oxford: Oxford University Press, 2017.

Cullmann, Oscar. *Christ and Time*. London: SCM, 1951.

———. *Salvation in History*. London: Harper & Row, 1967.

Bibliography

Davies, J. P. *Paul Among the Apocalypses? An Evaluation of the 'Apocalyptic Paul' in the Context of Jewish and Christian Apocalyptic Literature*. London: T. & T. Clark, 2016.

———. "Why Paul Doesn't Mention the 'Age to Come.'" *Scottish Journal of Theology* 74 (2021) 199–208.

Davis, Joshua B., and Douglas K. Harink, eds. *Apocalyptic and the Future of Theology: With and Beyond J. Louis Martyn*. Eugene, OR: Cascade, 2012.

De Boer, Martinus C. "Apocalyptic as God's Eschatological Activity in Paul's Theology." In *Paul and the Apocalyptic Imagination*, edited by Ben C. Blackwell et al., 45–63. Minneapolis: Fortress, 2016.

———. *The Defeat of Death: Apocalyptic Eschatology in 1 Corinthians 15 and Romans 5*. JSNTSup. Sheffield: JSOT, 1988.

———. *Galatians: A Commentary*. Louisville: Westminster John Knox, 2011.

———. "Karl Barth, Theological Exegesis, and the Apocalyptic Interpretation of Paul." *Zeitschrift für Dialektische Theologie* 37 (2021) 11–37.

———. "Paul and Apocalyptic Eschatology". In *The Encyclopedia of Apocalypticism*, edited by John J. Collins and Bernard McGinn, 345–83. New York: Continuum, 2000.

———. "Paul's Mythologizing Program in Romans 5–8." In *Apocalyptic Paul: Cosmos and Anthropos in Romans 5–8*, edited by Beverly R. Gaventa, 1–20. Waco, TX: Baylor University, 2013.

———. "Paul, Theologian of God's Apocalypse." *Interpretation* 56 (2002) 21–33.

———. *Paul, Theologian of God's Apocalypse: Essays on Paul and Apocalyptic*. Eugene, OR: Cascade, 2020.

Derrida, Jacques. "On a Newly Arisen Apocalyptic Tone in Philosophy." Translated by John Leavey Jr., In *Raising the Tone of Philosophy: Late Essays by Immanuel Kant, Transformative Critique by Jacques Derrida*, edited by Peter Fenves, 117–71. Baltimore: Johns Hopkins University Press, 1993.

DiTommaso, Lorenzo. "Apocalypses and Apocalypticism in Antiquity (Part I)." *Currents in Biblical Research* 5 (2007) 235–86.

———. "Apocalypses and Apocalypticism in Antiquity (Part II)." *Currents in Biblical Research* 5 (2007) 367–432.

Downs, David J., and Matthew L. Skinner, eds. *The Unrelenting God: God's Action in Scripture: Essays in Honor of Beverly Roberts Gaventa*. Grand Rapids: Eerdmans, 2013.

Driel, Edwin Chr. van. *Rethinking Paul: Protestant Theology and Pauline Exegesis (Current Issues in Theology 17)*. Cambridge: Cambridge University Press, 2021.

Dunn, James. *Galatians*. Black's New Testament Commentary. Peabody, MA: Hendrickson, 1993.

———. *The Theology of Paul the Apostle*. Grand Rapids: Eerdmans, 1998

Eastman, Susan. "Apocalypse and Incarnation: The Participatory Logic of Paul's Gospel." In *Apocalyptic and the Future of Theology: With and beyond J. Louis Martyn*, edited by Joshua B. Davis and Douglas K. Harink, 165–82. Eugene, OR: Cascade, 2012.

———. "Ashes on the Frontal Lobe: Cognitive Dissonance and Cruciform Cognition in 2 Corinthians." In *The Unrelenting God: God's Action in Scripture: Essays in Honor of Beverly Roberts Gaventa*, edited by David J. Downs and Matthew L. Skinner, 194–207. Grand Rapids: Eerdmans, 2013.

———. "Double Participation and the Responsible Self in Romans 5–8." In *Apocalyptic Paul: Cosmos and Anthropos in Romans 5–8*, edited by Beverly R. Gaventa, 93–110. Waco, TX: Baylor University, 2013.

Bibliography

———. *Paul and the Person: Reframing Paul's Anthropology*. Grand Rapids: Eerdmans, 2017.

———. *Recovering Paul's Mother Tongue: Language and Theology in Galatians*. Grand Rapids: Eerdmans, 2007.

Fortna, Robert T., and Beverly R. Gaventa, eds. *The Conversation Continues: Studies in Paul and John in Honor of J. Louis Martyn*. Nashville: Abingdon, 1990.

Fowler, Alastair. *Kinds of Literature: An Introduction to the Theory of Genres and Modes*. Cambridge, MA: Harvard University Press, 1982.

Frey, Jörg. "Demythologising Apocalyptic?: On N. T. Wright's Paul. Apocalyptic Interpretation, and the Constraints of Construction." In *God and the Faithfulness of Paul*, edited by Christoph Heilig et al., 489–531. Minneapolis: Fortress, 2017.

Gathercole, Simon J. "'Sins' in Paul." *New Testament Studies* 64 (2018) 143–61.

Gaventa, Beverly R., ed. *Apocalyptic Paul: Cosmos and Anthropos in Romans 5–8*. Waco, TX: Baylor University, 2013.

———. "The Cosmic Power of Sin in Paul's Letter to the Romans: Toward a Widescreen Edition." *Interpretation* 58 (2004) 229–240.

———. "Neither Height nor Depth: Discerning the Cosmology of Romans." *Scottish Journal of Theology* 64 (2011) 265–78. (Revised as "'Neither Height Nor Depth': Cosmos and Soteriology in Paul's Letter to the Romans." In *Apocalyptic and the Future of Theology*, edited by Joshua B. Davis and Douglas K. Harink, 183–99. Eugene, OR: Cascade, 2012.)

———. *Our Mother Saint Paul*. Louisville: Westminster John Knox, 2007.

———. "Thinking from Christ to Israel: Romans 9–11 in Apocalyptic Context." In *Paul and the Apocalyptic Imagination*, edited by Benjamin C. Blackwell et al., 239–55. Minneapolis: Fortress, 2016.

Goff, Matthew. "The Mystery of God's Wisdom, the *Parousia* of a Messiah, and Visions of Heavenly Paradise: 1 & 2 Corinthians in the Context of Jewish Apocalypticism." In *The Jewish Apocalyptic Tradition and the Shaping of New Testament Thought*, edited by Benjamin E. Reynolds and Loren T. Stuckenbruck, 175–92. Minneapolis: Fortress, 2017.

———. "Wisdom, Apocalypticism and the Pedagogical Ethos of *4QInstruction*." In *Conflicted Boundaries in Wisdom and Apocalypticism*, edited by B. G. Wright and L. M. Wills, 57–67. Atlanta, SBL: 2005.

———. *The Worldly and Heavenly Wisdom of 4QInstruction*. Leiden: Brill, 2003.

Griffith-Jones, Robin. "Beyond Reasonable Hope of Recognition? *Prosōpopoeia* in Romans 1.18–3.8." In *Beyond Old and New Perspectives on Paul: Reflections on the Work of Douglas Campbell*, edited by Chris Tilling, 161–74. Eugene, OR: Cascade, 2014.

Gunkel, Hermann. *Schöpfung Und Chaos in Urzeit Und Endzeit: Eine Religionsgeschichtliche Untersuchung Über Gen 1 Und Ap Joh 12*. Göttingen: Vandenhoeck und Ruprecht, 1895. [ET *Creation and Chaos in the Primeval Era and the Eschaton: A Religio-Historical Study of Genesis 1 and Revelation 12*. Translated by W. J. Harrington. Grand Rapids: Eerdmans, 2006.]

Gupta, Nijay K., and John K. Goodrich, eds. *Sin and its Remedy in Paul*. Contours of Pauline Theology. Eugene, OR: Cascade, 2020.

Gurtner, Dan and Loren Stuckenbruck, eds. *T&T Clark Encyclopedia of Second Temple Judaism*. London: T. & T. Clark, 2020.

Hanson, Paul D. *The Dawn of Apocalyptic: The Historical and Sociological Roots of Jewish Apocalyptic Eschatology*. Philadelphia: Fortress, 1979.

Bibliography

Harink, Douglas K. "J. L. Martyn and Apocalyptic Discontinuity: The Trinitarian, Christological Ground of Galatians in Galatians 4:1–11." *Journal for the Study of Paul and His Letters* 7 (2017) 101–11.

———. "Partakers of the Divine Apocalypse: Hermeneutics, History and Human Agency after Martyn." In *Apocalyptic and the Future of Theology: With and beyond J. Louis Martyn*, edited by Joshua B. Davis and Douglas K. Harink, 73–95. Eugene, OR: Cascade, 2012.

———. "Paul and Israel: An Apocalyptic Reading." *Pro Ecclesia* 16 (2007) 359–80.

———. *Resurrecting Justice: Reading Romans for the Life of the World*. Downers Grove, IL: InterVarsity, 2020.

———. "Time and Politics in Four Commentaries on Romans." In *Paul, Philosophy, and the Theopolitical Vision: Critical Engagements with Agamben, Badiou, Žižek and Others (Theopolitical Visions)*, 282–312. Eugene, OR: Cascade, 2010.

———. "'Who Hopes for What is Seen?': Political Theology through Romans." In *The Unrelenting God: God's Action in Scripture: Essays in Honor of Beverly Roberts Gaventa*, edited by David J. Downs and Matthew L. Skinner, 150–71. Grand Rapids: Eerdmans, 2013.

Hays, Richard B. "Apocalyptic *Poiēsis* in Galatians". In *Galatians and Christian Theology*, edited by Mark W. Elliott et al., 200–219. Grand Rapids: Baker, 2014.

———. *Echoes of Scripture in the Gospels*. Waco, TX: Baylor, 2018.

———. *Echoes of Scripture in the Letters of Paul*. New Haven, CT: Yale University Press, 1989.

———. *Reading Backwards: Figural Christology and the Fourfold Gospel Witness*. London: SPCK, 2015.

Himmelfarb, Martha. *Ascent to Heaven in Jewish and Christian Apocalypses*. Oxford: Oxford University Press, 1993.

Hogan, Karina Martin. "Mother Zion and Mother Earth in 2 Baruch and 4 Ezra." In *Intertextual Explorations in Deuterocanonical and Cognate Literature*, edited by Jeremy Corley and Geoffrey David Miller, 203–24. Berlin: De Gruyter, 2019.

Humphrey, Edith. *The Ladies and the Cities: Transformation and Apocalyptic Identity in Joseph and Aseneth, 4 Ezra, and the Shepherd of Hermas*. JSPSup 17. Sheffield: Sheffield Academic, 1995.

Hunsinger, George. "*Mysterium Trinitatis*: Karl Barth's Conception of Eternity." In *Disruptive Grace: Studies in the Theology of Karl Barth*. Grand Rapids: Eerdmans, 2000.

Jenson, Robert W. "On Dogmatic/Systematic Appropriation of Paul-According-to-Martyn." In *Apocalyptic and the Future of Theology: With and beyond J. Louis Martyn*, edited by Joshua B. Davis and Douglas K. Harink, 154–61. Eugene, OR: Cascade, 2012.

Jervis, Ann. "Did Paul Think in Terms of Two Ages?" Unpublished presentation, SNTS annual meeting, Athens 2018.

———. "Promise and Purpose in Romans 9.1–13: Toward Understanding Paul's View of Time." In *God and Israel: Providence and Purpose in Romans 9–11*, edited by Todd D. Still, 1–26. Waco, TX: Baylor University Press, 2017.

Käsemann, Ernst. *Commentary on Romans*. Grand Rapids: Eerdmans, 1980.

———. *New Testament Questions of Today*. London: SCM, 1969.

BIBLIOGRAPHY

———. *On Being a Disciple of the Crucified Nazarene: Unpublished Lectures and Sermons.* Edited by R. Landau. Translated by Roy A. Harrisville. Grand Rapids: Eerdmans, 2010.

———. *Perspectives on Paul.* London: SCM, 1971. [ET of *Paulinische Perspektiven* Tübingen/London: Mohr Siebeck/ECM, 1969.]

Keck, Leander E. *Christ's First Theologian: The Shape of Paul's Thought.* Waco, TX: Baylor University Press, 2015.

———. *Echoes of the Word.* Eugene, OR: Cascade, 2015.

———. "Paul and Apocalyptic Theology." *Interpretation* 38 (1984) 229–41.

———. "Paul as Thinker." *Interpretation* 47 (1993) 27–38.

———. *Romans.* Nashville: Abingdon, 2005.

Kerr, Nathan R. *Christ, History and Apocalyptic: The Politics of Christian Mission.* Theopolitical Visions. Eugene, OR: Cascade, 2008.

Koch, Klaus. *The Rediscovery of Apocalyptic.* Translated by Margaret Kohl. London: SCM, 1972. [*Ratlos vor der Apokalyptik: Eine Streitschrift über ein vernachlässigtes Gebiet der Bibelwissenschaft und die schädlichen Auswirkungen auf Theologie und Philosophie.* Gütersloh: Gütersloher Verlagshaus Gerd Mohn, 1970.]

Kynes, Will. *An Obituary for "Wisdom Literature": The Birth, Death, and Intertextual Reintegration of a Biblical Corpus.* Oxford: Oxford University Press, 2019.

Long, D. Stephen. *Hebrews.* Belief Theological Commentaries on the Bible. Louisville: Westminster John Knox, 2011.

Longenecker, Bruce W. *The Triumph of Abraham's God: The Transformation of Identity in Galatians.* Edinburgh: T. & T. Clark, 1998.

Longenecker, Richard. *Galatians.* Word Biblical Commentaries. Grand Rapids: Zondervan, 2015.

Lowe, Walter J. "A God Nearer to Us Than We Are to Ourselves." In *Apocalyptic and the Future of Theology: With and Beyond J. Louis Martyn,* edited by Joshua B. Davis and Douglas K. Harink, 51–72. Eugene, OR: Cascade, 2012.

———. "Prospects for a Postmodern Christian Theology: Apocalyptic without Reserve." *Modern Theology* 15 (1999) 17–24.

———. "Why We Need Apocalyptic." *Scottish Journal of Theology* 63 (2009) 41–53.

Macaskill, Grant. "History, Providence and the Apocalyptic Paul." *Scottish Journal of Theology* 70 (2017) 409–26.

———. *Living in Union with Christ: Paul's Gospel and Christian Moral Identity.* Grand Rapids: Baker, 2019.

———. *The New Testament and Intellectual Humility.* Oxford: Oxford University Press, 2018.

———. *Revealed Wisdom and Inaugurated Eschatology in Ancient Judaism and Early Christianity.* JSJSup 115. Leiden: Brill, 2007.

———. Review of *The Deliverance of God* by Douglas Campbell. *JSNT* 34 (2011) 150–61.

———. "Wisdom and Apocalyptic in the Gospel of Matthew: A Comparative Study with 1 Enoch and 4QInstruction." PhD diss., St Andrews University, 2005.

Marcus, Joel. *Mark: A New Translation with Introduction and Commentary (Anchor Bible)* (2 vols.) New Haven, CT: Yale University Press, 2002.

Marcus, Joel, and Marion L. Soards, eds. *Apocalyptic and the New Testament: Essays in Honor of J. Louis Martyn.* Sheffield: JSOT, 1989.

Martyn, J. Louis. "Afterword: The Human Moral Drama." In *Apocalyptic Paul: Cosmos and Anthropos in Romans 5–8,* edited by Beverly R. Gaventa, 157–66. Waco, TX: Baylor, 2013.

Bibliography

———. "The Apocalyptic Gospel in Galatians." *Interpretation* 54 (2000) 252–60.

———. "Epilogue: An Essay in Pauline Meta-Ethics." In *Divine and Human Agency in Paul and his Cultural Environment*, edited by John M. G. Barclay and Simon J. Gathercole, 173–83. London: A. & C. Black, 2006.

———. "Epistemology at the Turn of The Ages: 2 Corinthians 5.16." In *Christian History and Interpretation: Studies Presented to John Knox*, edited by W. R. Farmer et al., 269–87. Cambridge: Cambridge University Press, 1967.

———. "Events in Galatia: Modified Covenantal Nomism versus God's Invasion of the Cosmos in the Singular Gospel: A Response to J. D. G. Dunn and B. R. Gaventa." *Pauline Theology* 1 (1991) 160–79.

———. *Galatians: A New Translation with Introduction and Commentary.* Anchor Bible. New York: Doubleday, 1997.

———. "The Gospel Invades Philosophy." In *Paul, Philosophy, and the Theopolitical Vision: Critical Engagements with Agamben, Badiou, Žižek, and Others*, edited by Douglas K. Harink, 13–36. Eugene, OR: Wipf & Stock, 2010.

———. Review of *Paul the Apostle: The Triumph of God in Life and Thought* by J. Christiaan Beker. *Word and World* 2 (1982) 194–98.

———. *Theological Issues in the Letters of Paul.* London: T. & T. Clark, 2005.

Matlock, R. Barry. *Unveiling the Apocalyptic Paul: Paul's Interpreters and the Rhetoric of Criticism.* JSNTSup. Sheffield: Sheffield University Press, 1996.

McCormack, Bruce. "Can we Still Speak of 'Justification by Faith'? An In-House Debate with Apocalyptic Readings of Paul." In *Galatians and Christian Theology*, edited by Mark W. Elliott, Scott J. Hafemann, N. T. Wright, and John Frederick, 159–84. Grand Rapids: Baker, 2014.

———. "Longing for a New World: on Socialism, Eschatology, and Apocalyptic in Barth's Early Dialectical Theology." In *Theologie im Umbruch der Moderne: Karl Barths frühe Dialektische Theologie,* edited by Georg Pfleiderer and Harald Matern, 135–49. Zürich: Theologischer Verlag, 2014.

McKnight, Scot, and B. J. Oropeza. *Perspectives on Paul: Five Views.* Grand Rapids: Baker, 2020.

Morse, Christopher. "'If Johannes Weiss is Right . . .' A Brief Retrospective on Apocalyptic Theology." In *Apocalyptic and the Future of Theology: With and beyond J. Louis Martyn,* edited by Joshua B. Davis and Douglas K. Harink, 137–53. Eugene, OR: Cascade, 2012.

Najman, Hindy. *Losing the Temple and Recovering the Future: An Analysis of 4 Ezra.* Cambridge: Cambridge University Press, 2014.

O'Regan, Cyril. "Two Forms of Catholic Apocalyptic Theology." *International Journal of Systematic Theology* 20 (2018) 31–64.

Portier-Young, Anathea. *Apocalypse Against Empire: Theologies of Resistance in Early Judaism.* Grand Rapids: Eerdmans, 2014.

Reynolds, Benjamin E. *John Among the Apocalypses: Jewish Apocalyptic Tradition and the "Apocalyptic" Gospel.* Oxford: Oxford University Press, 2020.

Reynolds, Benjamin E., and Loren Stuckenbruck, eds. *The Jewish Apocalyptic Tradition and the Shaping of New Testament Thought.* Minneapolis: Fortress, 2017.

Rowland, Christopher. *The Open Heaven: A Study of Apocalyptic in Judaism and Early Christianity.* London: SPCK, 1982.

Rowland, Christopher, and Christopher R. A. Morray-Jones. *The Mystery of God: Early Jewish Mysticism and the New Testament.* Leiden: Brill, 2009.

BIBLIOGRAPHY

Sasse, Hermann. "Αἰών, Αἰώνιος." In *Theological Dictionary of the New Testament* edited by Gerhard Kittel et al., 206. Grand Rapids: Eerdmans, 1964–.

Schreiner, Tom. *Galatians*. Zondervan Exegetical Commentary on the New Testament. Grand Rapids: Zondervan, 2010.

Schweitzer, Albert. *The Mysticism of Paul the Apostle*. London: A. & C. Black, 1931. [ET of *Die Mystik Des Apostels Paulus*. Tübingen: Mohr-Siebeck, 1930.]

———. *The Quest of the Historical Jesus*. Tübingen: Mohr-Siebeck, 1906. [ET of *Von Reimarus zu Wrede: Eine Geschichte der Leben-Jesu-Forschung*. Tübingen: Mohr-Siebeck, 1906.]

Scott, James M. *The Apocalyptic Letter to the Galatians: Paul and the Enochic Heritage*. Minneapolis: Fortress, 2021.

———. "A Comparison of Paul's Letter to the Galatians with the Epistle of Enoch." In *The Jewish Apocalyptic Tradition and the Shaping of New Testament Thought*, edited by Benjamin E. Reynolds and Loren T. Stuckenbruck, 193–218. Minneapolis: Fortress, 2017.

Shaw, David. "The 'Apocalyptic' Paul: An Analysis and Critique with Reference to Romans 1–8." PhD diss., University of Cambridge, 2020.

Smythe, Shannon N. "Karl Barth in Conversation with Pauline Apocalypticism." In *Karl Barth in Conversation*, edited by W. Travis McMaken and David W. Congdon, 195–210. Eugene, OR: Pickwick, 2014.

Stone, Michael E. "The City in 4 Ezra." *JBL* 126 (2007) 402–7.

Stone, Michael E., and Matthias Henze. *4 Ezra and 2 Baruch: Translations, Introductions, and Notes*. Minneapolis: Fortress, 2013.

Stuckenbruck, Loren. "Overlapping Ages at Qumran and 'Apocalyptic' in Pauline Theology." In *The Dead Sea Scrolls and Pauline Literature*, edited by J-S. Rey, 309–26. Leiden: Brill, 2014.

———. "Posturing 'Apocalyptic' in Pauline Theology: How Much Contrast with Jewish Tradition?" In *The Myth of Rebellious Angels: Studies in Second Temple Judaism and New Testament Texts*, 240–56. Tübingen: Mohr Siebeck, 2014.

———. "Prayers of Deliverance from the Demonic in the Dead Sea Scrolls and Related Early Jewish Literature." In *The Changing Face of Judaism, Christianity, and Other Greco-Roman Religions in Antiquity*, edited by Ian Henderson and Gerbern Oegema, 146–65. Gütersloh: Gütersloher Verlagshaus, 2006.

———. "Some Reflections on Apocalyptic Thought and Time in Literature from the Second Temple Period." In *Paul and the Apocalyptic Imagination*, edited by Benjamin C. Blackwell et al., 137–76. Minneapolis: Fortress, 2016.

Sturm, Richard E. "Defining the Word 'Apocalyptic': A Problem in Biblical Criticism." In *Apocalyptic and the New Testament: Essays in Honor of J. Louis Martyn*, edited by Joel Marcus and Marion L. Soards, 17–48. Sheffield: JSOT, 1989.

Tigchelaar, Eibert J. C. *Prophets of Old and the Day of the End: Zechariah, the Book of the Watchers, and Apocalyptic*. Leiden: Brill, 1996.

Tilling, Chris, ed. *Beyond Old and New Perspectives on Paul: Reflections on the Work of Douglas Campbell*. Eugene, OR: Cascade, 2014.

Vielhauer, Philipp. "Apocalypses and Related Literature: Introduction." In *New Testament Apocrypha*, edited by W. Schneemelcher, 581–642. Philadelphia: Westminster, 1964.

Way, David. *The Lordship of Christ: Ernst Käsemann's Interpretation of Paul's Theology*. Oxford: Clarendon, 1991.

Bibliography

Wasserman, Emma. *Apocalypse as Holy War: Divine Politics and Polemics in the Letters of Paul.* New Haven, CT: Yale University Press, 2018.

Webster, John B. "Reading Scripture Eschatologically (1)." In *Reading Texts, Seeking Wisdom: Scripture and Theology,* edited by David Ford and Graham Stanton, 245–56. Grand Rapids: Eerdmans, 2004.

Weiss, Johannes. *Jesus' Proclamation of the Kingdom of God.* Translated by Richard Hiers and David Holland. Minneapolis: Fortress, 1971. [*Die Predigt Jesu vom Reich Gottes.* Göttingen: Vandenhoeck & Ruprecht, 1892.]

———. *Der Erste Korintherbrief* Göttingen: Vandenhoeck & Ruprecht, 1910.

Westerholm, Martin. *The Ordering of the Christian Mind: Karl Barth and Theological Rationality.* Oxford: Oxford University Press, 2015.

Wright, Benjamin, and Lawrence Wills, eds. *Conflicted Boundaries in Wisdom and Apocalypticism.* Atlanta: SBL, 2005.

Wright, N. T. "Apocalyptic and the Sudden Fulfilment of Divine Promise." In *Paul and the Apocalyptic Imagination,* edited by Benjamin C. Blackwell et al., 111–34. Minneapolis: Fortress, 2016.

———. *History and Eschatology: Jesus and the Promise of Natural Theology.* The 2018 Gifford Lectures. Waco, TX: Baylor University Press, 2019.

———. "Hope Deferred? Against the Dogma of Delay." *Early Christianity* 9 (2018) 37–82.

———. *Interpreting Paul: Essays on the Apostle and His Letters.* London: SPCK, 2020.

———. "A New Perspective on Käsemann? Apocalyptic, Covenant, and the Righteousness of God." In *Studies in the Pauline Epistles: Essays in Honor of Douglas J. Moo,* edited by M. S. Harmon and J. E. Smith, 243–58. Grand Rapids: Zondervan, 2014. [Reprinted in *Interpreting Paul: Essays on the Apostle and His Letters,* 1–17. London: SPCK, 2020.]

———. "Paul in Current Anglophone Scholarship." *The Expository Times* 123 (2012) 367–81.

———. *Paul and His Recent Interpreters.* London: SPCK, 2015.

———. *Paul and the Faithfulness of God.* London: SPCK, 2013.

———. *Paul in Fresh Perspective.* Minneapolis: Fortress, 2005.

Ziegler, Philip G. "'Bound Over to Satan's Tyranny': Sin and Satan in Contemporary Reformed Hamartiology." *Theology Today* 75 (2018) 89–100.

———. "The Fate of Natural Law at the Turning of the Ages: Some Reflections on a Trend in Contemporary Theological Ethics in View of the Work of J. Louis Martyn." *Theology Today* 67 (2011) 419–29.

———. "The First and Final 'No': the Finality of the Gospel and the Old Enemy." Paper delivered at the Annual Karl Barth Conference, *The Finality of the Gospel: Karl Barth and the Tasks of Eschatology,* Princeton Theological Seminary, June 19, 2019. [Forthcoming as Ziegler, Phil, and Kait Dugan, eds. *The Finality of the Gospel: Karl Barth and the Tasks of Eschatology.* Leiden, Brill: 2022.]

———. *Militant Grace: The Apocalyptic Turn and the Future of Christian Theology.* Grand Rapids: Baker, 2018.

———. "Some Remarks on Apocalyptic in Modern Christian Theology." In *Paul and the Apocalyptic Imagination,* edited by Benjamin C. Blackwell et al., 199–216. Minneapolis: Fortress, 2016.

www.ingramcontent.com/pod-product-compliance
Lightning Source LLC
Chambersburg PA
CBHW031427150426
43191CB00006B/434